GETTING OFF

A criminal lawyer's Road to Redemption

VERONIQUE PERRIER MANDAL

GETTING OFF

Perrier Mandal, Veronique

    Getting Off/Veronique Perrier Mandal

ISBN 13: 978-0-9880132-1-6

Disclaimer: Some of the names of people in this book have been changed at the request of Don Tait

Cover design: Veronique Mandal and Jessica Jagmin

Printed and bound in the USA

Middlebranchpublications@gmail.com

For Marguerite and Richard
Barbara and Nick
Iris and Ron

Foreword

The disappearance of mercurial lawyer Don Tait in the winter of 2000 presented The Windsor Star with the type of journalistic challenge that defines a newsroom.

If someone else found him first – a well-heeled competitor such as the Globe and Mail, for instance – we would be humiliated. I was squarely on the horns of that dilemma. So, I challenged the staff to find him, get him to talk, and we'll send you anywhere in the world to tell the story. It became known as the Tait Bounty.

Within weeks, to the surprise of no one, Veronique Mandal was packing a bag for Costa Rica. She had found him using means that to this day remain somewhat of a mystery to me. She would travel alone to the capital San Jose where Tait had reportedly become a local raconteur. Her only security blanket was metro editor Mike Frezell, tracking her whereabouts with a GPS unit from the safe confines of the newsroom. What we would do if Mandal encountered danger was a bit less defined.

We collectively breathed sighs of relief when she returned to Canadian soil. Upon seeing the fruits of her labor – colourful, poignant and often sad reflections by Tait coupled with compelling accounts of his new life and surroundings – we knew that our readers were in for the ride of a lifetime.

We instructed Mandal to work from home and I edited the stories from my basement office. Tait had obviously bared his soul. It was in turns tragic, for those sympathetic to the plight of an alcoholic, and maddening for those he had stiffed before fleeing Canada. Mandal had so much material that we decided to spread the account over two days, producing front pages that to this day I consider among our best.

In awarding Mandal the 2000 Ontario Newspaper Award for Enterprise Reporting, Toronto media lawyer Bert Bruser, the category judge, called the Tait coverage a "compelling yarn" and a "clear winner in a strong field of entries." He said Mandal's "dispassionate account of Tait's life in Costa Rica exposed the pathetic depths to which he had fallen."

1

Why was no one surprised that Veronique Mandal claimed the Tait Bounty? In my more than three decades in the newspaper business, I have rarely encountered a journalist who so embodied the traits of tenacity and courage. On a daily basis she would be challenged with delivering the toughest interview, and never disappoint.

And now, nearly two decades later and having followed Tait to Africa, that tenacity and courage is once again on full display. In an age of short attention spans and "fake news" admonitions, it's a rare pleasure to see a story so exhaustively and honestly mined.

Marty Beneteau
Former Publisher, The Windsor Star

Author's Note

AS A JOURNALIST, I am most familiar with writing about people without any trace of me or my opinions in the story – as it should be if the time-honoured rules of fair and balanced journalism are to be upheld.

Most biographies also avoid reference to the author; however, there are notable exceptions, as in the case of Humphrey Carpenter's biography of J.R.R. Tolkien. Carpenter included himself because it was pertinent to the work, which is the only time an author should dare insert him or herself into someone else's personal journey.

Writing this story about Don Tait is one of those exceptions. The decision to include myself in parts of this biography was not an easy one. In the end I had to be finally persuaded by Tait himself, because he was adamant that so much of this tale could not be told any other way.

Tait insisted if this book was to be written it had to include some of my interactions with him, which he believed helped move the narrative at various points in the story. He explained, quite emphatically, that because I was the only one to witness some of the crucial transitions in his life, taking myself out completely would result in "weird disconnects" that wouldn't make sense to readers. Therefore, the inclusion of this perpendicular pronoun is not a product of vanity, but merely an element in the continuity of Tait's journey.

Don Tait was already a media favourite when I became a junior reporter at the Canadian Broadcasting Corporation in 1985. His high-profile clients had him appearing on radio and television and on newspaper front pages almost on a daily basis. I paid attention to him only when assigned to cover one of his court cases. In those days it was far more interesting to me to cover health and entertainment stories about "real" people. The likes of Tait were, to me, media-fodder, seen more often as objects of "good copy" for the evening news.

It might therefore appear that I would be an unlikely person to write Tait's biography. That would be true were it not for several encounters with him in the intervening years that were to eventually lead me, as a reporter, to chase him down after he absconded from the law and the taxman. Finding him - a broken down, pathetic drunk - in Central America gave me a new and surprising perspective into the character of the man. In many ways the piteous wretch I found was a nicer character than the one most often braying to the media. The time spent interviewing him in San Jose lead to stories about his volcanic downfall, keeping readers on both sides of the Canada - U.S. border alternately fascinated and appalled.

"If you live and ever return to North America, and if you have any brain cells left to remember this conversation - and will allow someone to write your story, give me a call," were my parting words to him before leaving Costa Rica. It would be almost five years - after Tait had gone to rehab several times, gone to jail, left the country to live in Africa and suffered a near fatal heart attack - before I heard from him again.

That unexpected phone call, spurred by a guest on the Oprah Winfrey Show, led to this biography. While I began the book as a dispassionate journalist, I was also affected by Tait`s story and what he was becoming and that also led to writing style changes in the progression of the work. Little did I know that in the writing of Tait's personal journey my own life would reach a new level of spirituality.

Now, more than a decade since that call, and in the last years of his life, Tait's existence is a spiritual one. He has found the love, peace and kind of respect as a human being he couldn't find as a high flying legal eagle. Tait is a dichotomy – pre-and post-Africa. This story is based on his extraordinary life.

BEHIND BARS

Saturday, January 10, 2001

EVEN BEHIND BARS, Don Tait's celebrity status had been working for him. He wasn't subject to searches and didn't have to share a cell. But a complaint from a couple of his fellow inmates was about to change his smug entitlement. Tait's coming humiliation was being discussed in the guard duty room.

Cavity searching prisoners is not a fun way to start a work week. It was something rookie jail guard Adam Sorwell dreaded. But today, senior guards peg the quiet spoken rookie to cavity search the jail's most illustrious prisoner. His buddies Pete and Steve find it amusing.

"You going in to see the lawyer Adam?"

"Yep. Guess it's my turn."

"He's pretty famous or infamous around here."

"No kidding. His face is always on TV."

"Always defending the big shot guilty ones."

Pete laughing. "Yeah, and often gets them off. Good luck."

"Sure you don't want to take this one Pete."

"This one's all yours."

"Steve?"

"Not a chance. We're supervising."

Adam picks up his small black bag and goes to see one of the city's most well-known criminal lawyers. It's not something

he's been looking forward to. His buddies start "tossing" Tait's cell, shaking the pillow and overturning the mattress.
"Morning Mr. Tait."

"Good morning."

Adam hesitates.

"Well, come on. Let's get it over with."

"Ah...ah...you need to..."

"I know."

Don Tait unzips his orange jumpsuit and lets it fall to the floor. He bends over at the waist. Far enough so that the cheeks of his rear end spread open. He feels the uncomfortable scrutiny of the young man charged with ensuring there is no illegal contraband hidden in his anal cavity. Most of all he feels abject humiliation.

"Sorry Mr. Tait. It's regulations."

"Yeah."

Monday, January 12, 2001

(The Windsor Star newsroom)

"You going to see Tait?" one of the night editors ask as I'm heading out of the newsroom.

"Probably on my way home."

"Well, say hi for me."

"Sure."

"Hey, say hi for me too," shouts another reporter from across the newsroom.

"From me too," from another. "Tell him he gave me some of my best quotes."

Ten minutes later I pull in to the parking lot of the Windsor Jail. It's an interesting old building and its history flashes through my mind, having read about it several days earlier in The Windsor Star. Constructed in 1925, it opened in 1929 as the Windsor Essex Gaol, with a capacity for 147 but had become decrepit. It was replaced by a super jail in 2014.

This isn't my first visit to the jail. It's a regular stop for reporters on the trail of a good story. But I am usually there to talk to clients, not the lawyers themselves. Identifying myself to the guard on duty, I'm buzzed in to the visiting area and take a hard chair in front of the plexiglass visitor's wall. In front of each sitting position there is a small round hole in the glass to speak through. I'm not sure what condition Tait will be in when he appears but the fact he is still alive astounds me. This visit feels strangely unnerving – like waiting to talk to someone you know should be dead. A guard arrives to tell me Tait will be delayed, asks if I would like to wait. I would.

I get up and walk across the room to sit by a window. I think about what I've learned about Tait and his life. Looking up at the bars on the windows I can't help but wonder how the hell does an expensive criminal lawyer end up here?

THE FUGITIVE

THE DISAPPEARANCE of one of the city's most famous criminal lawyers is big news and editors in print and broadcast newsrooms are anxious for one of their reporters to crack the story. The editor of The Windsor Star issues a challenge: Anyone who finds Don Tait can travel to interview him, wherever he is.

Having written the stories leading up to and following his disappearance, I was determined the "anyone" was going to be me. I wasn't sure why I wanted to go after Tait – maybe it was because of the publicity my stories would get, or maybe it was something else, something I couldn't quite put my finger on.

People on both sides of the Canada – U. S. border wanted to know Tait's story. There was the usual voyeuristic fascination for anything that speaks of intrigue and hardship for the rich and famous. But, there were also many people who had a stake in his whereabouts, not the least of whom were his clients and the taxman. Finding Tait, I decided, could be career changing.

Police agencies on both sides of the border were on the lookout for the fugitive. Canada had a warrant out for his arrest and the Americans were keeping an eye out for him to help their Canadian counterparts. His legal colleagues wanted to know where the hell he was and when, if ever, he'd be back. With more than fifty of Tait's clients waiting for justice, they weren't happy to be left to clean up the chaos. The clients were out a lot of money and wanted their day in court. Tait's departure had caused one heck of an uproar. Perhaps my determination to be the reporter who found Tait was fuelled by the intrigue of seeing how far he had fallen this time. I had been interviewing Windsor's legal star on and off for fifteen years; had a strange encounter with him in the courtroom in the 1980s and subsequently discovered he had been lying during my interview with him in 1997 when he discussed the surgery that had saved his voice and boasted his life was under control.

For some unfathomable reason I had a strange feeling our destinies were linked and wanted to see this through to the end, whatever that end might be. That strange incident in a courtroom many years earlier revealed a chink in his armour. During a recess that followed a harsh gruelling of a witness, Tait walked over to talk with reporters. As they were scribbling down the pithy quotes he gave them, Tait suddenly looked at me and said "She hates me. I can tell. I just know she hates me. But I had to do it for my client." He stopped the emotional outburst and walked back to talk to his client. Wow, I thought. That was peculiar.

Now, after almost twenty years, I was on the hunt to find him to learn more. Gathering information was like pulling teeth. His legal colleagues and buddies all said they didn't know where he'd gone, but were worried about him. Cop friends and those he'd defended over the years said they hoped nothing bad would happen to him. Police Chief Glen Stannard was close to Tait. One afternoon, over coffee, he talked about the lawyer he'd come to know and respect.

"This is really unfortunate, but he has to come back to face the court and try to get back on his feet. He's a good guy and a talented lawyer. I don't know what's gone wrong but yeah, I'm worried about him. Very worried. I have a bad feeling about how this could turn out," Stannard told me.

The Chief recounted the many times Tait had defended Windsor police officers in court and how difficult it was for them to see him now as a criminal. He said they all truly believed his alcoholism was causing most, if not all, of his problems. Leaving Stannard that afternoon, bracing myself against a vicious cold wind, I went to meet Tait's biker buddy Bill O'Reilly. We were meeting at a no name bar on Wyandotte Street, in a neighbourhood where many hookers I'd interviewed over the years plied their trade. I looked down at my clothes - black pants and black pea coat - hoping I wasn't too well dressed for the bar yet dressed in a way not to be mistaken for one of the "girls."

The bar was dim and gloomy. Two men sporting long ponytails, tattoos, beards and heavy jean jackets with biker-type logos I couldn't make out, were sucking back beer and arguing. O'Reilly was sitting alone at a corner table with his back to the wall. He was drinking coffee and appeared agitated - tapping the fingers of his right hand against the mug. We shook hands, but he didn't get up, gesturing to the chair to his left.

"So, what do you want to know?" He wasn't a guy for small talk.

"Where I can find Tait."

"Want a drink?"

"Sure. Black coffee." He yells the order to the bartender.

"What makes you think I know or that I'd tell you if I did?"

"I think he would agree with you telling me. I think he might also agree to talk to me."

"What makes you think that?"

"He knows I can be trusted."

"How do I know that?"

"You'll have to take my word for it or you can ask him. Can I ask you a few questions?"

11

"Depends on what the questions are."

"Does he intend to come back?"

"Maybe. It depends."

"On what? The court? His girlfriend? His health?

"Yeah."

"How is his health?"

"Bad."

"How bad?"

"Bad." I can see O'Reilly is worried. I give him my most sympathetic look and tell him I'm sorry to hear it. No response.

"So, where is he?" I ask hopefully.

"I don't know if I can tell you."

"Which country? Tell me that."

"South. No. Don't ask."

"Are you selling his belongings?"

"Yeah."

"Are you sending him the money?"

"What money?"

"Look, I'm not going to talk to the taxman."

"I'm helping him out."

"What are you going to do? Is he drinking?"

"What do you think?" he barks at me. By this time, a couple of the guys at the bar are paying more attention to our conversation than they are to the bartender. It's unnerving.

"You've been a good friend for a long time."

"I'd kill for him."

"Have you?" That really gets him annoyed.

"You got any more questions?"

"When will you let me know where he is?"

"After I talk to him."

"When do you..."

"After I talk to him."

"Can I call you in a few days?"

"Sure."

He concentrates on his coffee. I stand up and stick out my hand.

"Thanks a lot. I appreciate your time." My mouth is really dry. He looks at my hand.

"Yeah." He takes it. Holds on to it.

"One other thing. Stay away from the clubhouse. You can run into trouble asking questions out there."

"Yeah. Sure."

I leave, feigning an air of confidence and fake a smile at the tough guys watching me. They give O'Reilly an enquiring look that says, "new meat?" I nearly run into the door. They all laugh. The cold air is a balm after the skanky stale air in the bar. I'm not sure how much I just learned but I had the feeling more might soon come to light.

Taking a stroll down Wyandotte to see if any of the girls who had agreed to interviews in the past might be around, I strike out. One I don't recognize saunters up. "I hear you're looking for Don Tait?"

"Yeah. He's hard to find."

"I hear he might be in South America." She struts away.

"Where? Hey! Thanks." She doesn't look back.

A "might be" from a street walker is not the best evidence and there are many places to hide in South America. But you never know. I file the nebulous tip. My next targets were Tait's daughters. Over the next two months I would have conversations with Melanie and Barbara, hoping if they trusted me they'd be willing to ask their father to talk to me. Meeting Melanie always made my heart ache. We often met in coffee shops and restaurants. The youngest Tait daughter was elfin-like with her long dark hair always hanging loose. Her pretty face was marred by a drug and alcohol-filled youth and young adulthood. Her thin fingers often trembled as they attempted to hold on tightly to the warmth of her coffee mug. She was sad and while it was clear that her childhood had been far from normal and she resented her mostly absent father, she also loved him and yearned for more of his care and affection.

One Tuesday morning after a non-productive meeting with Melanie, I called Barbara who was married with children. She too was the product of a household of extreme excesses and appeared to be coping with her own brand of demons. Yet, she was sufficiently together to raise a couple of young daughters of her own. The telephone conversation was brief and I learned nothing more, but she agreed to talk again and perhaps set up a meeting.

Conversations with Tait's ex-wife Johanna and his most recent ex-girlfriend and fiancée Sandra Martin, helped me understand how those women became besotted and emotionally unglued during their relationships with him. And then there was the unfathomable loyalty to a man who had abused them both.

The first meeting with Johanna was at Lazares Furs where she was employed. Her shoulder length blond hair was tied back in a ponytail. She was slim and pretty and also intelligent and thoughtful. It was obvious why Tait would have been attracted to her. A lot of water had passed under the bridge in the five years they had been separated but she was as concerned about Tait as she would be if they were still together. She also feared that this could be the end of his life.

"You know, he's a very troubled man with a lot of mental and health problems. He brought them on himself but that doesn't matter. I am really worried he may not recover from this one."

"You still care about him?"

"Yes. I do. He's caused me a lot of pain, but I don't want anything bad to happen to him."

"Do you know where he is?"

"I hear rumours, but I don't really know. I just know he's not in the country."

She picks a non-existent fleck off her skirt and looks away, leaving me to suspect she really does know but I decide not to pursue it, at least not then. We shake hands and I leave thinking about the woman who had captivated Tait's heart for so long, who appears to be a genuinely lovely person. What, I wonder, could have possessed Tait to throw her over?

Martin began turning up at the Star, wanting me to hear her side of the story and to understand she did not want to see Tait in jail. She insisted he had not meant to have her break her nose when he pushed her into a sink during their drunken brawl. She still wanted a future with him. A week later I received a tip from police that Tait had sneaked into Windsor from Detroit in the trunk of Martin's car.

15

After a violent argument, Martin had called police complaining that Tait had assaulted her and stolen her jewellery. On February 11, 2000, Windsor police charged Tait with assault and theft, in absentia. She didn't tell them where Tait had come from. I file the information on that tale. It will be one of the many things to talk to Tait about once I find him.

In late February Melanie called and asked if she could meet for coffee at our usual spot. "I have a file for you," she says before hanging up. Grabbing my coat, I ran the four blocks to the Tim Hortons coffee shop. Melanie wasn't in a hurry to hand over the legal-size file sitting to her right on the table and it took prompting to remind her why we were meeting.

"Oh, yeah. Dad asked me to give you this." She slides the file across the table. It is filled with police reports – all complaint calls from Tait's home, mostly involving violent outbursts by Martin. It was great stuff.

Melanie said her father had asked her to make sure the file was delivered to me. I was curious.

"Why? Why does he want me to have this?"

"I don't know. He just asked me to make sure you got the file and asked that you read everything in it."

"Has he agreed to see me? Can you tell me where he is?" I was hopeful.

"Look, he just said to give you the file and for you to read it. OK?"

"Sure. "

She was getting agitated and I didn't want to push her too far. We finish coffee over inane chatter about there not being much to do in Windsor and the weather.

"Want another cup?"

"No. Thanks. Gotta go." She was suddenly anxious to get away.

"Sure. Thanks for this." I was just as anxious to leave and get back to the newsroom to go through the file. Time was passing and the hunt for Tait was intensifying. National news organizations were on the prowl for information and I did not want anyone to get to Tait before I did.

Two weeks later, on Friday, March 3, Chris Vander Doelen, the then automotive reporter (and my husband) answered the city desk telephone at the Windsor Star the same time my phone was ringing.

"Hello, Windsor Star. It's Veronique."

"Hey kid. It's Tait."

"Tait? Hey." I scramble to connect the tape recorder to the phone. My heart is in fibrillating with excitement. "This is a surprise."

"I hear you want to talk to me." Tait is nonchalant and laughing.

"Sure do. "

Vander Doelen begins waving his hand. I ask Tait to hold on. "I've got Don Tait's daughter on the phone for you."

"I've got Don Tait on the phone," I tell him quietly. 'Tell her I'll call her later. Don't tell anyone who I'm talking to." He nods assent. I lower my voice. Given the close proximity of reporters in the newsroom, I don't want anyone overhearing the conversation and certainly don't want anyone knowing who is at the other end of the phone.

"Sorry about that. One of your daughters wanted to talk to me."

"Probably Melanie. I told her I would call you. So, what do you want to know?"

We talked for more than three hours. The tape ran out after an hour and I made copious notes.

"I hope I can use all of this."

"Sure. Absolutely."

"I've been taping the conversation."

"You can't use what we've just talked about."

'You just told me I could." I felt panic rising.

"I'll tell you everything and you can use it, but you have to come down here and talk face to face."

"Where is 'here?'"

"Costa Rica. San Jose."

"OK." I look at my day book. Today was Thursday. "I'll be there Sunday."

"Call me and give me your arrival time."

"How do I reach you?"

"Call the La Gran Via hotel."

I put down the receiver and stared at the phone, hardly believing what had just happened. Looking around, I got up, walked over to the assignment editor and knelt on one knee close to his chair.

"Lefty, I have to go to Costa Rica on Sunday."

"Oh yeah."

"Seriously. I have to be in Costa Rica for an interview."

"Who's in Costa Rica?"

I whisper "TAIT."

"Fuck. Get in here." He practically dragged me into the board room demanding details, then told me to wait and called in the editor, Marty Beneteau. Once Marty heard the news they both demanded absolute secrecy. I am told not to tell anyone, not even colleagues in the newsroom. This was the scoop of the decade and they did not want it leaking to other media outlets.

Beneteau had his executive assistant book my flights and hotel in secrecy. They used Lefty's credit card. Then there's a wrinkle. The Easter Seals Telethon weekend broadcast was starting Saturday night and I was one of the television hosts. While the editors salivated over the scoop they were getting, I got on the phone and began calling journalist friends who were not already appearing on the telethon. The problem was I had to ask them to take my place but not to ask why I had to bow out so urgently. My first thought was radio reporter Patti Handysides who wouldn't be fazed by a TV camera, but she wasn't home. The next five colleagues - print and radio - said "No way. Not a chance. Sorry." I try Patti again. She answers.

"Patti, would you take my place at the telethon without asking why I can't do it?'

"Sure. No problem. What do I do?" Now I could breathe again.

The next call was to Tait's daughter Barbara to tell her I was going to see her father.

She asked me to come to her home Saturday morning. While she was welcoming and gracious, she was also guarded. Over mugs of tea we talked about Barbara's life as Don Tait's daughter and, as with Melanie, it was clear she loved her father but was equally blunt about his shortcomings as a parent. His womanizing and lifestyle didn't leave a lot of time for two young girls. Also like Melanie, she battled with booze and suffered bouts of depression. Slightly overweight at the time, with short blond hair, she was attractive and smart.

She was also worried her father would die in Costa Rica and obviously understood the seriousness of his mental and physical state of health. She said she despaired he might not seek help in time to save himself. The conversation was friendly and she repeated several times that she wanted me to know she loved her father, despite their rocky relationship. Barbara and her daughter had written letters to him and she produced a photo album she had put together the night before, hoping it would please him.

"Give him a hug for us and tell him we love him," she said as I was leaving. "Tell him we'd like him to come home."

On Sunday at 11 a.m., as I boarded an American Airlines flight from Detroit, Michigan, I was excited and worried. There was no telling how Tait would react, whether he would be coherent and whether he would remember a reporter was coming to interview him. While people around me dug into their airline lunches, I leaned back and closed my eyes, partly in exhaustion but also with some anxiety. I replayed the tapes in my head of everything I knew about Tait and his life and all that had transpired over the previous four months. I couldn't help but worry he might not show up, depending on his state of sobriety. I glanced at the TV screen which showed the plane flying over the Gulf of Mexico. I'd soon be finding out.

COSTA RICA – TELL ALL

(March 6, 2000)

A HOT RAY OF SUN slides over the mountain, across the dusty barrios and down into the dirty streets of San Jose. It searches relentlessly, finally making its way across a small balcony and into an open window. Ignoring the worn carpet, cheap furniture and stained bedspread, it finds its target.

A worn, swollen hand rubs a tired eye, trying to swat it away. Puffy lids, sticky with sleep dust, open a fraction, then quickly close. Using both hands to protect the bloodshot eyes inside, the hulking figure beneath the paper-thin sheets brings himself to life. He rubs his nose, misshapen because of the many times it's been broken. Daylight. He's still alive. Fuck.

He tries to roll over, away from the hot ray, but his bloated body won't let him. He reaches out, blindly searching for his two-dollar watch. An alcohol soaked brain cell remembers when it would have been a Rolex. The hands tell him it's 8 a.m. He wonders why it's important. His bladder demands relief. At a snail's pace he moves his swollen legs across the bed, plants his feet on the floor and forces his naked body upright. He staggers into the tiny bathroom.

"Not much good for anything but pissing," he laments to his flaccid penis. Another brain cell remembers marathon sessions when he was hard for hours. Catching sight of his pasty skin stretched to gargantuan proportions, he doesn't recognize the body as his own. Where was the hard, lean muscle that women lusted after and left husbands for?

He needs a drink. The forty-ounce Smirnoff bottle on the cheap dresser is empty. Beads of sweat appear on his forehead and under his nose. Soon, rivulets are running down his ruddy cheeks. The shakes make it difficult to pull clean underwear from a drawer. He should shower. He sits on the bed, staring at the watch. "Fuck." He remembers. A Windsor Star reporter is showing up at 9:30.

Painfully, he showers. Dressing is laborious, given the state of his legs. Not to mention the aggravating tremors and generalized body pain. Wanting to look decent for the interview, he chooses his one cheap, black and white check suit and dark green shirt and tie. Used to be Armani or nothing. He squeezes his swollen feet into a pair of black loafers. Thinks about flip flops. Concedes to pain and style, at least what's left of any semblance of style. Total cost of the ensemble, including shoes: $180. His total wardrobe is worth about $600. He combs his sweat soaked grey hair forward, picks up his wallet and slips on the watch. Checking the time, he dons dark glasses to hide his crippled eyes and leaves his room.

Out in the street, I pay a cab driver while my photographer from the local paper, La Republica, gathers his equipment. Shouldering my heavy handbag and briefcase, we begin walking the two blocks to Tait's hotel. I had asked the cab driver to drop us off some distance from the hotel in order to get an impression of the place that was harbouring, or sheltering, the Canadian lawyer who was on the fugitive list of Canadian and U. S. police.

I try to recall when it was that I had last seen Tait. Then remember it was three months before on a street in downtown Windsor. He had gained weight and looked like a man in a deep alcoholic depression. He nodded briefly and walked on, obviously not wanting to talk. Who would I find here in San Jose – Tait the powerful, bombastic lawyer or, as I expect, a broken man.

Taking a deep breath, I follow the photographer cross the Plaza Coutura heading to the La Gran Via Hotel. It's hot and people are scurrying in and out of quaint shops lining the Plaza. We stop in front of La Gran Via which is not all that grand. Having known Tait at the pinnacle of his career, when his physical prowess was the envy of many, when his handsome, chiselled jaw made him stand out in a crowd and his razor-sharp mind kept friends and foes alike on their toes, the sight of him coming out of the lobby of a cheap hotel in San Jose was shocking.

The man walking towards us was badly weathered by his long, protracted bouts with the bottle. His once broad smile, set against rows of perfectly white teeth, was engaging, but was now forced from a face puffed by alcohol. He looked seedy. His legs in his cheap suit looked like tree trunks. Sweat ran in angry beads down the sides of his face and his grey, thinning hair was combed forward, aka Friar Tuck, and stuck to his scalp. He held out a wet, bloated hand.

"Hey kid."

Oh my God, I think, where the hell is Don Tait?

Then the old charm. The warm, infectious laugh as he mocks his appearance and surroundings. He's aware of his guest's gob-smacked scrutiny and wants to prove he still has the Tait "thing."

"Come on in and see when I live." He leads us through a narrow doorway and in to the lobby of La Gran Via. We take the elevator to the third floor then follow Tait as he unlocks the door to his room and ushers us inside.

"Not exactly what I've been used to but it's home," he says jokingly, looking around with some embarrassment at his $500 a month 12 x 20-foot room. The small, double bed is neatly made and the shabby green rug is somewhat clean, despite its apparent age. A dresser with a mirror sits along one wall. The bathroom is small and clean, with nothing but a brush, toothbrush and toothpaste in sight. Tait opens the closet door to show off his motley collection of clothes. A far

23

cry from his preferred Armani, he describes each of the seven pieces in his sparse wardrobe.

"Shorts, shorts, t-shirt, t-shirt, shirt, shirt, shirt, shirt. Those and the suit, shirt and shoes I'm wearing? All about a hundred and fifty bucks. I usually just wear shorts and a t-shirt and sandals. Got this suit to meet you. What do you think?" He's laughing.

"It's not Armani."

"Don't need Armani here. I just don't need Armani. Period. I'm done with that. All of it. Want to sit outside. It's pretty hot in here." He's sweating. Sitting on the balcony overlooking the Plaza Coutura, Tait agonizes over his decision to flee – leaving his clients without representation, his friends and colleagues distressed and his daughters without their dad. He laments that his 13-year-old granddaughter, Courtney, is being harassed at school because everyone wants to know where her grandfather is. "Guess they'll all know once you write this story," he quips. "They hear so many rumours and read so many bad things about me. I don't consider myself a fugitive. I'm not on the run. I'm here. They know where to find me. Let them come and get me."

As Tait talks it is clear that his downfall is as much a tragic love story as the tale of a superstar on the skids. He blames bad relationship decisions for bringing him to his emotional and economic knees. After nearly an hour of talking his lips begin to quiver. Once the poster boy for alcoholic rehabilitation at Windsor's Brentwood Recovery Home, Tait has barely made it to 10 a.m. and it's evident that the alcoholic demons are pecking at his insides. He wipes a river of sweat off his head and face with a tissue and apologizes. His speech is slow and measured, not the rapid-fire barbing reporters came to expect from a sharp witted and talented legal mind. He unwraps the small photo album from Barbara and smiles at photos of his two daughters. He finds a photo of himself with his mother when he was about five and his eyes fill with tears.

"I think of her fifty times a day and she's been gone fifteen years. If she was still alive I would have listened to her and maybe all of this wouldn't have happened," he says with unbridled sadness. He tucks letters from his daughters and Courtney inside his jacket pocket, too emotional to read them in front of visitors. Courtney calls him "Faffy," he says smiling and it's obvious he adores the young teenager.

Tait fidgets. The demons of alcohol are howling and he suggests going for lunch in the third-floor restaurant of the hotel. There, Jorge the waiter and Rita the cook make a fuss over Tait, whom they call Senor Don.

"Jorge. C'm here. C'm here. Café por favor." Tait laughs heartily at his meagre attempt at Spanish.

"Si, Senor Don."

"I do a lot of arm waving, gesturing and eye movements. I plan to take lessons." He's jovial. The Jack Daniels has kicked in. Hotel manager, Albaro Montero, comes over to greet one of his favourite tenants.

"He is a good man and we look after him," Montero says of Tait. "We protect him."

Montero and his staff screen Tait's calls and accept only those on the approved list. Two more double Jack Daniels and Tait is ready to move on. He leads the way out of the hotel and into the stifling early afternoon heat. Strolling across the dusty, cobblestone street into the Plaza Coutura – the hub of Costa Rica's national capital – Tait walks with a stilted, painful gait. Each step is obviously excruciating and he nearly loses his balance. Arriving at the Gran Casino Hotel he chooses a table on the veranda restaurant. The long marble veranda with large columns and the casino adjoining it have a 1940s feel, not unlike vintage Casablanca.

Tait pulls his wrought iron chair closer to the table and wipes a gallon of sweat off his brow. The waiter asks if he wants a

25

"double." Tait says "yes, a double vodka." He wants to talk about his new life and his new self, much of which is clearly an illusion. He laughs often but the constant tremor of his hands grows more noticeable and his lips tremble when he talks about the loneliness that often assails him when he thinks about the turn his life has taken. Tait appears more philosophical and resigned. He says he believes he is having a spiritual awakening and seems perplexed by this new feeling.

"I'm seeing things differently. I look at people differently. I look for the good in people and don't judge them. Not that I'm anyone to be judging anyone else. There are good people here. I've made friends. They don't care that I used to be someone. I joke with people and tell them 'I use to be someone, a big shot. Now I'm a big shit.'"

He says when he left Windsor he was humiliated, now he's just humble.

"People don't know who I am. They don't care who I am and know nothing about me. I don't have the pressure of living up to the Don Tait image and it feels good. I don't have to live a life of pretence, always trying to prove myself and dealing with that fat, insecure boy inside me."

He insists he is now able to more clearly see the good in people, something he said Brentwood's rehab director Father Paul Charbonneau always told him to do.

"Because of all the bad things in my life it's taken me a long time to realize how good people can be. I want to wind out the rest of my life enjoying people who don't expect you to be anything more than what you are." Tait points to the casino manager as an example. "See him. He's a great guy. Takes care of me."

Alvaro Gonzalez approaches and leads Tait inside the casino, to his favourite spot at the Blackjack table. Tait says he comes for the company and "watches his money." Sometimes he wins several thousand dollars, sometimes he loses. Sometimes, they give him $200 or $300 when he loses because they know he'll be back. With only eight tables and thirty slot machines, a regular stands out, especially one whose flirting days are not behind him.

"Mr. Don is a good man," says Gonzalez. "A very nice man. We look after him."

In many ways this Tait appears to be a nicer person than the one most journalists would remember, but journalists were seldom exposed to the real Tait – they were always shown the slick, sassy, quick-witted lawyer whose life was a cover up. The real Don Tait had friends in Costa Rica he would not have acknowledged in his former life. What is strikingly different is the deference he pays to everyone – from the hotel manager to a hawker in the Plaza Coutura, his favourite spot to watch people. He gives them his time and wholehearted attention. They are people who would not have received a nod from Tait "the star." I do wonder if Tait would continue this persona stone cold sober.

Before Tait makes his first bet, his new friend Ray Petti, a hairdresser from Florida, arrives. They have the easy banter of two men who understand each other. Petti is wearing white pants and a green, short-sleeve Hawaiian shirt. Soon after, Petti's fiancée, Helen Copez, arrives dressed in white Capri pants and a pink cotton pullover with a large boat neck a la American movie star Annette Funicello-style. They decide the little group should visit the national museum across the square.

Tait, ever the charmer, is in his glory. He throws back another double vodka. He laughs and jokes and is obviously at ease with Petti and Copez, two people he admits he would probably not have taken the time to know in his old life. After a tour of the museum Tait, Petti and Copez agree to meet later in the evening in a restaurant on the outskirts of the city. Back at the hotel, Tait perches on a colourful stool on his balcony and gazes across the Plaza Coutura, past the American fast food outlets and points to the Sierra Madre Mountains. They are his favourite topic of conversation. But when his poetic waxing of the mountains wanes, he talks about the pain he has caused and those he believes have betrayed him. The betrayers include people who "went looking for my ties" when he gave away most of his wardrobe before fleeing the country. "Like I was dead."

Tait produces coffee brought to his room by a waiter, sits back and reminisces about the high-flying life he's led. It is certainly a life usually reserved for works of fiction. Even his short stay in Costa Rica has been filled with typical Tait intrigue and over-the-top manoeuvrings. Those, not surprisingly, mostly involved his ex-girlfriend Sandra Martin. With a swashbuckling akin to Errol Flynn, Tait regales his visitors with descriptions of how he risked capture by American and Canadian law enforcement officers, pulling off capers no sane minded person would contemplate. His first tale adds more detail to the story the Windsor cops released about one of his clandestine visits to Windsor.

Just two weeks into his stay in San Jose he wanted to see Martin and used his return ticket on American Airlines to go to Detroit, supposedly on family business. He checked into a Hilton hotel, called Martin and they spent the weekend gambling heavily at the MGM Grand Casino. Tait said good-bye to Martin on Monday and returned to Costa Rica.

Several weeks later on February 11, wanting to see Martin again, he took another flight out of the capital. This time Martin met him at Detroit's Metro airport where he expected to be met by men in uniform with handcuffs at the ready. He is relieved and surprised when the immigration officer returned his passport and allowed him to enter the U.S.

"I went there to tell her I still loved her and wanted to send for her to come to Costa Rica. In spite of everything I wanted her to be happy. I was even picking out an expensive, over the top place for us to have a wedding reception in San Jose. She kept begging me to come to Windsor with her and I kept explaining I had to get back to Costa Rica and I promised to send for her. But she was drinking and threatened to turn me over to Windsor police if I didn't come to Windsor with her."

Her behaviour convinced Tait it was time to really pull the plug on the relationship. Her threat to turn him over to the cops, he says, is the "last straw." Hoping to retrieve expensive jewellery he had given her, he agreed to go to Windsor with her. With his small case, Tait squeezed himself into the trunk of Martin's car and they headed for the border. He was sweating, stinking of alcohol and the temperature was below zero. As they pulled up to the Immigration booth Tait held his breath, praying the officer at the gate wouldn't check the trunk. He heard Martin telling the officer she had been visiting friends and within minutes, undetected by Canada Immigration, she had him across the border.

In the trunk, Tait is relieved but freezing. His swollen, painful legs are killing him. It's February in Canada and he is wearing only a thin suit jacket. The car stops and Tait waits for Martin to let him out. He waits. And waits. He's frustrated but doesn't want to bang on the trunk in case someone hears him. After about five minutes the car starts up again. Then stops. Another five minutes passes. They start moving again and twenty minutes later Martin pulls into the $1,600 a month home he was renting for her in the upscale neighbourhood of Southwood Lakes.

Martin opened the trunk. Tait, with stiffened muscles and skin starting to turn blue, demands to know why it took so long to get from the border and what she was doing when she stopped the car. He is furious when she blithely admits she was hungry and went through the McDonald's drive thru to get a burger. The yelling and screaming continued as they let themselves in to the house.

Despite the angry exchanges, the one thing that united this pair was their drinking and they began to consume copious amounts of wine and vodka, and continued arguing. Tait picked up a large diamond ring, diamond bracelet and necklace and several other pieces of jewellery from Martin's dresser. He tells her he is fed up with her nonsense and is taking the jewellery and leaving. The fighting intensified. By now they were shouting and hitting each other. Tait took a knife from the kitchen drawer.

Martin ran into the bedroom and jumped on the bed. He threatened her and stabbed the knife into the pillow, he says, to "frighten her." In a frenzy, Martin started scratching her neck, face and arms until they bled. She then ran screaming down the driveway to call a neighbour. Tait panicked, grabbed the jewellery and ran from the house. The neighbour called the police and reported that Martin told them Tait had attacked her with a knife and had stolen her jewellery. An All-Points Bulletin was issued for Tait's arrest on charges of assault with a weapon, robbery, threatening and three counts of breaching bail conditions which had been imposed months earlier when he assaulted Martin in a domestic brawl.

In the meantime, Tait, blind drunk and without his jacket, was stumbling along the roadside and fell into a ditch. He crawled along in the dirt until he was able to drag himself out and headed for a nearby gas station where he knew he'd find a payphone. Fumbling in his pocket for a quarter, he called a cab, planning to go to the MGM Casino in Detroit. As they were driving into the downtown area of Windsor towards the border, the cab driver's cell phone rang and judging from the tone of the conversation, Tait realized the driver was being asked to describe his fare. Tait was spooked. He grabbed the cabby's cell phone, told him he had a gun – a lie – ordered him to stop and ran from the cab.

He attempted to get into several downtown bars but was turned away because of his intoxication. He eventually found a bar with a doorman who let him inside. He ordered a vodka and sat and cried. A big Greek guy, around fifty years old, sitting at the bar noticed the pathetic man crying in his vodka and asked if there is anything he can do to help. "Can you take me to Detroit?" The Greek, Sam, a Detroiter, called his ex-wife Marnie, a woman in her late forties, and they agreed to smuggle Tait back across the border, in the trunk of their car.

In Detroit they helped Tait check into a hotel. He was barely able to walk because of his grossly swollen legs, but they managed to get him into his room and did what they could to take care of the hapless lawyer. They helped him undress and get into bed. Over the next three days and nights they worked in shifts. They bathed his legs, keeping cold cloths on them until he is able to walk and the pain from the DTs has settled. On the fifth day Tait took a call on his cell phone from O'Reilly telling him the police were closing in. O'Reilly told his friend to "Get the hell out of there." The ex-wife called her boyfriend who agreed to drive them to the airport in his car – just in case. They run out of the hotel barely half an hour before police turned up at his room. Now sober, Tait figured he had only hours before the cops tracked him down. He was frightened he wouldn't make it out of Detroit this time around.

His good Samaritans took him to Metro airport and there, constantly looking over his shoulder, he purchased a ticket for San Jose. Tait is on edge, fully expecting immigration officials to have his picture, ready to turn him over to police. He couldn't relax until the plane had lifted off and he knew they were out of Detroit air space. He arrived in Costa Rica without detection and still marvels at having pulled off the daring escapade.

In San Jose life resumed pretty much the way it was before he left, with Tait seeking comfort from Jack Daniels and other alcohol stalwarts. With a brain addled by booze, he decided to run yet another risk of being caught or confronted and on March 1, took another flight back to Detroit on "family" business. This time, when he changed planes in Miami, he had an uncanny feeling he was being watched. Maybe, he says, it was just his imagination because he wasn't arrested. He spent a week gambling in Detroit, winning $20,000 at the Blackjack tables. While O'Reilly remembered the incident, Tait has little memory of this visit and no memory at all of O'Reilly finding him on the roof of a hotel near Metro airport.

As O'Reilly arranged to get Tait on a plane back to San Jose, he worried there would be another suicide attempt he won't be around to prevent. O'Reilly refused to discuss details of the incident and how he could cross the border when he was under a ban by U.S. immigration. In a sober moment on the plane, Tait said he wondered how long his luck would hold before he was captured on one of his clandestine visits.

Tait rubs his eyes. The emotion of the interview is tiring. The urgency that was his very existence is gone, replaced by a worn body and tired mind, wanting a quiet place to hide. He grows restless and decides to take his guests on a tour of his favourite areas of San Jose. He calls a cab and we set off, driving through crowded streets, with Tait providing a docent-like commentary on the state of the economy, the social structure, the country's lack of a military, the city and country history and politics.

After a brief visit to one of his friend's homes - a well-appointed apartment in a middle-class neighbourhood - he gave the cabby the address of the restaurant in an upscale neighbourhood where Petti and Copez were waiting. Out on a patio surrounded by lush vegetation under a moonlit sky, Petti and Copez once again greeted Tait like a long lost, beloved relative. Tait ordered a double vodka. He appears happy and at ease. There's no pressure. No one is gushing over the great Don Tait. He insists on ordering for his media guests. He eats quickly. During a period when his friends are speaking in Spanish, Tait again talks about the regrets in his life. He says he accepts responsibility for everything he's done and wishes he could fix it.

The hurt feelings, regrets, loneliness and fear of the future all come tumbling out in a torrent of recriminations and tears from a man struggling to hold his life together. He insists he can fix his life if he stays in Costa Rica. He says he plans to stop smoking and go to English speaking AA meetings. On that note he orders another double. He often makes joking comments about his lost libido, trying to make light of something that clearly bothers him considerably. Tait dries his eyes and wipes the teardrops off his hand. Seeing his distress, his friends hug and reassure him. In spite of his fears, the redoubtable Tait is soon laughing and talking with people at other tables. The kind words, the charm and the Tait smile serve as magnets. He's always reaching out. The fat little boy of his childhood, wanting to be liked.

Several more rounds, a final double vodka and Tait was ready to go home. It had been an emotional day and he was tired. There were still so many questions I wanted to ask but it was clear he was in no condition to be persuaded. His friends agreed to take him back to his hotel. Before he leaves, Tait takes my hand. "I trust you," he says, giving me a half-hearted hug. I tell him to call me if he survives, just in case he'd be willing to let me write the story of his life. He smiles. I watch him walk away on legs now so swollen he drags them along like dead weights. It's a pitiful sight.

I stared at the retreating cab and smiled at the thought that this broken, almost seedy Don Tait is probably more likeable than the arrogant, ego-driven sex symbol who lived the kind of life most mortals only dream about, but one so filled with unbelievable tales it reads like fiction. The following morning, I was off to Canada to write a story that would be read by people across the country and bring me national job offers and newspaper awards. There's a strange relief that there was never a sexual attraction between us but there's an equally strange premonition that our paths will continue to cross.

Flying home, despite being focused on the great scoop I was about to unleash, I couldn't help but wonder about the story that wasn't being told. The story about who Don Tait really was and what in his life had shaped him into the man everyone thought they knew.

THE EARLY YEARS

Fredericton, New Brunswick

January 1943

DON TAIT WAS PUSHED kicking and screaming into the world on a sub-zero morning January 11, 1943 as death and destruction caused by a World War, consumed people around the globe. Little did Dorothy Emma Hawkins Tait know her son would lead a life that was to leave an indelible mark on his chosen profession, the women in his life, his children and a legion of addicts who would encounter him through the course of his own addictions.

But this was a time to celebrate. Dorothy took her small son home to her parents' comfortable house in the small community of Nashwaaksis on the east bank of the Saint John River just outside Fredericton in the province of New Brunswick. Tait's father was stationed with the army in Petawawa, Ontario on officer training duty.

Dorothy adored her curly haired boy who could have given the Gerber baby a challenge. The bond they formed from the time of his birth was to last until her death in 1985. Don Tait was an admitted momma's boy and dearly loved this tall, slender woman with the long dark wavy hair reminiscent of starlets in post-war Hollywood movies. She was vivacious and fun loving, liked by everyone. During Tait's early childhood years his father was away most of the time working in Quebec on construction sites, so he and his mother lived with her parents in their home on the edge of a forest in Naskwaaksis, and on the banks of the Nashwaak River where his grandfather operated a sawmill. James Hilton Hawkins was a wealthy man whose family lived well for the times and even though he lost money in the stock market crash of 1929, and subsequent depression, Tait said his grandfather always "did ok."

Their two-storey wooden home had been built by his grandfather between 1895 and 1900. Sitting on a large stone basement, the first floor was surrounded by a veranda held up by large round columns and fancy wooden rails. Inside, there were two kitchens - one for summer and one for winter. The winter kitchen was heated by a large wood stove. In the big pantry, his grandmother kept stores of household staples. She filled huge wooden bins with flour, potatoes and other root vegetables to last through the winter months. Large quantities were required because everything they ate was made from scratch. The main feature in the living room was a floor-standing radio with brass knobs and it was there the family gathered in the evening to listen to music, comedy shows and news reports from journalists and politicians about the war.

Their life with luxuries included being the first family in the area to own a car and they had a new Packard every year. They were also the first to boast an indoor toilet when everyone else still used outhouses.

The front entrance foyer was home to the old-fashioned ringer telephone and led into the sitting room. It was also where his grandmother would herd the family during lighting storms. They would sit without speaking in the darkened room, all wearing rubber boots. This ritual was adopted after her brother was struck and killed by lightning while sitting in their kitchen and no amount of persuasion could make her do otherwise.

Upstairs had three bedrooms, a sewing room, bathroom and lounge area. His grandparents slept in separate bedrooms and Tait was allowed to sleep with his grandmother. The house overlooked a creek where his grandfather had built a dam, creating a natural pool where they could swim. The dam was used to produce hydroelectric power to light their home. They fished and went hunting with BB guns in the nearby forest. For Tait it was a child's Shangri-La.

It was also the place where he took his first drink. One afternoon his grandparents and mother found him flush faced. As they were trying to figure out what might be wrong, he passed out. The family doctor arrived and pronounced the three-year-old Tait drunk. They found an empty quart container of beer in the pantry. He had consumed it all. It could be considered an omen for what was yet to come. But life with his grandparents was everything a small boy could want. Tait remembers: "It was idyllic. My life was perfect. They were extremely loving to me and I had lots of friends to play with. We played hockey on the creek in winter and spent hours in the forest. It was a fantastic time in my life."

And it was also here, many years before, in 1919 his mother Dorothy Hawkins was born. In high school she was attractive and popular. She preferred dancing to scholarship, but managed to graduate, albeit last in her class. She had no ambition other than as a wife and mother. She dated many suitors, but only those who were prosperous and up and coming from well to do families in Fredericton. It is important to note that there were no alcoholics in the Hawkins clan.

While Dorothy made her son feel safe and loved, he also felt safe in the arms of his tall, muscular, athletic father, Rayfield MacDonald Tait who, ironically, would also be the cause of Tait's problems with self-esteem and his image. Tait says, however, that although he always felt his father was disappointed in him, it was never something his father expressed and Tait admits that his perceptions of filial disapproval probably stemmed from his own insecurities.

Rayfield (who was always called Don) was scouted by the Montreal Maroons NHL franchise hockey team while he was captain of the Fredericton Capitals. "Tiger Tait" did everything well, including playing rugby, baseball and football, which earned him the Tiger moniker. His wife pronounced it Tagger and always called him Tag. Born in 1916, he was smart and did well in school. He was a handsome man about town and dapper - owning 25 tailor-made suits –

all of which his brother Bill sold while Ray was fighting in WWII.

Ray was popular, sang in the church choir and was studying Engineering at the University of New Brunswick when war was declared in Europe. He enlisted in 1942 and was sent overseas to England as a private and rose to the rank of lieutenant. While overseas he won the Middleweight Boxing Championship in the Canadian Army. He returned to Canada, received more training at military bases in Kingston and Petawawa and was promoted to captain. Throughout the rest of the war he was stationed in Brockville, Ontario.

Ray's father had died when he was only seven years old. The head of the Tait clan had been a hardworking, easy going man who was well respected in town. His death did not cause financial hardship because his widow, Cassie Forbes, came from a wealthy family. As the only sister of John and Roy Forbes who owned the Forbes & Sloat Construction Company, they made sure she and her three children were well looked after. Their great-grandfather Forbes, considered a hellion and a drunk, had been sent packing from Scotland to North America with a pension on condition he never return to Scotland. The great-grandsons, John and Roy, were both drunks. Ray was a drunk and the gene would be passed to Ray's son Don.

Ray was John Forbes' favourite and the one in line to take over the business. Brother Bill, the youngest, was a lazy drunk who was always in trouble and as an adult died from diseases caused by his alcoholism. However, Ray's older brother Mac was jealous of Ray's favoured status with uncle John and wanted to be first in line to inherit. Ray began working for Forbes & Sloat and for several years things were going well. Tait recalls a sense of excitement in the air every time his father returned home from a construction job. There were special treats and some of the most memorable were the rides Ray and the train engineer would take him on, travelling from St. John to Fredericton. They went to parties and the future seemed to be set on a predictable, positive path.

However, Ray's early promise for success was never to be realized. John, for some unknown and never understood reason, did not approve of Ray's marriage to Dorothy Hawkins, even though they were of equal social and financial status. In 1951 the two self-willed, stubborn alcoholics became embroiled in a bitter quarrel. Neither would back down nor apologize and John cut Ray out of the company. They never spoke again for the rest of their lives. It was a decision that changed the course of Ray and Dorothy's life and certainly the life of their young son, Don.

Ray and Dorothy had married at the Hawkins' home in 1942. Dorothy wrote in her dairy she had married her dream man.

"The day I always dreamed about has finally arrived. And the most wonderful part of it all is that I am not just marrying anyone, I am marrying the only person I will ever want, the only person I will ever love, Tager, all my Tager now."

In the early years of their marriage Tait's parents were happy and in love with never a cross word between them. During that time the young Tait felt happy, safe and loved. However, once Ray left Forbes he began moving around Eastern Canada from one construction job to another - to wherever he could find work. He was always away, always drinking and never able to achieve his potential because he could never get sober. Life became a financial rollercoaster, to say nothing of the emotional turmoil that comes from having a drunk for a husband and father.

The carefree pleasures Tait experienced while living with his grandparents were gone. His parents were constantly fighting and his dad would be physically abusive. Yet, despite their volatile relationship Dorothy remained loyal and loving. They would have huge fights but she would also comfort, encourage and support him.

"I often think the Tammy Wynette song 'Stand By Your Man'

was written about my mom," Tait often said. The Taits moved from their idyllic life in Naskwaaksis to an apartment building in St. John. Tait hated their new home.

"It was a brick post war building built on a rock. There were no trees and it was bleak. St. John was always foggy and I hated it. I missed my Grammie. Everything that was familiar to me was now gone."

On Tait's first day in grade one at St. John Public School in September, 1949 he was afraid and didn't want to go so his mother walked with him every morning until he would walk alone. Then, in March, 1950, before the end of grade one, Ray moved them to Amherst, Nova Scotia where Tait entered Amherst Public School and completed first grade. A photo of him with his father standing in front of their house in Amherst shows Tait was beginning to get fat. In the summer of 1950 they moved again, but this time it was back to Naskwaaksis. Tait was overjoyed to be home with his grandparents and friends.

"It was just like before. Dad had taken a job in Seven Islands, Quebec as a construction superintendent for a railway that was being built and was gone for months."

Tait started grade two in Naskwaaksis. His mother spent many hours helping him with school work and encouraged his learning. She taught him about Mexico and how to spell and pronounce the name of a particular volcano – Popocatepetl. The memory of it is so clear he has never forgotten the name or the spelling. He did exceedingly well, standing first, second and third in his classes. In September 1951 he started grade three and within weeks his perfect life was shattered yet again. His father announced he had taken a job in Niagara Falls and would be moving Tait and his mother there after Christmas. He was working on a hydro project that was going to take years to complete and wanted his family with him. Tait begged them to let him stay with his grandparents. But in late December he and his mother stepped off the train at Union Station in Toronto.

"I remember clearly stepping out at Union Station and looking up at the Royal York Hotel. It was the biggest building I'd ever seen and I felt very tiny, very alone and very afraid. This wasn't just a different place, this seemed like a different world. Another school to get enrolled in, new teacher, new classmates. I was terrified."

He started school in January in Niagara Falls at the Kitchener Street Public School and it didn't take long for cruel kids to begin chanting "Fatty fatty two by four couldn't get through the bathroom door so he did it on the floor." He often wept, wanting so badly to be back with his friends in New Brunswick. His new home didn't help. It turned out to be a renovated attic in an old house in a rundown area of town. Tait remembers it as a "terrible, disgusting place," next door to the Nabisco Shredded Wheat factory. He longed to roam through the forest of his grandparents' place where he felt safe. The move didn't appear to be making his parents any happier either and they were fighting more often than they were civil to each other.

The taunting about his being fat was also creating a deep pain and insecurity that made his young life miserable. It was so profoundly wounding it was to affect him throughout his adult life, causing an obsession about his body and keeping it in rock hard shape. Labelled a "fat kid" he became hyper sensitive and paranoid about what people might be saying about him, suspecting everyone who crossed his path of ridicule.

"One day I was walking home from school and there were a couple of men sitting on a porch and as I passed they started laughing and I was convinced they were laughing at me. It was a horrible feeling. I was alone. I had no friends and I wanted to get out of that place."

His mother consoled him and told her son he was better than the bullies who taunted him, but, for a young boy with a poor self-image, it didn't assuage his feelings of hurt and self-disgust. And, more than sixty years later, the memory of how he felt during those times is still vibrantly clear. It may have

40

helped, he says, if he had a father who acted like a normal dad. However, when his father came home, except for an odd time when there was peace in the home and it felt like a normal family, there was constant chaos. Ray's alcoholism was getting worse. He would make empty promises he would not or could not keep. His temper always got the better of him and the fighting would start. The young Tait would often blame his mother for causing the fights.

"When he would start I'd beg mom not to say anything. I couldn't stand the fighting and would hide under the bed. Then I'd blame her for causing it because she would get angry and egg him on. I reasoned that if she didn't say anything he would stop."

Although his father had a violent and explosive temper he never struck his son. But while he was not physically abused, Tait suffered the abuse that comes with living in an alcoholic home. To cope, Tait used to dream about the kind of home he so desperately yearned for and when they moved to St. Catherines, Ontario several months later, he found one not far from where he lived. Visiting it became a ritual he kept hidden from his parents.

SAD BOY

As DUSK FALLS ON the Carleton Street neighbourhood in St. Catharines, a sad little boy crawls out from under his bed where he goes to hide from the raised voices, drunken violence and chaos that constantly surround him. He pretends to disappear.

Then, as if drawn by a magnet, he pulls a sweater over his chubby body and quietly leaves the house. Taking his bike from its perch in the yard, he pedals along the street until he sees it. It is his favourite place, even though coming here also makes him sad. The 1950s style home made of stained wood is surrounded by a perfectly cut lawn but most importantly, it has a big picture window. He always comes here at this time of day because he knows they will all be sitting down to dinner. He can see the mother and father and two children. They are his perfect fantasy family, behaving to each other the way he longs for at home. He watches as they pass dishes across the table to one another. He imagines they are being kind and funny and telling stories, not yelling or screaming or accusing each other the way his parents do whenever they sit down for a meal.

"I would stop on the road outside this home and hide behind a tree. I could see the family sitting at the dining table. They would be talking and laughing. I had no brothers or sisters and in a strange way it made me feel good. But then, I would go back to my dysfunctional home with a thirst for something I couldn't have. In some ways it was a torture for me but I couldn't help myself. I wanted what they had so badly," Tait remembers.

Tait's parents moved to St. Catharines from Niagara Falls in the summer of 1952 and lived there until 1965. Tait was enrolled in yet another elementary school, this time at

Maplewood School in Lincoln County. Christmas 1954 was one of the saddest of his life. He was devastated by news of his grandmother's death from a stroke. He was ten and old enough to understand that life for him would never be the same again. While his grandmother lived he could dream of one day going back to live with her. But now, the only stable force in his ever-shifting life was gone forever.

The turmoil in his life was having a deteriorating effect on his school work and the low marks he was getting were in stark contrast to the success he achieved when attending school in Naskwaaksis. Because his father's drinking continued out of control and he couldn't keep a job, they were always broke. His mother, who never knew from one week to the next if they would have money coming in, had to constantly borrow from finance companies to help pay the bills.

One company, Niagara Finance, was always calling because they had not made payments. When his mother could afford to put money on a loan she would send Tait on his bike to take payments into the finance office. The payments were more regular once she got a job as a salesperson in the basement of the T. Eaton Company.

"Life was just tough and they saw their dreams disintegrating. She'd complain and he'd get violent but she never once considered leaving him. She hung in 'till the very end of her life."

His father was Dr. Jekyll and Mr. Hyde – not unusual in an alcoholic. During times when he was sober he was optimistic, hope was high and things would be good for a while. But it never lasted more than a month or two.

"I never hated him. It was worse. I was ashamed of him and his hard drinking and because people had started talking about him. It was starting to show on him and my mom."

Dorothy became pregnant and at eight months developed severe toxaemia which caused her to suffer a miscarriage. Ray was away working and at a time when she needed emotional support, needed her Tager, Dorothy suffered alone. Tait was twelve years old and would have had a baby brother named James. Without the constant presence of a father figure, Tait was grateful for the kindness of strangers. Their apartment building was owned by Stan Syzmanski, a Polish man who had two sons - Walter, 18, and Eugene, 20, who was attending the University of Western Ontario.

The Syzmanski family also owned a convenience store and a large fruit orchard. Walter taught Tait, then nine years old, how to drive the tractor. The workers called him "killer Tait" and the nickname stuck until he was around twelve. The men filled the roles of big brother and father. When a new Olympic size swimming pool was built in town in 1954, Tait landed a job as locker attendant and during the next six years obtained his senior lifesaver certification and the bronze and silver medallion with the Royal Lifesaving Society. He taught swimming to youngsters in the mornings and on weekends, worked as locker room attendant in the afternoons and evenings and eventually became a lifeguard and swimming instructor. Because Tait never felt good about himself, he began to blame himself for what was going on in the family. He would ask himself "What's wrong with me? What can I do to be more of what my dad wants me to be? Maybe if I could be that, it would make things better."

But his father never asked him to be anything. When he played hockey his father told him he was an "OK" player but came to watch fewer than half a dozen games. That was just fine because his son never wanted him there because the extra flesh hanging over his bones fed his insecurity and didn't make him feel "OK." He just felt like a fat boy and a bit of a loser. His increased sports activity, however, began to pay off when he began to slowly shed the fat from his young body. At 13, trying to overcome his crippling shyness, he pretended he was cool. He idolized James Dean and Elvis Presley and attempted to look like them by copying their hair style and wearing a "rebel look" jacket.

44

He would ultimately lose his "fat boy" status, but unlike most children who are able to move on from the distresses of childhood, for Tait the scars were to last a lifetime. That "fat little fucker" as Tait still refers to him, would be a lifelong companion, always there in moments of triumph and depression. No one knew that every triumph he was to experience was accompanied by an acute wave of fear of failure. This type of scenario would become all too common, even in later years when he was at the top of his profession:

After a gruelling court case where he performed brilliantly for his client and emerged victorious, Tait would strut into Plunkett's Bar and Grill on Chatham Street in Windsor, Ontario awash in accolades from several dozen legal types, fawning women and hangers-on gathered for their post court libations. As he downed his first vodka and savoured victory, the "fat boy with a pitchfork" would whisper "You're a fraud, you're not as great as you think you are. They'll all find out you're a fraud." Only the rest of a forty-ouncer would quell the psychological berating, help him focus and make him feel like he was king of the world. Now, he was in charge. The taunting devil was gone. Until next time.

Tait entered Linwell High School and hated grade nine. Besides the normal angst of eighth graders who suddenly find themselves at the bottom of the heap – following a year on top of the heap – Tait wasn't popular and the cute girls in grade nine were interested in cute boys in grades eleven and twelve. But on a positive note, he says, he was no longer obese. Self-conscious but not obese.

At fourteen he joined the air cadets and won a scholarship which paid for flying lessons that allowed him to get his pilot's licence. He wanted to join the Canadian Air Force so that he could get another four years of instruction and experience in order to become a commercial airline pilot, but was dissuaded by his mother who wanted him to go to university. In high school his insecurities saw him hanging out with the kind of kids most parents tell their teenagers to stay away from but

Tait was drawn to their bravado, don't give a damn attitude.

"I knew I could be accepted with them. The other types, the Ivy Leaguers, came from good homes in better areas of town. They came from happy, well-adjusted parents who obviously had good incomes. I knew they were better than I was and there would be no point in attempting to invade their territory."

He managed to pass grade nine with grades in the low 70s but ended up in a grade 10A class with all the brightest students - those Ivy Leaguers. He adopted a rebellious attitude and dress to hide his insecurity and fear, and became a troublemaker. Mimicking other rebellious students he began slouching in his seat, keeping his foot in the aisle, not paying attention, not handing in homework and skipping the odd day of school.

One day, as a joke, his buddies from shop division - the hard rocks - dared him to run for class representative on student council and to the dismay of his principal he was elected. Realizing the council was nothing more than a rubber stamp for the administration, he played his favourite character, James Dean, and began refusing to agree to suggestions from the teacher-counsellor. Whether they were suggestions about holding activities or becoming more involved in school affairs, he would "show attitude" and ignore her.

Tait wanted to learn to drive but his mother wanted him to wait until his father came home. However, there was no telling when his father would be home and Tait was impatient. He began sneaking the car out of the garage without telling his mother. He practiced his driving for a few weeks, took the test and passed. His licence soon made him a popular guy. During the day when his mother was busy helping customers at the Eaton store, Tait would pick up girls who wanted a ride to school. They would smoke and chatter as they enjoyed Tait's free taxi service. He felt like a king. The parents of his female classmates were delighted with the Tait boy who was driving their precious cargo to and from school each day. One had the temerity to compliment Dorothy on the qualities of her "sweet boy," extolling the virtues of a teenage boy who was "so nice" about picking up her daughter every morning and driving her and her friends to school. It was a revelation to his mother.

Tait's first sexual experience came when he was fifteen. It wasn't a romantic romp but something he shared with several of his buddies when they were on their way home from a hunting trip. They stopped to pick up a pretty hitchhiker who turned out to be a lusty young woman who had run away from home. She told the boys she was more than willing to satisfy the sexual urgings of awkward teenage boys and accompanied them to an apartment where they all became sexually acquainted.

She had no place to stay that night so Tait told her she could sleep in his car. They drove back to Tait's house, parked the car and the young woman bedded down in the back seat. Tait had a restless night and "couldn't wait to get at her" in the morning. He did and she hit the road. Two days later Tait felt an itch that crept through his groin like a cuddle with a porcupine. The doctor called it crabs. It would be an unforgettable first sexual encounter.

AN ALCOHOLIC IS BORN

ONE OF THE MOST SEMINAL events in Tait's life happened
the year he was in grade ten. Tait and his pals liked to turn up
at school dances "acting tough" in black leather jackets, low
wellington boots and GWG jeans. It was a typical teenage
dance where girls lined up along one wall in the gym and boys
on the other. He would watch as one guy after another
screwed up courage and ventured across the floor in
expectation. And continued watching as the question "wanna
dance" came tumbling out. Silence. Then the big rejection and
the return walk of shame and humiliation. Even though there
were twins he wanted to ask to dance, Tait was determined it
would never be his fate to be shot down so publicly.

"I said there would be no way I was going to get rejected like
that. So, I never danced. I was actually scared to death,
insecure and afraid and convinced I didn't really measure up.
I certainly didn't measure up to my father when he was young.
I was no athlete. I was no lady killer and not much of a fighter."

However, things were about to change. One night before a
dance, his friend Roy Zaluski, who lived across the street, stole
a bottle of whisky from his father's liquor cabinet. Prior to this
Tait had tried beer but had never felt the effects of alcohol.

"Roy and I went out into the parking lot with two bottles of
coke. We threw out half and filled the bottles up with whiskey.
We probably had five or six ounces each. Roy got really sick
and started vomiting. Not me. I had a personality change. In
that moment my genetics from my alcoholic father kicked in
and magic happened. It was the beginning of a new me. It was
the day I started my life as an alcoholic."

Pumped and fearless, Tait marched into the dance, cock-
walked around the gym a couple of times, spotted the twins

across the room, boldly walked over and asked one of them to dance. She said "yes." Not only did she dance with him the rest of the night, she let him walk her home.

"Alcohol took away all my fears and inhibitions. My friend Roy was obviously not an alcoholic because it didn't change his life, but for me, I had found my solution to fear and insecurity. Alcohol allowed me to do all the things I was afraid to do. It was a magical solution."

When Tait drank he became the antithesis of that scared little boy who haunted him. Later in his life, in Moot courts or jury trials, Tait knew exactly what he had to do to perform. In a jury trial he would go to the Top Hat Supper Club on University Avenue in Windsor, sink three double vodkas and a beer chaser and was "ready to kick ass." Alcohol, he determined, just as it did that night at the dance, not only took away fear and insecurity, it also allowed him to be successful.

Tait and his friends, all age sixteen, started going to bars twenty minutes away in Niagara Falls, New York, where the drinking age was eighteen. He also started going to other dances, particularly at the United Autoworkers Hall where he would get in fights – always "full of booze." He and the pretty twin he'd asked to dance in the school gym went dancing several weeks later at a club on the outskirts of Buffalo. Driving home in his father's '52 Chevy "under the influence," he drove off the road and the car flipped over on its side. When help arrived, the drunk teens were unhurt and "making out" under the car. That was the end of the relationship.

The second girl he took to bed – well, to his parents' couch – also caused him some discomfort of a different sort than the porcupine variety. She was Carolyn, a nice girl whose father was an industrial lawyer and who lived in a house in the swank area of Niagara-on-the-Lake. Her older sister was married to NHL star Bobby Hull. In the middle of one lusty encounter in the family room his father walked in, took one look, turned and walked out. He never mentioned the intrusion to Tait. This was the second of Tait's five sexual encounters during high school.

Surprising, some might say, for a man who was to become known for bedding hundreds of women, so many he would say years later, that he "lost count."

Tait did not ease gently in or out of high school. During his first attempt at grade eleven in 1959 he missed sixty-five school days. The principal refused to allow him to write exams because of the missed days and the fact he had written several dozen false notes from his father excusing his absence from school.

He wasn't a tough guy but, because he wanted to be, he continued to hang around with the local tough guys who always seemed to be having fun. He was scared to death of them most of the time but never backed down from a fight. All of which he lost. The tough guys liked his attitude and eventually stopped beating him up. They liked him so much they even included him in their crime sprees.

That got him arrested, along with three of his tough guy friends, after they broke into a clothing store and nicked a "whole lot" of men's clothing. They spent the night in jail and were charged with breaking and entering. His friends' parents hired criminal lawyers who understood how to deal with such cases. Tait's mother got him a corporate lawyer. He pleaded guilty and was placed on 18 months' probation. There is no record of his arrest.

Not surprisingly, he was eventually expelled. Not that it bothered him. He was fed up and wanted to quit school but his mother was determined her only son would get an education and make something of himself. Despite their near poverty status, she found the $25 a month to send him to St. Catharines Collegiate the following September. Had they lived on the opposite side of Carleton Street he would have gone to the school free of charge. Tait had now developed an interest in only one career – being an airline pilot.

Tait fell in love for the first time with Mary Lou, a stunner who was dating a university student. He met her at St. Catherines Collegiate where they were both repeating grade 11, but Don could never understand why someone as smart as Mary Lou had failed. His academic performance had deteriorated from being an A student in grade nine and ten, to a C student by grade eleven. They would pass notes in school, go to the movies together and Tait took her flying – but not to bed. He was madly infatuated with Mary Lou and although they kept in touch for a time when he was at university, it ended when he met the girl he would eventually marry.

"We never had sex but I was like a boy in love and I think it was what I thought was a deep love. I'll never forget the feeling I would get every time I dropped her off. She would go to the window to watch me leave and wave at me. It was just something she did and I can still remember how that made me feel."

After graduation from SCCI and Vocational School, Tait was not interested in more education but his mother remained adamant he was getting a university education. He agreed to go to university to please her but never wavered from his dream of flying. In 1962 he entered the science program at the University of New Brunswick and hated it. Chemistry was fine but the math taught in New Brunswick was at a higher level than in Ontario and it was killing him. He dropped science and entered the second year of a four-year honours arts program.

Tait was exceptionally poor and rarely had money for cigarettes. Outside lecture theatres there were ashtrays filled with sand where students would quickly butt their partially smoked cigarettes before going to class. After school, Tait would take a bag and collect the longest butts. He took them back to his room in residence, removed the tobacco, placed it onto a long paper and rolled cigarettes with a cigarette maker.

It was not lost on Tait that his station in life was a stark contrast to some of his classmates who included John Bassett, the son of a newspaper baron and Thor Eaton whose father headed Canada's powerful T. Eaton family.

"They had some wild parties. One of the frat parties was a Pig Party. It seems terrible now, but it's what happened in the sixties. You had to bring an ugly girl and have sex with her at the party and there was a prize for the guy who brought the ugliest girl. I had sex on the floor with the girl I brought and she was eating an apple through the whole thing. There was a lot of drinking at those parties, but no drugs."

In February 1963 Tait and several university buddies went to a high school dance to check out the girls. They cut fine figures in their red leather UNB jackets and the high schoolers were suitably impressed with the older, cool guys. Tait took a shining to a petite, attractive blond who was standing around with her friends. He walked up to 17-year-old Brenda Atcheson and asked her to dance.

They began dating and were soon going steady. Like most teenagers of the day they were doing some heavy petting under cover of darkness, particularly in a parked car. But, as anyone who has tried it knows, the contortions required are not conducive to romantic sex. One afternoon when Brenda's parents weren't home, she took him to the unoccupied basement apartment in their house. There was something about sneaking into the apartment that added to the excitement of their romp.

Being more satisfying than the car, the basement became their frequent meeting place. Almost every evening after supper, as soon as she could escape her parents, Brenda would sneak down into the empty apartment, open the basement window and Tait would slither in for a few hours of pleasure. They weren't always quiet in their pleasure pursuits and one night, as they were enjoying lustily loud sex, Brenda's mother came to see what the noise was all about. Panicking, Tait hurried to get into his hastily discarded pants while listening to a bombardment of screaming condemnations. He was unceremoniously ordered out of the house.

What Tait didn't know was that several years earlier, Brenda had been sent to a home for unwed mothers in Nova Scotia to take care of an unwanted pregnancy. Her parents did not want the shame of a daughter giving birth out of wedlock. It was what many parents did in those days, especially those who lived in small towns. Tait was amused to discover a close connection to Brenda's pregnancy. "The irony of this is that the father of Brenda's child was Bill Tait who was my first cousin. So, I was actually related to Brenda's child." Tait and Brenda continued to sneak around. They were having too much fun to give up on sex.

In the summer of 1963, a year after he started school at UNB, Tait went home to St. Catharines to work for $50 a week in the local graveyard. His job included measuring and digging graves, cutting grass and helping with funerals. Several weeks into the job, he was grateful to get a call to work in the local paper mill for union wages – as much as four times the money he made in the graveyard. Tait had to earn money to pay his tuition, since it was the only way he could afford to finish university. After long gruelling hours in a factory he had to go home where his parents were still constantly at war with each other. He wanted to get away from them and he missed Brenda, whom he had not seen for several months.

Boarding a train one Friday after work he set out for New Brunswick. Once there he borrowed a friend's '53 Chevy Bellaire and he and Brenda went to McLeod's Hill, parked and there, on the back seat of the Chevy, conceived their daughter Barbara. Tait returned to Ontario and before the end of summer Brenda called. She was pregnant. She said her mother gave her turpentine and wanted her to drink it to abort the baby. She declined the offer.

"Her mother was an unpleasant and extremely controlling

53

woman who controlled her father Tom who was an art teacher. I couldn't believe she was willing to give that kind of shit to her daughter. It could have killed her. But I guess she was still pretty mad about the first pregnancy."

The best option and right thing to do, Tait reckoned, was to get married. In late August 1963, just before the beginning of the school year, they were married. He was twenty and Brenda seventeen. Tait wore a dark suit and tie with a white shirt and Brenda a white summer frock that wasn't a wedding dress. About ten people attended the event – all friends of Tait's parents. Brenda's parents stayed home. The young couple spent their honeymoon weekend in Niagara Falls and returned to New Brunswick where they spent the next three years living Brenda's parents' basement apartment – a place they were more than familiar with.

On November 22, the day U.S. President John F. Kennedy was shot and killed in Dallas, Texas, Tait smashed up his 1950 Monarch and luckily escaped injury. He replaced it with a Volkswagen he would drive until it disintegrated under him. Brenda went into labour in February,1964. Tait drove her to the hospital and stayed to support his young wife. Despite the shotgun wedding caused by the pregnancy he welcomed the arrival of their new daughter.

"Barbara was such a beautiful baby and even though I had not planned to be a father yet, I didn't feel trapped. I was excited actually. In the end it turned out to be a terrible marriage, but it wasn't surprising because we were babies ourselves in many ways and unfortunately, when we grew up we grew apart."

Summers, when the young couple lived at the Tait home, were not pleasant for Brenda because she and Tait's mother did not get along. She was resentful of the bond they shared. She took to drawing cartoons of Tait's mother holding up a chain that was secured around her son's neck. That relationship was one of the few things the young couple argued about in the early and later days of their marriage. Tait worked hard during the summers between semesters at UNB. His father, a superintendent, got him a job on a construction crew building the Skylon Tower in Niagara Falls in 1964 and the following summer he worked in the paper mill in Thorold, earning enough money to pay their bills and save tuition money.

In 1966, following graduation with a four-year BA in history and economics, his flying obsession still front and centre, he applied to become a pilot with United Airlines at a time when they were getting rid of their propeller planes and wanted to make their jet fleet the biggest in the world. Tait saw an ad in a magazine asking people to write aptitude tests to determine if they were pilot material. Tait drove from Fredericton to Boston to write the first series of exams for UA and success there led to a trip to New York for a final set of exams which he also passed. Then came the news he was waiting to hear - he was to go to Denver, Colorado in late 1966 to train as the third person in the cockpit. Tait could hardly believe his good luck. He would be flying from Denver to LA and Hawaii. He started studying for his commercial pilot's licence.

While Tait was riding the high of seeing his dream of wearing a pilot's uniform close enough to grasp, politics in the United States would make the joy short lived. Because men in the U.S. were being drafted and sent to the war that was raging in Vietnam, there was a shortage of workers. Thousands of men from across the globe were flocking there and had no trouble getting work permits. But complaints had started from a number of quarters that veterans returning home were not able to find work because jobs were being taken by foreigners. A new law, supported by then President Lyndon Johnson, decreed that anyone living in the U.S. with a work permit would be subject to the draft. Accept the draft or be deported.

In August 1966 United Airlines sent Tait a "Dear John" letter telling him they did not want to spend huge money training him with the spectre of the draft hanging over his head. They put his application on file. Just as his dream was about to come true, it was blown to pieces.   It was a devastating disappointment but Tait, with the optimism of youth, believed it would be only a matter of time before the war was over and he was called back. He went to work with his father as a labourer on a construction site in Kitchener, Ontario. He had a degree and no plans.

One evening while drinking with several buddies from Guelph, Ontario, they told him they were going to law school. Because he had no plans he decided to apply to law school himself to "kill time." He applied to three well respected Ontario universities – Queen's, University of Toronto and the University of Western Ontario in London. He was accepted by all three but chose Western. Still figuring the Vietnam War would soon end he thought he would wait it out in law school. He had no interest in becoming a lawyer, none whatsoever.

He checked the mail every day, waiting, and picturing himself in a United Airlines uniform. He needed something to brag about because he was still living in the athletic shadow of his father.

No call came from United and he was beginning to accept that it never would. He relinquished the dream and moved his family to London where they rented a small, cheap one-bedroom apartment on Richmond Street. A year later they moved into a two-bedroom apartment on Oxford Street where they lived until after his bar admission exams.

Tait was now making great money working at London Raceway as an odds calculator for American Totalizator. He worked the evening race card calculating bets and posting them on the boards. His daily pay for three to four hours of work was $100 – a princely sum in those days. During the summer months he worked on construction sites with his father and at American Totalizator in the evening. Brenda worked in the university library where she was making her own friends. They were getting along but a distinct rift was developing between them.

"Brenda appeared to be coming unglued – emotionally and mentally. She wasn't a particularly good wife or mother and had become bitter and nasty. We had a lot of friends and we partied with couples. Marijuana was becoming part of the party scene along with the drinking."

Tait was also becoming a "miserable son-of-a-bitch" of a husband and mistreated Brenda shamefully. "I blamed her for a lot of things, anything that went wrong. I constantly put her down and fucked around on her."

Women had discovered Tait's assets and, fuelled with liquid courage, he was not refusing their advances. "When I went out with the boys I had no intention of seeing any particular woman, but there was always a woman available. It was the times and it was there for the taking. Woman thought nothing about asking if you wanted to go outside to fuck, even women you knew for 10 minutes. It was a very different time."

While he portrayed an image of a man of bravado, he was haunted by feelings of inadequacy and low self-esteem. So that people would not know how hard he studied, he became fanatically organized. He would study hard, learning what he needed to know to get consistently high marks then head to the CPR hotel (The Ceeps) where university students drank. He had to always be proving himself and needed the praise that came with classmates being amazed he could get such high marks and still party hard. At the Ceeps they would lay bets on how much he could drink in a short period of time – getting plastered on 12 shots of whiskey downed in 15 seconds. But he was young and his liver still relatively new.

His lust for life, particularly the part that included alcohol and women, lured him to hard drinking parties with fellow law students who had no idea their party buddy Tait was a closet hard-working student. He had become ambitious and realized he was good at law and consistently at the top of his class. But trouble was on the horizon. One night Brenda became disoriented and dizzy and couldn't walk properly. The symptoms disappeared but it would be an omen of serious health problems to come.

LEGAL WIN AND SEXY PAYOFF

TAIT WON MANY PRIZES in law school for standing first in many of his corporate, tax and evidence classes. His dream now was to become a corporate commercial lawyer. He had offers from several firms but chose to article at the Robarts law firm in London because John Robarts was premier of Ontario and therefore well connected. Near the end of his articling days with the firm he was to come to an epiphany that would change the course of his career. Having absolutely no desire to ever enter a court of law defending criminals, Tait balked when Jeff Flynn, one of the firm's partners, suggested it was important for him to have experience in all aspects of the law, including criminal law. He asked Tait to take on a pro bono case defending a young female client on an impaired driving charge.

The woman was in her late twenties, single and sexy with long black hair. Tait didn't notice her good looks at first - he was too concerned and overwhelmed by the idea of going to court. In fact, he was "scared shitless" and the anti-ego devil on his shoulder wasn't helping. He was terrified of being a laughing stock so he worked his ass off and spent several weeks sitting in on court cases to watch how criminal lawyers conducted their trials. He prepared and rehearsed for hours, determined not to make a fool of himself and more importantly, to win. When his client's court date came up he walked in to the courthouse with no idea that this day was to be a turning point for him on many levels.

During the cross examining of a police officer Tait began to feel a swell rise inside his chest, his heart raced and he felt the power of performing before an audience. He wowed them, he won and it was magical. He was hooked and was left wanting more. The client was grateful and impressed. So much so she

59

took the tall, muscular, dark-haired legal eagle to a nearby motel and as he fondly remembers, spent many hours thanking him profusely. This win took him to a level of emotional success he had never experienced. It was about getting off on the exhilaration of winning, getting off on the approval of his colleagues and friends and getting off on the gratitude expressed by his client. As it would be for the rest of his life and career, the solution to any of his problems would be about things outside himself and never taking the treacherous step of looking inwards.

Corporate and tax law went out the window. Criminal law was sexy. Criminal law was about performance and the payoff could be mind-blowing. Criminal law was a psychological hiding place for the scared, insecure boy living inside him. In Don Tait, criminal lawyer, that boy disappeared. The bravura he craved had surfaced and not giving credit to a possible talent, he was convinced he had been able to fool the judge and fool the audience. That convoluted mindset would prove a blessing and a curse.

Following his graduation from law school in 1969, Tait and Brenda drove to New Brunswick on vacation. Tait rolled the car on the highway and took out part of the windshield. Brenda refused to drive back to London with him and took the train. Tait drove the more than one thousand miles in the damaged car, despite having bugs stuck in his teeth much of the time because of the missing windshield. It was about this time Tait was beginning to realize his drinking might be "abnormal." One weekend when Brenda was visiting her mother he went to the liquor store and bought two forty ouncers of vodka. At home, he went into the bedroom, pulled the drapes, turned on the television and stayed there for two days, sinking into an alcoholic stupor that felt so good.

"It gave me a sense of freedom and I loved it. I knew I could drink more than anybody but I also realized I had a greater recovery capacity than most. There was a faint thought that this might not be a good thing but I blew it off because I knew

it gave me the courage and feeling of power I couldn't get
without it."

SETTING UP PRACTICE — FINDING DODGE CITY

IN LATE 1970, Tait moved the family out of their apartment on Oxford Street in London to live with his parents while he prepared for and wrote the bar admission exams. He was called to the Bar in May,1971 and was ready to strike out on the next leg of his career, acknowledging a final farewell to the picture he had of himself in a pilot's uniform. Brenda was pregnant with their second child, Melanie

Tait was one of ten legal graduates invited to be wined and dined by representatives from some of Toronto's biggest law firms. During festive rounds of eating and drinking he was offered jobs at several large, respected firms including Thompson Rogers but decided he didn't want to work in a law office that functioned like a factory. It was well known that they provided rooms with beds for young lawyers who had to stay all night working on cases. He also decided he did not want to live in the big city.

He and his classmate Ian Fisher – who was also married - began driving across Ontario looking for a city where they could set up a law practice. After visiting Thunder Bay, Sudbury, Toronto, London and St. Catharines, Kitchener and Guelph they decided Windsor would give them their best opportunity. Fisher wanted to practice family and real estate law, Tait was hooked on defending criminals. He was familiar with Windsor because his parents had lived there several years while his father worked on building the city's largest mall. They lived in the Le Goyeau apartments on Riverside Drive and Tait often visited with Brenda and the children. On a cool morning in May, 1971, he packed his family into their "rusty hunk of junk" – a Maroon coloured Volkswagen - and moved to the loopy, rough border town known as the automotive capital of Canada. The river provided a barrier and there were casual immigration checks, but for all intents and purposes, the border with Detroit didn't exist.

The twin auto towns of Canada and the United States were like the Wild West. Both were always in a state of boom or bust, depending on where oil prices were at the time and what the Japanese were up to. Visitors couldn't believe the heroic levels of local drug and alcohol consumption and the regularity of biker killings. The Outlaws and Hells Angels were locked in an ongoing turf war about who owned the cross-border drug trade and local strippers, so people were getting shot. A lot of them. The Lobos were also established in Windsor, population 193,000, and added to the murder rate and general mayhem. It wasn't unusual for cops passing through Windsor at the time to return home with lurid tales of having been to "Dodge City."

It was a wild party town and even some of the city's top judges were piss tanks who hung out at the local Top Hat Supper Club after court, to watch big name American entertainers and drink themselves into a stupor. Several of them became embroiled in a major prostitution scandal and eventually three of the city's seven judges were booted off the bench. Two were from the criminal court and one from family court. Tait began taking legal aid cases. Legal Aid is Canada's free legal service for the poor and underemployed. With his first paycheque he went to a gas station on Wyandotte Street East and for the first time was able to say "fill 'er up." When the gas tank was two-thirds full it fell off the car. Tait got out, closed the door and left it. He went to Dan Kane's General Motors dealership located near the courthouse and bought a Caprice.

He and Brenda and their daughters moved into a low-income townhouse in Amherstburg, about half an hour outside Windsor. One night in early April 1971, only months after their arrival in the city, Brenda became quite ill. Tait put them all in the car and drove to Metropolitan Hospital in a snow storm. Brenda was admitted and tests the following day confirmed a diagnosis of Multiple Sclerosis. Neurosurgeon

Victor Kleider told Tait his wife was in "bad shape."

Tait's father attended his Bar Admission ceremony while his mother looked after Brenda. Soon after, knowing she would not be able to rely on a husband who was busy trying to set up a law practice for the constant care and attention she required, Brenda took the children to live with his parents in London. Tait visited his wife and daughters every weekend and to save money he left the townhouse and moved in with Ian Fisher, sleeping on the couch in his Le Goyeau apartment. That wasn't the most convenient arrangement, so Tait bought a sleeping bag and air mattress and slept in a closet in his office in the downtown TD Bank building. For more than a month he would get up early, take one of his two good suits and go to the YMCA to shower and shave. He moved back in with Fisher for several more months and eventually rented a bungalow on Riverside Drive in Tecumseh.

After moving out of the townhouse he had begun receiving letters from Leon Paroian's law firm threatening a lawsuit over breaking a lease. Lawyer Bob Ash sent the letters on Paroian's behalf. Tait called to tell him to "go fuck himself." The firm dropped the threats. They later became friends and Paroian offered jobs to both Tait and Fisher. He also sent them clients. Tait and Fisher were making $25 an hour doing duty council work. Fisher hated it and soon switched to real estate law. In their new offices they flipped for a room with a window. Tait lost. But in so many other ways, Tait had begun a winning streak. Slowly but surely, he was beating a path to success and never passed on an opportunity to make an impression. One particular invitation set the stage for Tait's future.

The director of Legal Aid invited him to an Ontario Provincial Police retirement party in the sleepy, agricultural town of Harrow, Ontario, about half an hour south of Windsor. He said it would be an opportunity for the young, brash lawyer to drum up referrals. There, while drinking and eating muskrat, he met the city's most renowned criminal lawyer at the time,

Frank Montello.

Montello knew his way around and was no slouch when it came to using whatever legal means possible to defend a client. He courted the judges. They were pals and when the scales could be tipped one way or the other, they tipped Montello's way. Tait didn't score major victories at the party but he was able to show his face to the people he wanted to remember him, especially Montello. It didn't hurt that Tait oozed a natural charm. From the get go he looked expensive, like he'd fallen off a GQ page. He moved like a panther, aware of his effect on his prey, particularly women. His thick hair and brows offset wide set dark eyes that were quick to laugh and left one with the feeling there was something he wasn't telling you. It didn't hurt that his full lips surrounded a blinding white smile.

With Brenda out of town he began seeing other women who were mostly one-night stands and none developed into a relationship of any significance. He was constantly looking for approval, especially from women. They assuaged his insecurities and made him feel good about himself. They helped keep the inferiority demons at bay. But the focus on his libido could not match his devotion to the law and he never let his drinking and womanizing get in the way of his court performance. His drinking buddy Judge Gordon Stewart, knowing he had very little money, gave him six suits that he had cut down to size. They were good suits but still second hand and Tait vowed it would be the last time he would need a hand-me-down suit. Armani was soon to become his trademark and he never appeared without that expensive look, even in his backyard, even when he wasn't making Armani money.

He knew what he wanted and that it was only a matter of time before he got it. He knew criminal law could bring prestige and money and he didn't have long to wait. Only weeks later, when Montello had to be in London, Ontario to defend a rape case, he remembered the eager young stallion and called, asking Tait if he would take care of his remands for the next few weeks. Tait could hardly believe what he was hearing. Here he was, a young kid lawyer who would be doing all of Montello's high-profile cases that had been earlier postponed. He would use this opportunity for all it was worth and it would be worth plenty.

He made sure he did a good job and when Montello returned he took the young Tait under his wing. Tait began hanging out in Montello's office, sitting in on his preparations with clients. The bottle of scotch would come out, clients filled the waiting room and Tait lapped it up. He got to know the clients, Montello trusted him and he was soon one of the only lawyers out drinking with Montello and the judges. When Montello had a co-accused, Tait got the case. Within six months out of law school he was doing jury trials. In the criminal arena, everyone saw Tait was becoming busy. He wasn't winning big murder cases, but he was building a reputation.

However, he was made acutely aware of the distance he had to go to compete with Montello during a visit by his mother Dorothy in 1972. Wanting to see him in court, in his robes, she attended a jury trial where both he and Montello delivered addresses to the jury. At the end of the day Tait, happy with his performance in court that day, asked what she thought. Without hesitating she answered, "That Frank Montello is quite a lawyer." She said nothing about her son. It's a story that still makes him laugh out loud. It was partly true. Compared to the seasoned Montello, Tait admits he had no style, but he was learning fast and getting lots of publicity. Montello represented the Satan's Choice and Lobos biker gangs and Tait tailed along, taking it all in. Most of his clients still came from Legal Aid but he knew he was building a reputation and more importantly, getting noticed.

In fact, both he and Fisher were growing reputations. The Paroian law firm came calling again as did Morris Kamin who was considered the "main guy" in personal injury law. Tait and Fisher talked it over and decided to join Kamin. They formed the Kamin Tait Fisher and Burnett law firm.

Tait continued to hang out with the judges and Montello. He would go to the private Windsor Club and would often have to drive Judge Stewart home after a night of suicidal drinking. In later years he sponsored Stewart in a 12-Step AA program but in the heyday of the 1970s their lifestyle was part of their persona – hard drinking and in charge. They drank and partied and it all seemed perfectly normal to Tait. For a guy with alcoholic and addiction tendencies, this was nirvana. He was swept up into the life and he thrived on it. You had to be a particular breed of person to survive in that atmosphere. He was that breed. He was driven and ruthless and those around him could see he was something unique and special, a rising star among them.

Within his first two years in practice he acted in five murder trials – an unprecedented record for a young lawyer. While he lost many of those early cases, the losses were becoming fewer and fewer. Clients who couldn't afford Montello were hiring Tait. His mentor also taught him that while winning was good, what really mattered – win or lose – was to make sure the media spelled your name correctly. That bit of sage advice was also echoed by another rising legal star - Patrick Ducharme, who also once said "...even on his worse drunken day Tait could perform better than most and be impressive."

The media loved the new addition to the legal community. He was becoming quoted so often there was a rumour that Montello was getting pissed off with his protégé's hogging the spotlight. Some said Montello was accusing Tait of poaching clients. Both, who have remained close friends, have always maintained nothing was farther from the truth. There were sufficient numbers of bad guys for both of them.

Criminals from both sides of the border who were committing crimes in Windsor began hiring the new legal star. His reputation was growing because of his defence of cops and biker killers alike. In the forgotten world of 1970s rustbelt

North America, Tait was becoming notorious. If you were dead-nuts guilty and couldn't do the time, you took your chances with Tait. It wasn't unusual to see half a dozen lawyers sit in on one of his cases. His performance could be mesmerizing – for those observing and a hapless witness. From that vantage Tait was formidable. The audience was rarely disappointed. He had a special performance to intimidate a witness:

 Like a cat stalking his prey, Tait stands well back from the witness box. He touches his index finger to the right side of his nose. He quietly asks a question. His eyes are focused like lasers on the witness. He moves a little closer and asks another question. This time a bit louder. He moves closer and asks another question. The witness is transfixed on Tait who repeats this performance with three or four more questions until his voice is at a crescendo and he is almost in the witness's face. The witness is rattled. Tait's client ultimately gets off. It's great theatre. He makes it look easy.

But what no one knew is that Tait, his insecurities always bubbling near the surface, would get to work at 5 a.m. and spend hours studying a case and rehearsing his performance. He would watch himself in the mirror as he repeated the script he will deliver flawlessly later that day. He knew the law, he knew how to use it to get the best deal for his clients and he understood the nuances in the system that could often tip the law in favour of his client – the guilty and the innocent. It didn't matter which because it was all about winning.

Tait preferred jury trials because he had an innate ability to read the twelve peers of the accused who sat in two rows to the left of the judge on the bench. He knew how to manipulate them, to get them on side – his side, not necessarily on the side of the accused. If there was any way of getting a win he would use whatever manoeuvring he had at his disposal. He had little tricks. One of his favourites was to pull the tail of his shirt out through a small opening in the fly of his trousers. He would face the jury until someone, usually one of the women, would get his attention and gesture, while smiling slyly, to indicate his fly was down. Tait would feign surprise, flash a broad smile at the woman and tuck his shirt inside and adjust the zipper.

It seemed Tait could do no wrong and appeared invincible. He was brilliant. But what his colleagues and the public didn't see was the constant battle he was having with the demon fat boy on his shoulder, always picking at his brain, reminding him he wasn't all that good and taunting that one day the jig would be up. He'd be found out and everything would come crashing down around him. The frenetic rehearsals were an attempt to quell the fear of not being good enough and to cover that fear with a polished arrogance. To quell the beast he drank. After work and after a court performance that had men and women alike crying on the witness stand, he'd head to a nearby watering hole and drink double vodkas, convincing himself he really was the best. Morning would come, the demons would be at work but a few belts helped get him focused.

More than anything, he wanted approval and there were three ways to get it. Money. Sex. Alcohol. He wanted it all and as much of it as he could get. He wanted it so badly the line between the defence attorney on the right side of the law and his close association with his lawless biker clients often began to blur. To keep that approval, he had to keep winning and if the scales of justice were to tip one way or the other he was determined they were tipping in his favour. While he used every trick in the book to get a client off, he always did it within the parameters of the legal system. However, he did it so well those watching often found it hard to tell if he was crossing the line and they came away baffled or mesmerized.

One late afternoon in 1972, as was his habit, Tait was sitting in his office above the Toronto Dominion Bank at the corner of Wyandotte Street and Ouellette Avenue, drinking. His last visitor of the day was Father Paul Charbonneau, a short, burly, foul-mouthed, cigar chomping Roman Catholic priest who ran the local drunk rehab, Brentwood. He rarely dressed in priest's clothing, choosing instead a golf shirt, pants and ubiquitous pair of sunglasses. Tait wanted to call Charbonneau as a witness for a client who had gone through the Brentwood program but Charbonneau didn't like going to court and wanted to personally deliver a report on the man to Tait. It was Tait's first encounter with Charbonneau and he had no idea that afternoon just how important this man was going to become in his life.

By 1973 his alcoholism was in full swing. While he had some friends among the cops, most of them hated him. He was belligerent to them and would flip them the finger when he'd drive past a police car. On one occasion when he was in the police station "ranting and raving" about some issue, two burly officers of the law - one who was head of the drug squad who eventually became a client - picked him up by the underarms and threw him out the door where he landed on his ass. After a particularly harsh grilling by Tait in court the cops would be on the lookout for him.

"They would watch me come out of a bar where we all hung out, follow me and stop me. They got me once for impaired and I lost my licence for three months. I can see now why they had it in for me. I used to taunt them. I was nuts."

His relationship with the cops changed after the first time he defended one of them in court. When the officer in trouble needed a lawyer there was no contest. After being grilled by him in court, he wanted Tait. The cops may not like him but they weren't stupid. "I learned a lot and I learned that cops had a philosophy like gang members. They circled the wagons around each other when threatened and took care of their own."

Many cops he grilled in the witness box became friends. Retired Inspector Ian Chippett came to have a grudging respect for Tait.

"You could never outsmart him. But you could tell he had to win and win all the time. He also had a heart of gold. But, winning was everything and he knew no boundaries," Chippett recalls.

That lack of boundaries, when fuelled by alcoholic bravado, saw Tait often hanging out with his least savoury clients.

His relationship with the bikers began during an interview in Morris Kamin's office with a group of about ten Satan's Choice bikers, which was also when Tait met the outlaw who would become one of his most supportive friends. Bill O'Reilly was born in the Northern Ontario town of Sudbury near the Quebec border. His membership in a gang in Sudbury led him to the position of enforcer with the Satan's Choice Motorcycle Club in Windsor. They were to eventually merge with the International Outlaws club, as did most members of the Windsor motorcycle gang, the Lobos. Some of the Lobos joined Hell's Angels. It was obvious to Tait that O'Reilly, who had once been jailed for a robbery he did not commit, was not a fan of lawyers.

"He kept making sarcastic remarks and letting us know he had an attitude when it came to lawyers and no wonder. He was an obnoxious prick. I didn't like him and he didn't like me."

That distrust thawed over the next few years when Tait represented him in court on minor charges, mainly traffic-related cases by cops who were constantly keeping close tabs on the local bad guys. Much of the really "bad shit" committed by Reilly, who Tait said "offed" many people never reached court. Throughout history there are many cases that never reach a court of law, for one reason and another, some morally ethical, others not so much.

Tait was held on retainer by the Outlaws to defend its members. In the 1970s and '80s O'Reilly was leader of the pack and he had money. Lots of it. He had a home in a prestigious, upscale neighbourhood known as South Windsor. The five-bedroom home boasted an indoor pool and oversized garage housing a late model Cadillac and a room for manufacturing amphetamines. O'Reilly also had a stable of women who worked for him, plying their trade as strippers and prostitutes. The nubile young women came and left at all hours of the day and night. On summer days they lounged nude in the back yard, providing titillating entertainment for males of all ages who lived in the surrounding two-storey homes.

O'Reilly was supplying many members of Windsor's professional class with women and there were benefits from that line of work. In one case O'Reilly was being sentenced before a well-respected judge when he and Tait employed a devious strategy to sway the verdict.

"O'Reilly invited several of his girls to come to court for the sentencing and when the judge sat on the bench he could see them sitting in the front row. Three of them were all too familiar to the judge and Bill didn't go to jail. That's the way things were done."

Even though Tait knew what O'Reilly did for a living and that he was quite capable of putting a bullet between the eyes of an enemy, Tait never had a qualm about having him in his home and never feared he or his family would be in danger. The same could not be said for O'Reilly. One afternoon when O'Reilly was sleeping in the hull of his yacht on Crystal Bay a Hells Angels hit squad pumped him full of holes with a machine gun. He took seven bullets and during his recovery in hospital became addicted to morphine and codeine. Tait's friendship with O'Reilly was ultimately sealed the day he turned up to visit the biker in his hospital room. O'Reilly was taken aback by the unexpected visit and grew a very warm spot in his heart for Tait with whom he would forge a lifelong friendship.

"He was riddled with bullets and some of them couldn't be removed because they were too close to main organs. I visited him in hospital and for some reason it changed everything between us. Bill became really loyal to me after that."

O'Reilly became Tait's ipso facto protector. While he could talk and act like a typical bad-ass biker, Tait found that O'Reilly was a news junky who read newspapers and kept up on what was going on in the world. He was a devout, traditional Roman Catholic who wanted the church to continue delivering the mass in Latin. O'Reilly endeared himself to Tait.

Those who knew Tait well, knew he was a sucker for an underdog and throughout his career would hand out money if the sob story was plausible. People who didn't know him well, disliked him or were jealous of the high-flying lawyer, wouldn't believe it. Perhaps it's because everything that happened to Tait seemed to take on a larger-than-life aspect. He lived large. While most ordinary humans treated a hospital stay as something private, for Tait it became a raucous circus. During a week-long stay in hospital awaiting lower back disc surgery, his private room was party central. Staff watched as a constant parade of bikers, cops, lawyers, crown attorneys, doctors and nurses and other hangers on made the pilgrimage to the celebrity lawyer's bedside. The nurses brought him buckets of ice for the copious bottles of booze consumed by him and his guests. On surgery day, the unending consumption of alcohol prior to his procedure made the anaesthetic difficult to administer.

Although Tait paints himself as a selfish prick, and he is probably correct in many instances, particularly when applied to his treatment of his wife, there were many friends and acquaintances during those years who were recipients of his generosity. If you needed a hand out or a leg up, Tait didn't quibble about the cost. He may have been selfish in his constant search for gratification, but would be the first to pick up a tab. There are many lawyers in Windsor who owe their careers to Tait, either because he brought them into his firm and saw to it that they prospered or because he paid their tuition to law school. None of those payments were ever expected to be returned, and most were never offered.

But in the waning years of the 1970s Tait's life began spinning out of control. When Brenda and the children returned to Windsor, Tait was spending more time working on his career and less time at home. He and Brenda were not getting along and it was only a matter of time before the writing that had long been on the wall was finally acted on and they would split. Brenda was bitter about her disease, bitter about the lack of attention paid to her by her husband and bitter about having to raise their daughters with an absent father.

"She wasn't a great mother but she did the best she could. I wasn't a particularly great father and I always felt sorry for myself that I had a sick wife and responsibilities at home. I'd often tell myself 'I don't need this shit.' I understand her and myself more now and certainly have more compassion about what she was suffering. But at the time I was selfishly thinking about me and my career and my needs and wants."

Tait would occasionally make love to his wife, but his lusty libido was generally satisfied in other bedrooms. His escapades were many. A woman he was seeing in Detroit was yearning for marriage and children and threatened Tait, telling him he either made a commitment or she would marry a doctor she was also seeing. Tait explained he was already married and perhaps she should choose the medic. But she wasn't ready to let Tait go, not just yet. They decided to have a farewell dinner at a favourite restaurant and when she was getting out of the car at the end of the evening she invited him in to her apartment to have sex one last time. In a sexual frenzy they hit the bed.

Later, as Tait was getting dressed to make himself scarce she suddenly shrieked as she remembered her chosen beau was coming for a nightcap. Just as Tait was tucking his tie into a jacket pocket the buzzer rang. "Be right there." She said into the intercom. Tait was unceremoniously shoved towards the bathroom and ordered to be quiet as she frantically tidied the bed and hauled on a robe. Seeing his shoes under a chair she tossed them in the closet. Tait jumped into the bathtub and hid behind the heavy shower curtain, invoking a prayer to a long-neglected deity.

The chosen suitor, who had arrived early, was told to "just sit down" while his lady love went to the bathroom to get ready. To her dismay and Tait's horror the attentive beau decided to accompany her and sat on the toilet seat while she freshened up. Behind the curtain Tait was sweating and getting wet from a dripping shower head.

"He was literally six inches from me and they were in there for minutes. I was afraid to breathe. I'd decided if he stuck his head in I would smash it. Honest to God. I knew I would have to do something drastic. When they eventually left the room, I crawled out through the bathroom window. Thank God it was on the first floor." His shoes probably ended up in the garbage.

OUTLAWS. BOOZE. SEX. DRUGS- Recipe for a fall

THE SOUND OF GUNNING Harley-Davidsons fills a farmhouse yard. On the veranda a lean, handsome man wearing cowboy boots and an expensive three-piece Armani with wide lapels swigs out of a bottle of Jack Daniels. He smiles at a dozen partying bikers wearing Outlaws colours hollering and drinking beer and spewing dirt in the yard like big kids. He takes another swig and kicks open the clubhouse door.

Inside are more bikers around a table doing lines of coke. Girls lounge in the background. "Nice work, man. That fuckin' judge never knew what hit him," one biker says to the suit, setting up more lines. "Want some blow? Meth?"

"Not now – got another court appearance in two hours," says the man in the suit. He slams the half empty bottle on the table, smiling. "Next time don't be so sloppy with the gun and I won't have to charge you a hundred grand." The bikers all laugh.

Tait strides out, fondling a tall blonde on his way out the door. He guns his big grey battleship of a Cadillac out of the dusty yard and steers back to the city. The towers of downtown Detroit are barely visible through the hazy, polluted sunshine. It's all becoming so routine. He doesn't see the incongruity, the danger. They're like the tough guys he impressed in high school. They just kill lots of people. He knew their girlfriends and families. He was "just having fun." He was a legal gunslinger and acted the part. The demon is at rest. Tait is inebriated but it doesn't matter. He can still perform and he will – in court and later with a stunner who won't be his wife. His reputation for representing bikers and cops is growing and the money is rolling in – lots of it. If they were dead nuts guilty they came looking for him. He knew every legal trick in

76

the book for getting them off or at least keeping them out of jail. He never repeats a mistake and has learned to take cues from his cop friends, especially when he grills them on the witness stand. He has become their "go to" lawyer and has made friendships among the ranks that will last a lifetime. Retired chiefs and officers speak about him with affection and awe.

When he's sober he wonders how he fools them all. Don't they realize he is just a little shit from New Brunswick? Most of them probably don't even know where that is. While he's terrified of failure most of the time, jacked up he doesn't care, at least not as long as the money is rolling in and there's booze, drugs and women. By 1975 Tait's drinking had become a serious problem. He would try to quit every once in a while but it never lasted more than a few days. One recovering alcoholic lawyer suggested Tait go to AA. He reluctantly went to one meeting and later told his well-meaning friend "They're a bunch of old fucks talking about God. I'm not going there again."

Tait's crazy, out of control life continued to get crazier. For sane people watching it was the stuff of fiction, but to Tait it was his reality. One sunny afternoon - Father's Day - Tait was having a few beers around the pool at his home on Cabot Street in LaSalle. His daughter Barbara, then nine years old, came out to tell him some people wanted to see him. He looked up and walking through his garage into the yard were three men with known serious criminal records, who were also known drug addicts and killers and who were associated with the Lobos biker gang.

"They were all jacked up on PCBs and horse tranquilizers. I wanted them off the property so I said, 'let's get in the car,' and I left with them - me barefoot and in my bathing suit. Ronald Lauzon who was a clean cut, not bad looking psychopathic killer crazy bastard, was driving and saying, 'We're all going to heaven today and I want a good lawyer with us.' I knew their reputation and I was scared. I knew I was in serious trouble and this could be curtains for me, so I stayed close to the car door with my hand on the door handle. The next traffic light we stopped at I jumped out, ran behind a school and started running home through the back streets.

"Once I got there I realized I had a problem. I couldn't call the cops because of what this might do to my legal career because I defended those guys in court and if I called the cops I would be seen as someone who was ratting them out. So, I called Tony Rainone, told him what happened and asked if he could help me out. He said he had Mafia connections and would come to see me. He showed up with a big black guy who was a one-eyed contract killer called 'Toute Suite' and gave me a .357 Blackhawk Magnum for protection. These guys carried semi-automatics. As this is all happening I'm still drinking and getting drunker by the minute."

Rainone, then in his fifties with snow white hair, was wealthy, having made "a lot" of money from his many and varied "activities." He was very powerful because of being well connected to the criminal element in Detroit. He told Tait to call Lauzon and tell him they would meet at Kamin's office on Pitt Street and for him to come alone. Tait, Rainone and "Toute Suite" took off in Rainone's panel van, with Tait driving. They abducted Lauzon outside Kamin's office and all returned to Tait's house. In the living room they stared each other down, guns drawn. Lauzon kept saying "I'm Jesus Christ and I want Don Tait," prompting "Toute Suite" to ram a pistol into his mouth and blood started flying.

"If you're Jesus Christ I'm the devil. Now what's your name asshole?" demanded "Toute Suite."

"Rodney Lauzon."

Tait yells at them "Jesus, don't kill him in my fucking living room."

They tell Lauzon he can't be "doing that kind of thing" to people and since he called himself Jesus Christ they were

78

taking him to Yawkey Bush to "crucify" him. Getting back into the van they take him to the woodlot in the west end of Windsor, pistol-whip him and leave him passed out on the ground. After that things are somewhat of a blur for Tait. He woke up the next morning with the .357 lying next to him on the bed. That day he moved his family out, sending them to stay at Crown Attorney Duncan McIntyre's house. It was Monday and he had to appear in court to defend a client.

"I have to go to court and I'm scared. I take a bottle of vodka and the gun and stick them in my briefcase. I'm in court with this. I opened the briefcase and one of the detectives saw the gun. He said, 'Holy shit what are you doing with that?' I told him what had happened and he told me to 'Be careful.' Well, I didn't get arrested."

Lauzon let the Lobos know what had been done to him and the bikers let Tait know they had a contract out on him because of what had happened to Lauzon. One afternoon biker Ernie Filiault, a man with a lengthy criminal record who had been acquitted on a recent murder charge, called to tell Tait he just "wanted to talk." Tait, aware of Filiault's criminal history, invited him to come to his office after hours. Filiault strutted in sporting the stereotypical long beard with hair down his back. A tough and mean fighter, he cut an intimidating figure in his black shirt, black jeans and full Lobos colours.

"He said he was surprised I agreed to meet him and I told him the cocksucker Lauzon deserved what he got and if anything, I saved his life because they wanted to kill him and told him the whole story. I pulled out my gun and put it on the desk. We started talking quite friendly."

By the end of the conversation Filiault was on Tait's side. "He stood up and said 'It's over. I'll take care of it.' And I knew he'd be as good as his word."

From then on Tait's reputation as a lawyer who could be trusted but who stands his ground was cemented with the bikers. He was the kind of guy they liked and not only was he now their lawyer of choice, he was firmly on their permanent party guest list. It wouldn't necessarily be something to be proud of and although his friends and colleagues were constantly warning him not to get too close to his unsavoury clients, it was not something Tait wanted to hear so he ignored their concerns. Years later when Filiault's young son, who was about nine years old, needed help, Tait felt sorry for the boy so he and his second wife Johanna took him into their home for several months.

"The kid wasn't responsible for his father's lifestyle and I couldn't just let him flounder on his own. I wanted to make sure he got on the right track."

Tait's clients in the Outlaws gang were constantly at war with his clients in the Hells Angels. They would be flying in and out of Montreal with bombings and assassinations following in their wake. He drank and snorted cocaine with them and partied with Satan's Choice at their clubhouse on Hickory Street in Windsor. He attended their funerals, drawing media attention. He carried a .38 pistol with a permit from Sandwich police. He sported a big white fedora. The first time he tried coke was in the bathroom of a local strip club with O'Reilly. Tait recalls he was loaded drunk at the time but the cocaine "sobered me right up." They introduced him to biker speed but he decided he didn't like it.

One thing Tait came to understand about this group of clients was their volatility and unpredictable behaviour. One day they turned up at his home with a special child size "chopper" they'd built for Tait's daughter Barbara when she was around nine years old. They, and Barbara, were delighted with the bike. When Rainone, a Windsor boy with "connections" sought out Tait's services to help him beat a major fraud charge, he was to discover that defending clients when there was Mafia involved added scary elements to the picture.

"When we went to court on the fraud charge against him the Crown had lined up a bunch of witnesses from Detroit to testify against him. But on the first day of the hearing Tony had cars with hit men stationed around the court house and not one witness showed up in court that day. Word got out that the boys were circling so none of the witnesses would testify for the Crown."

Tait knew nothing at the time about the shake down of witnesses and that they were too scared to show up in court and found out about it much later, after the case was over.

"Tony and his wife really liked Brenda and me. Even though his wife made it clear she wanted me sexually I knew it was suicidal to do anything about it. It might have been tempting but hey, we're talking about the Mafia and besides, she was seriously addicted to prescription drugs and had a lot of issues."

JOHANNA

TAIT'S ROVING EYE WAS a female tracker beam and in 1975 while defending a client at a jury trial in Stewart's courtroom he couldn't keep it off court reporter Johanna Pruyn, a stunning blonde. Tait was smitten. He found her "incredibly sexy" and flirted shamelessly. She, on the other hand, was slow to respond and at first, was not overly impressed by the thought of hanging out with Tait.

"I told myself I would never, ever go out with him. He was a known womanizer, he drank and he was married. And I wasn't raised to go out with someone like him. I had just been divorced two months and I said 'No, no way.' But he had that charm and charisma and I and everyone else enjoyed having him in our courtrooms."

She eventually allowed him to persuade her to go to lunch with him at one of the best-known fish restaurants frequented by Windsorites – Joe Muer in Detroit. He was charming and she was captivated, but reticent because he was still not divorced from Brenda, although Tait assured her the marriage was over.

"I was really, really, crazy in love with her and knew more than anything I wanted to get a divorce and marry her."

Tait's pursuit of Johanna intensified and he sensed she was beginning to enjoy the relationship as much as he was. He took advantage of a Law Society event to invite her to Toronto for a weekend. It was to be the beginning of a passionate affair that would ultimately lead to Tait's divorce and then marriage to Johanna. After their weekend in Toronto, Tait began spending more time with Johanna at her apartment in the Le Goyeau building than he did on Cabot Street. It was then that

Johanna began to get a taste of what life with Tait might be like. It wasn't pretty. His biker clients were always doing him favours but in biker style. One major drug dealer told Tait he would take his Corvette and get it repainted for him. Tait handed over the keys. Two weeks later the Corvette and the dealer were still AWOL so Parent and Filiault said they would hunt them down. As was their fashion, they found the guy who took it and proceeded to "chastise" him. But they chose to do the chastising – a sound pistol whipping - in Johanna's apartment. "Go downstairs to your friend's apartment, they ordered her, until we take care of this." The Corvette was returned in good shape, but not repainted. It is only in retrospect that Tait sees how frightening their behaviour was for Johanna.

"She saw a lot of bad shit. Stuff she never imagined she would have to and never should have been subjected to. It was beyond bad."

Brenda suspected her husband was having a serious affair with the young court reporter and one evening when Tait arrived at Johanna's apartment carrying a bottle of vodka, Brenda was there telling her side of the story. It wasn't a pleasant visit for any of them. In 1977 Johanna was in hospital having surgery when Brenda moved out of the Cabot Street home. Tait's father picked Johanna up from hospital and she moved in to the house.

Soon after, Brenda returned to London, leaving her two daughters with Tait. Tait's parents had been living with them and because Brenda, who was dealing with the effects of MS, needed help, Dorothy virtually ran the household. This was awkward for Johanna and, as it had between Dorothy and Brenda, the relationship with her mother-in-law hit a sour note.

"I was an intruder. Melanie was only six and confused because she couldn't understand why her mother didn't take her. Barb and I got along very well and she treated me like a mother. She would call me and ask, 'have you heard this song?' I'd sit and listen, then we'd talk. Later, when things got really bad with Don, we'd protect each other."

While things were going well for Tait on the love front, his legal life was in bad shape. He was drinking heavily and couldn't get it under control. As soon as he opened his eyes in the morning he took a big slug from a twelve-ouncer of vodka, waited until he could feel warmth seep into his blood, showered and dressed and went to court. He would drink enough to get over the shakes but not enough to be drunk. If a trial started at 10 a.m. he would be good for about one hour before the shakes started again. He would take his briefcase into the bathroom and slug down another two to three ounces before continuing in court. His consumption of breath fresheners and use of eye drops must have shot profit margins of the products through the roof.

On occasion, Johanna had to stop at the liquor store on their way to court where she was instructed to buy a mickey of booze. He would lie down on the back seat and glug several ounces before going in to represent his client. Judges and court staff in small towns outside Windsor, where Tait appeared for a number of his clients, started making sure that any case involving Tait would be scheduled for early morning. That's when they knew he was most likely to be sober. Later in the day – all bets were off. They all knew Tait was a drunk but he was a brilliant drunk. When he was part of a team of lawyers working a major case in the city of Toronto his colleagues there made sure anything he was presenting was also scheduled early in the day.

Everyone around him knew he was dissembling and by 1979 his behaviour became more bizarre. Planning to go to Bogota, get on a mule and go up into the mountains for reasons he absolutely cannot remember but suspects it was to be closer to a cocaine supply, he left Johanna and the kids and headed for Toronto. He checked into the Holiday Inn at Milton Airport and it was there some of his biker buddies found him in his room, comatose on drugs and alcohol. Tait has no recollection of being there or how the bikers found him. Johanna remembers Tait calling her and she in turn called O'Reilly and asked him to go help Tait and bring him back to Windsor.

"I was a total nut job," Tait recalls. "Total, out of it, nut job."

They got him to a hospital in Kitchener where doctors treated him for alcohol poisoning. His blood alcohol level was 0.50 per cent, a level that would kill most normal humans. According to medical literature, death commonly occurs with a blood alcohol level of 0.37 per cent and levels of 0.45 and higher are fatal to "nearly all individuals." Once doctors had his physical condition stabilized he was taken to Windsor and admitted to the psychiatric unit at Hotel-Dieu Hospital.

There they took all of his clothes and had him put on a pair of paper slippers and a "Johnny" shirt with no underwear and open at the back. Within hours of being admitted Tait was assuming control. At one point he commandeered a bank of payphones along one wall and for a time had phones held to both ears – talking to people at his office and home and others he can't remember.

"It was just absolute madness. Sheer madness."

A psychiatrist at the hospital arranged for him to attend a 28-day rehab program at a drunk tank in Brighton, Michigan. For the first week he was placed in a regular hospital bed in the detox wing and given pills to prevent seizures, with regular blood and liver function tests. After detox, he began taking part in the facility's rehab programs - attending meetings and meeting with a social worker and psychiatrist. He had a roommate but much of his time there is but a foggy memory, as are many details of his various sojourns in rehab. He does remember it was a high-end rehab with a golf course. Johanna came to visit, as did Brenda.

Rehab didn't take. Tait remembers he felt full of "fear and anxiety" and because he would not attend AA meetings had

85

nothing to help support his fight with alcoholism. He was embarrassed knowing his colleagues and friends were aware he had been in a psychiatric ward. For some strange reason he suspects probably had to do with his significant alcoholism, when he returned to Windsor he had developed a stutter that rattled him when he was addressing a jury. One morning he took a drink to calm his nerves and noticed that the stutter went away, so he continued drinking. He felt if he didn't drink he would go mad.

"I was constantly caught in a Catch 22 situation. Right from the beginning when I had three murder trials in my first year out. Even though I didn't win them and it was unheard of for a young lawyer to do that. I drank but didn't get drunk. It was just enough to allow me to be cool. If I stopped drinking the fear and inadequacy came back. I was dammed if I do or don't. It was a quandary and I was stuck. It was a no man's land for me."

And it wasn't only biker clients doing favours for Tait. On October 20, 1988, using his friendship with several judges, Tait had his divorce granted within one day. It was a Friday and on Monday he married Johanna in Judge Lloyd Henrickson's court with cop friend Bill Delaney as his best man and in the presence of his parents and his daughters. With a brain soaked in alcohol and having snorted cocaine before the ceremony, he promised to love and cherish his new bride. It was certainly not a magical wedding day for Johanna.

"He was loaded all day and we stayed that night at a hotel but he was out of it he was so drunk. The next day we went to Toronto for a few days but he was drunk all the time. That was our honeymoon. When we got back to Windsor things just went from bad to worse. I can't remember many nice times after that."

Living on the edge became a frightening, vicious circle. It was a lifestyle Tait was familiar with but something Johanna found took a lot of getting used to. She found herself riding a daily rollercoaster where the thrills were getting fewer and the number of frightening side effects were increasing. Tait's insecurities were so acute he became paranoid and jealous of Johanna's family. She couldn't talk about them because he would accuse her of "caring about them more than you care about me."

Tait just couldn't seem to understand why Johanna kept telling him she wanted their lives to be more normal, like other professional families. He would retort with "Look at everything I give you, the best of everything. You should be happy." But she kept reminding her husband that life wasn't all about money, that a normal life was more important to her. Unfortunately, it was becoming clear that what she craved most of all was something he could not give her.

Their home was certainly not that of a typical professional family, not by any stretch of the imagination. Few of the city's lawyers had hardened criminal bikers walking in any time of the day or night. Big time drug dealers and known killers and the omnipresence of O'Reilly had Johanna constantly on edge and with good reason. It was nothing to see one bad guy pull out a gun and threaten to "blow away" the bad guy sitting next to him during a disagreement. And mean it. One day when they were having an argument in the kitchen, Tait, in a violent, alcoholic rage, punched his fist through the glass door into the room. There was blood everywhere and Johanna had to take him to the hospital emergency room to get stitched up.

"Things were getting worse every day and I was finished. I'd had enough. I was telling a friend about what was going on and she took me to an Al-Anon meeting where I first met Father Charbonneau. He knew who Don was and told me nothing could be done until Don was ready to get help and wanted help and that would probably mean hitting rock bottom. But, in the meantime, Fr. Charbonneau told me I should keep going to Al-Anon and I did."

In another half-hearted attempt to get sober Tait took a second stab at rehab at Henry Ford Hospital in Detroit. The

DTs he was having were so bad Johanna stayed in his room, holding him in the bed over several days. Once they'd dried him out he was released and told by his doctor he would be fine if he only consumed an occasional glass of wine. They left the hospital and went directly to Joe Muer for lunch with a bottle of wine.

The rollercoaster life went into rocket mode. All of the shenanigans going on in Tait's personal and professional life were played out in court and at home. One of Johanna's more challenging experiences living with Tait came on a weekend when Filiault came walking in the door around midnight with another biker "all cut to shit." He woke Tait up and told him he needed Johanna's help. Filiault dragged the biker into the living room and deposited him on the couch. He howled in pain and Johanna could see blood oozing from under the cloth around his left thigh. Filiault explained that the biker had been trying to blow up a building when a gas explosion caused him to get blown through a plate glass window during the operation.

Filiault said "He needs medical attention. If I take him to hospital they'll question him. I need Johanna to fix him up or I'll have to kill him. Sew up his leg." It wasn't a request, it was an order. He had her get a needle and thread and told her to sew up the deep, gaping wounds made by the flying shards of glass. There was no way Johanna could have touched that ripped muscle and blanched at the sight of so much blood. She told them she wasn't going to do it but agreed to drive the guy to the nearest hospital. She got him into ER and sat and waited in her car.

It was one of the hundreds of surreal events she was to experience living with Tait in those early days. It wasn't unusual for him to insist that she come with him when he visited the bikers at their clubhouses. "She's OK, don't worry," he would tell the rag tag gang members gathered in the seedy hangouts as they stared suspiciously and ogled the petite blonde walking in the door.

"Not exactly what a young lawyer should be doing or having his new bride do, is it? I tell you it was a time of complete insanity."

The insanity never abated. Tait's life continued in a drunken haze and continued its downward spiral. When he drank he "got plastered" and on one occasion while attending a baseball game at Tiger stadium in Detroit he was so drunk he fell down a flight of stairs and cut his head open. He was also acting like his clients – brash and reckless. So much of his behaviour he now says seems like a dream, and no wonder. On a late Saturday night at the intersection of Eugenie Street and Ouellette Avenue a car filled with U.S. teens pulled out in front of him, then backed up. Tait, who could have blown eight times over the legal blood alcohol limit, pulled out his gun and shot six bullets into their car. He drove off and says he was never questioned by police about the incident.

In the meantime, Johanna was trying to give the girls as normal an upbringing as possible, given the circumstances of their lifestyle. She got them involved in a variety of activities outside the home – like horseback riding and modelling - she says, "to show them that they were important and worthwhile." Melanie was in elementary school and constantly in trouble. Johanna took her on regular visits to a psychiatrist. In grade eight, Barb was voted valedictorian of her graduating class but there was a bit of a wrinkle - she was in the psychiatric unit of a local hospital.

"I took her out of the hospital, bought her a lovely formal dress and took her to the graduation and then returned her to the hospital. What they were seeing and going through all their lives was really hard on them and it's no wonder they were always in trouble and had problems."

Because of their lifestyle and people she had to associate with, Johanna cut herself off from most of her friends. Those she saw were mainly couples with whom she and Tait would go to dinner with or they would take vacations together. However, before the really bad times, she said she remembers great

89

dinners and parties Tait would insist on paying for to celebrate a family Christmas, birthdays and special anniversaries for her parents whom he sent on a holiday to their native Holland.

"Everyone knew if you needed anything, if you needed money, Don would be there. Looking back, you realize that everyone was taking from him. No one ever asked if he or we needed anything. It was assumed he had the money so let him pay. No one has ever offered to pay for us. No one has been there for us except Frank. No one Don gave money to has ever offered to repay it."

But the good times were fleeting and were more often overwhelmed by too many bad times. The final straw for Johanna - and there were many - came one evening when Tait, an admitted nasty drunk, was wired on cocaine and alcohol. He was in a drunken rage and took his anger out on her. They were in the bedroom having a particularly vicious argument which included throwing things. Tait left the room and returned with his .38 calibre snub nosed Smith and Wesson. He cocked it and put it against Johanna's head threatening to blow her brains out. She lifted her arm and smacked his hand away. The gun went off, narrowly missing her ear and burrowing through the door into Melanie's bedroom.

"I saw grey, like being in a fog and I was stunned. I ran out of the bedroom and started running through the house to get away from him. He grabbed my foot but I managed to get away and ran to a neighbour's house. I had bruises everywhere. The neighbour said she had seen Brenda in that state before when Tait was drunk. He was crazy. He was so involved with the bikers he was acting just like them. I was afraid for my life in that house and afraid for my family."

O'Reilly asked her to come back to the house and told her not to worry, that she would be safe, that he would keep Tait in check. But Johanna decided in that moment it was time to get out, particularly since this incident came on the heels of a drunken Tait previously having threatened to blow up their house. Life was more than out of control. She was terrified for her life. It was an incident Tait recalls with abject remorse.

"I wasn't trying to kill Johanna. I was jacked up, loaded and I wanted to scare her, not kill her."

Johanna waited until Tait was out of the house one morning, sneaked out with her clothes and as many belongings as she could carry, and fled to her parents' home. Several days later they drove her to London to stay with her sister until she found a job. They were so scared that Tait might send some of his killer friends to find her they made her lie down on the floor of the back seat until they reached London. She got settled in London and soon found a job as a court reporter.

Just a few weeks after she left, on October 10, 1979, Tait's drinking reached a crisis point. In court he was defending a client in a complex criminal trial while battling his alcohol demons and acute depression. He was taking the antidepressant Librium and that evening, while washing the pills down with Jack Daniels, took an overdose. He was admitted to Hotel-Dieu Hospital under the care of psychiatrist Dr. Walter Yaworsky. The following day Yaworsky appeared in court and told the judge:

Mr. Tait was hospitalized last evening. He is under my care at Hotel-Dieu Hospital in Windsor. In my opinion I think the treatment of the acute phase of his condition will take about two to four weeks and then the second phase of the treatment might well take a further couple of months after that. So, in that regard he would not be able to work during that period - at least, this is my advice to him as his physician."

Tait's case load was taken over by his friend Guy Cotrell. He was discharged from hospital January 26 and immediately began drinking. In February 1980 Tait was in the fourth week of a major bender and, in a rare sane, but drunken moment, decided to go to the Brentwood Rehab Centre to see Charbonneau. It was 9 p.m. and Tait arrived with a forty-ouncer of vodka in tow. While he was waiting he began talking

91

loudly to one of the staff. Charbonneau, who had been up since 5 a.m., came out and seeing the bottle, lost his temper. Charbonneau remembers the rage he felt seeing Tait loaded drunk and waving the bottle around.

"I told him 'Get the fuck out of here. You're not ready for help. You're making too much noise and I'm tired.' He was absolutely out of it."

Charbonneau, a street smart take no crap kind of guy, wasn't about to push his well-meaning help on anyone. He'd wait. He knew it would be only a matter of time before he saw Tait again.

"I saw the look. I could smell it. This man was going down. Fast. I didn't know how it was going to happen but I knew he was coming to a sticky end. Whether he would be going to Brentwood or somewhere else, he'd be going somewhere for help. And soon."

Tait, who couldn't stand upright, dropped to the floor and promptly fell asleep. He woke up around 4 a.m., tried to stand up and pissed his pants. He left and drove home. Two weeks later, while he and two colleagues were involved in a major court case defending three teens charged with rape, Tait arrived at court every day so inebriated he was virtually non-functioning and his colleagues were trying desperately to hide his inebriation from the court.

One morning, still drunk, he was driving down Ouellette Avenue, Windsor's main drag, when a motorist behind him called 911 to report a drunk driver in a Cadillac. When he reached Tecumseh Road the cops had set up a road block and were waiting for the Cadillac. The cop who approached his car was a friend and told Tait to pretend he was having a heart attack. He called an ambulance and had Tait taken to Metropolitan Hospital. The physician who saw him told him there was nothing wrong, he was "just drunk."

Tait took a taxi back to the courthouse but it was clear to Judge

Larry Pinnell (affectionately known as "Weeping Larry" because of his soft heart) that Tait was so drunk he would not be able to function. Pinnell called a recess and told Tait's co-counsel - Ted Perfect and Cotrell - to say Tait was sick so that he would not have to hold him in contempt of court. Perfect called 911 and said Tait was having chest pains. Ambulance attendants arrived and took Tait, still in his robes, out of the courthouse on a stretcher.

Unfortunately for Tait they took him back to Metropolitan Hospital and to the same ER doc who has seen him earlier in the day. He wasn't happy to see the drunk lawyer again and threw him out, telling him he didn't want to see him back in ER. Tait drove to his office and because he was afraid the cops would be on the lookout for him, had his secretary drive him home.

While Tait was heading home, his daughter Melanie, now in grade three, was showing several police officers where her daddy kept his guns, which included the .357 Magnum. One was legal, several others were not. They were all loaded. As he came in the door of his home he was arrested for possession of a restricted and stolen weapon. He didn't know that the illegal gun given to him by one of the Outlaws had also been stolen. Tait was thrown in the Windsor Jail on Sandwich Street in the west end of the city and during the night went into severe withdrawal.

"I know Johanna called the cops because she knew Melanie was in the house and didn't want an eight-year-old finding the guns. Who could blame her?"

Montello, worried and realizing his friend and colleague had hit a new alcoholic low, went to Brentwood to see Charbonneau. At first Charbonneau thought Montello, who was looking a bit ragged with concern for Tait, was coming to sign himself in. Montello explained Tait's predicament and Charbonneau agreed to have him enter the rehab.

The following morning Tait, still barely sober, appeared in

court held up by two police officers to appear before a Justice of the Peace. Earlier, Montello had stopped at a drug store and picked up a prescription of Librium to prevent Tait from having a seizure during the court appearance. With Montello defending him at the hearing he was granted bail with the stipulation he attend a rehab program. (He would later plead guilty to having a restricted weapon and be given a conditional discharge. He received a pardon from the charge in September, 1980 with no criminal conviction registered)

Following his release on February 8, 1980, Charbonneau came to court and took him to Brentwood. Because of his prominent profile in the city, Tait's arrest led local newscasts and made front page headlines at the top of the fold of the Windsor Star newspaper.

"I was in a mess but the last place I wanted to be was there, in Brentwood. Melanie was brought in to say goodbye to me because she was going to live with my parents, Barb was in private school in New Brunswick, Johanna was gone. I was losing everything."

In London, Brenda had married the manager of the library at the University of Western Ontario. Tait had always suspected she was having an affair with him during the time she worked in a senior position at the library when he was in law school. Not that he could cast aspersions on his cuckolded wife. And there was more loss to come. While Tait spent the next two weeks in a withdrawal "fog," Montello was dividing his files among other lawyers and closing his office. His home and car were repossessed. It was all gone.

Tait spent his first few nights in Brentwood sleeping on a couch in the lounge because of lack of space. In Brentwood, Tait was "no big shit, just one of the drunks." He woke the first morning to see everyone else who had spent the night in the lounge on their knees praying. His first thought was "What the fuck have I gotten myself into here?" During the morning he attempted to play darts but found he had no coordination and could not throw as well as a three year old might.

94

For the next three weeks workers at Brentwood fought to control Tait's withdrawal symptoms. His body was on the verge of shutting down and he was closely monitored during the physical recovery period. He had been prescribed a variety of medications, including pills to keep his blood pressure down and keep him calm to prevent seizures.

Once he was considered physically stable, Tait was moved from the observation room into his own small room with a bed, table and desk. His mornings in rehab began with a shower and breakfast, followed by a lecture from Charbonneau whose arm waving, expletive-laced admonishments interspersed with puffs on his large Cuban, were legendary. Charbonneau believed in stripping people to the bare bone, then slowly allowing them to rebuild based on his insights and the tenets of AA. He took no crap, not from anyone.

One morning lying in bed Tait heard Charbonneau screaming, then a crash and seconds later a TV dropped past his window. Charbonneau was upset with a resident. Later, in a meeting with about twenty residents, Charbonneau noticed one of them sound asleep. He hurled his teacup at the guy's head, quickly getting his undivided attention. But he was effective and Tait cites him as the main reason he was able to get sober and stay sober for such a long period following this particular rehab stay.

Each morning in Brentwood Tait would take part in various group assignments and one-on-one counselling. In those early days he had a fantasy about getting out, heading to Las Vegas and becoming manager of a casino. He says, "All kind of weird things came into my brain."

His nine months in Brentwood became the first step in Tait's spiritual awakening, albeit a very small step but a beginning nonetheless. He attended AA meetings at night and spent many hours in discussions with Charbonneau who became a mentor and father figure.

"He really cared about me. Father Paul got in your face but I liked and respected him. There was always a twinkle in his eye and I was awed by the fact that he devoted his whole life to alcoholics. He and I got along well. I really believed in him and it was my belief and faith in him that made the difference for me and helped change my life. He taught me that the more I helped people good things happened. I did what I was told. "

But Tait did not embrace the program wholeheartedly and said it took some time for him to truly understand what it was all about. Yet, even though he thought he was buying in to the AA philosophy, he was misplacing the meaning of "higher power" and had no idea at the time that the missing spiritual piece would ultimately not make for a solid foundation in recovery.

"For months I would listen to what I considered mumbo jumbo about the solution being a relationship with God and I don't think I ever really believed any of it. I knew I was an alcoholic and the solution was not to drink. AA says you have to give yourself to a power greater than you and I did. I gave it to AA but more so to Father Paul. I made him the power greater than me. I relied heavily on him and developed a spiritual relationship with him."

Tait remembers his time in Brentwood as being "pretty uneventful," unlike many alcoholics who experience "the great awakening" or who have emotional or physical blowouts. While he was on friendly terms with many of the alcoholic residents, only one found a way into Tait's emotional psyche. In Dan Soulliere he found a lifelong friend. Soulliere had been working in a local factory but Tait saw something special in the man and suggested he go to law school. A good thought, but fairly impractical at the time, considering their circumstances. However, in later years Tait was to pay for Soulliere's law school tuition and following his graduation, hired him. He worked with Tait for several years and eventually set up his own independent family law practice. Now retired, he and Tait remain very close friends. Following the death of Charbonneau many years later Soulliere would become the rehab's director and has always professed gratitude and a deep affection for Tait.

"He was and is a good man, a talented criminal lawyer and a great friend. It was hard to see what he was doing to himself and feel helpless. What he did for me changed my whole life. Many people don't know half of the things Don has done for people. They just see the notoriety and excess but they don't know the real Tait. He's the real thing."

In March, about three months after Tait entered Brentwood, Johanna received a call from Father Charbonneau. He told her that Don was a changed man and was doing very well in recovery. He asked if she could find it in her heart to forgive him and give the relationship another chance. She agreed to come from London for a visit and in April, just after Easter, she and Tait spent many hours talking during her visits to Brentwood. They discovered that the love and lust still flamed between them and reconciled, making plans for when he would be released.

STARTING OVER– The Sober Years

IN SEPTEMBER 1980 a rejuvenated Tait packed his small suitcase, heaved a sigh of relief and went to say goodbye to the people he had formed a relationship with in the rehab. He was a drunk like them, but he was also a local celebrity and had an air about him that made people want to get closer. He could be profane and irreverent as easily as he could be elegant and sophisticated and perhaps it was this dichotomy that brooked no middle ground. People hated him or loved him.

Tait left Brentwood that fall morning with Johanna. They were going home together but not to the richly appointed housing they were accustomed to before rehab. Tait had lost everything and they were starting over. With daughters Melanie, home from living with her grandparents and Barbara, who was also home from Netherwood boarding school because the money had run out, they moved into a rented old townhouse on Chatham Street in a downtown Windsor neighbourhood. It was an inauspicious new beginning that would ultimately lead to years of sobriety and extraordinary success.

Fellow lawyers and judge friends, believing he had so tarnished his reputation he could never again be successful in solo practice, told him not to attempt it because it would only lead to disappointment. They were so convinced he would be a failure they suggested he get out of town and start over somewhere else. Charbonneau, however, disagreed and adamantly told Tait to ignore them and just do it.

He believed in Tait so strongly he gave him a $5,000 start-up loan which Tait eventually paid back with interest. He set up an office in the apartment next door and Johanna worked as his secretary. People who were fed up with his antics continued to tell him he would never make it in the city because of his now sordid reputation. And while Tait tried to remain confident that he could, and would be successful, there were times when their cautions had him worried.

He knew several cases he was working on before going to Brentwood that had been taken over by Montello, had not yet gone to court. Still a fan of the sharp-minded young lawyer, Montello met with Tait and passed the cases back to him. It was a slow start. Then, one day, in walked the Outlaw, Filiault.

"He wanted me to continue to act for him on a narcotics trafficking case that had not gone to court. To show me he meant business he tossed a briefcase on the desk, opened it and said, 'That's $25,000.' Here was a guy who at one time had put a contract out on me because of the beating one of his guys got for trying to kill me. Now, he wanted to hire me."

Cementing his reputation and earning him more biker business, Tait got the Outlaw off and never looked back. He could pay the rent and put food on the table. Tossing fear of failure to the wind, as much as his internal angst would let him, Tait was now convinced success was his for the taking. He would show the non-believers.

Still without significant cash flow, his accountant helped him buy a Toyota Celica and for the next year and a half his practice started picking up speed, which also meant the money started to swell his bank account. Two years to the month after being hauled into Brentwood, he and Johanna moved into a home on Snake Lane in the secluded area of River Canard in the town of LaSalle, a small bedroom community about thirty minutes from Windsor.

He swapped his Celica for a blue 1982 Cadillac which he quickly traded up for a gold 380, two-seater 1982 Mercedes SL. His spending excesses had begun. Money was taking the place of drugs and alcohol.

The media began covering his trials and seeking him out for legal comment. His bad boy makes a comeback image made him all the more interesting and in 1982 the Windsor Star published an elaborate profile of the dynamic, reformed lawyer Don Tait - extolling the virtue of his recovery. They took photos of the interior and exterior of his home and of him working in his study. He was sober and said while he would continue to defend his more unsavoury biker clients, he no longer hung out with them. The only biker in his inner circle was O'Reilly. Tait became the poster boy for Brentwood.

That year he also had a chance to say, "I'm sorry" to Brenda for the pain he had caused her. She was 37 years old and dying of stomach cancer. Tait had gone to see her during the last weeks of her life and the two "talked and made amends." He had brought her misery and her forgiveness assuaged some of the guilt he carried because of it.

Only three years out of rehab Tait was nominated by senior judges and peers to receive the honour of being named Queen's Counsel (QC) - awarded to lawyers appointed by letters patent to be one of "Her Majesty's Counsel learned in the law." The Attorney General of Ontario agreed with the many supportive letters written on his behalf and bestowed the moniker on Tait.

At the party to celebrate, almost the entire legal population, cops, politicians and all members of the local glitterati lined up to shake his hand and congratulate him. He received a letter from Judge Carl Zalev - one of the city's more elegant and reserved members of the bench - which read "In the last five years of appointments of QC, yours is the only one deserving." Those words from a judge of Zalev's stature resonated with Tait.

"I will never forget that letter. It was beautiful and it meant a great deal coming from Judge Zalev. He is someone I really respected. I never considered myself a great legal mind but I was a very effective lawyer."

He also received the prestigious U.S. - based Martindale-Hubbell Law Directory's highest rating for criminal lawyers in

Canada demonstrating a "very high ethical standard and legal ability."

With money now rolling in Tait began exchanging cars and homes, each grander than the one before. They moved from Snake Lane to a $250,000 home on the water in Amherstburg. Four years later they sold it for $750,000 in a house swap that saw them renovate the swapped house and ultimately sell it for $950,000 to a local lottery winner.

While Tait was getting off on his rise to the top again and couldn't get enough of the good life and the adulation that came with it, he was not making a home – at least not where Johanna was concerned. She liked nice things and appreciated the expensive gifts he gave her, but what she wanted more than anything was to have a normal family life with the man she loved. She enjoyed living in their home in Amherstburg and would have liked to stay there but Tait needed more and better. His parents had moved in with them again from New Brunswick and the two girls were in elementary and high school. Johanna was constantly called to the school where Melanie was in trouble because of her drinking and other problems.

"I was the one who attended the schools each time the kids were in trouble. I took care of everything."

In June 1991 he bought the last home he would own in Windsor - for a cool $1.05 million - from the now disgraced developer and German native Eric Brauss. It was the first home on Riverside Drive to sell for a million and was such an unprecedented sale it drew media attention. Tait and Johanna spent approximately $300,000 on improvements and in September 1999 Tait added $100,000 to the $586,000 mortgage.

A showpiece of stark, ultra-modern design, the two-storey house with its dark grey exterior became an iconic head turner. Inside, the upstairs had three bedrooms, several bathrooms and Tait's office. The master bedroom had the bed on an elevated platform and a mirrored ceiling. The dining and living rooms overlooked the Detroit River, as did the kitchen which boasted every top-of-the-line convenience that could be squeezed into the allotted space. The basement had a bedroom and fully equipped gym to rival some professional exercise facilities. While Tait loved his home because it had everything money could buy, Johanna found it sterile and cold. It never felt like home to her.

Tait's constant turnover of fast cars also drew public attention. He was the first person in Canada to own a restyled 1990 Mercedes 500 SL. He gave the white, classy vehicle to Johanna, leased a black Porsche 935 for himself and then couldn't resist owning the Porsche twin-Turbo wide fender 911 - white with a black convertible roof.

Behind the Riverside house he parked a 46 ft. Sea Ray - complete with expensive elevator-type lifts that brought it in and out of the water. A similar lift was installed for their matching sea-doos. He built a heated, air-conditioned dog house for his two beloved shepherds. They filled the house with expensive art – paintings, sculptures and glassware, sparing no expense. It was all about acquiring things and Tait wanting the best of everything.

Tait was doing back-to-back trials. Clients were clamouring once again to hire the reformed, legally brilliant bad boy of the court. He smelled of success and clients were more than willing to pay him $500 - $600 an hour. A sex assault case could bring in as much as $50,000. Mafia fees often came in cash. He wasn't squandering money on booze because he no longer drank and they seemed to want for nothing, but he had simply exchanged one addiction for another. Tait was leading a monster ego-charged life of excess.

"I wasn't drinking and I didn't hang with clients. I loved success and achievement, the feel of money and the things it could buy. I loved the admiration of people. I loved nice things. I bought nice things and went nice places. The first Rolex I ever saw was on me. I bought one for Johanna with diamonds on it. They were $8,000 in the early 1980s and that was a lot of money at the time. I liked being known in Windsor and Detroit, especially when I went to restaurants and people knew who I was. I loved that."

The Taits lived lavishly and took luxury vacations. But make no mistake about it, Tait earned those vacations. He worked an average twelve to fourteen-hour day and long hours on weekends. He was obsessed and hooked on the adrenalin rush court oratory brought him. Life was about achievement and success. The law was a means to an end, to be used to get what he wanted and what Don Tait wanted was getting approval and feeling the power and glory that comes with not just being the best but having everyone tell you that you are the best. He was focused on behaving in a way that earned everyone's approval. If there was something he knew he wouldn't do well, he didn't do it. There were many experiences in life he missed out on because he would never risk doing something if there was a remote chance it would not be successful. He also developed solid relationships with the police and powerful, connected people.

"I loved it. I lived for the moment I set foot in the courtroom and especially addressing a jury. It was natural to me and I loved being able to do the best for my client. I would often threaten them with a trial when they didn't see the reasoning in making a deal. We went to trial only when I could see a benefit to the client. I prepared and prepared and prepared. I made it seem like it was easy but that was because I spent so much time working at it. I enjoyed winning so much I knew I had to work harder than the other side in order to win."

Their wealthy lifestyle was possible in part because of the hundreds of thousands of dollars Tait earned from his defence of the bikers. But he also defended high paying people with connections to crime syndicates. As he often discovered, they could all be dangerous clients. One of his many such clients included Joe Marini who nearly got him killed. In court there are always two sides represented – the victim and the accused and often their extended families. Any or all aspects of the case presented by the defence can cause great resentment and anger among those family members. Tait was retained by the family to defend Marini on a charge of second degree murder in the death of the daughter of the Bortelli family, who were alleged by Marini and others to be connected to the mafia.

Marini had fled to Italy and Windsor police had to go there to have him extradited to Canada to stand trial. Things were not looking good since evidence put him at the scene of the murder and the forensic pathologist said the young woman appeared to have bruising on her throat consistent with a thumb print, indicating she was strangled. The Crown said they had "An overwhelming case against him." Even the judge told Tait "If you get this guy off I'll personally have a statue of you built outside the courthouse."

 Marini's version of the story had them having sex and later getting into a fight because he wanted to break off the relationship. He said the woman attacked him and when he pushed her off she fell against the coffee table and hit her neck. Police investigators found porn playing cards on a table, a dildo and other sex toys in the room. Tait's investigators turned up evidence that the woman had many sexual proclivities and owned a plethora of sexual toys including a double headed dildo, various sexual vibrators and the playing cards with porn images. All of these Tait presented as evidence that the sex was consensual.

Tait also called in Dr. Werner Spitz from Michigan. Spitz had become the darling of the legal communities in the U.S. and Windsor because of his expertise in forensics and the blunt, no bullshit delivery of his opinions. He had also written many of the textbooks on forensic pathology. In court, Tait made sure that Spitz's reputation and expertise were well documented for the judge and jury. He had blown up the photograph of the marks on the deceased woman's neck and disagreed that it was a thumb print. He did agree that the rectangular marking would suggest Marini was telling the truth when he said he pushed her and she fell, striking her neck on the night table, causing the carotid artery to go into spasm and killing her.

As Tait was parading each piece of damning evidence before the jury, the Bortelli family was in a rage because they saw it as besmirching their daughter's reputation. They would glare at Tait as he confidently strutted away from the witness box, his arrogant, cocky smile in their direction making them even angrier.

After the last presentation of evidence, the judge called a recess. He told Tait "Jesus Christ, looks like I'll have to build that statue." But this was no ordinary case, no ordinary client and no ordinary family of the victim. When Tait told Marini and his family he would in all likelihood get him off they were concerned. It was rumoured that the family of the deceased woman were well connected to the powerful mafia in Detroit and knew how things worked. Marini and his family were convinced that if he walked out of court free he would be killed in very short order.

Tait suggested they plead to manslaughter which would see Marini get a sentence of five years with parole after two spent in prison. Tait took the plea to the court and Marini got the five years. The deal worked well until he walked out a free man. Within days of his release he was found floating in Toronto Harbour. Tait got worried. He was even more worried after receiving a call from the police officer in Windsor in charge of the prosecution's office who told him their intelligence had revealed that he, Tait, was next on the hit list, but said he couldn't give him any details.

There was a contract out on him because he had trashed the daughter's reputation. O'Reilly started carrying a gun and wasn't far from Tait's side.

"I called Joe Cuffaro and asked what the fuck was going on, that I was getting it from reliable sources that I was supposed to be getting a hit from Detroit."

Joseph Cuffaro was alleged to be a powerful figure in criminal circles, allegedly referred to as the "Lee Iacocca" of the drug world, a reference to the brilliant mastermind behind the remaking of the Chrysler Corporation. Cuffaro's father was serving time for being a member of the mafia. Cuffaro was a client and Tait had flown to Montreal to pick up a "substantial" amount of cash to conduct Cuffaro's defence on drug charges. It was the kind of cash that had to be carried in a fair-sized suitcase.

"I said Joe, I have a problem here. I have a contract out on me. I'm next on the list. Well, he told me not to worry about it and that was the end of it. I was safe. Sometime later Bortelli's sister came to my office to let me know she wasn't an enemy."

Tait was winning and his ego driven personality began to let some of the lessons he learned from Charbonneau slip by the wayside. In the early years following his release from Brentwood Tait sat on the Board of Directors, following the AA principles of love and service. He became Chairman of the Board and still related to Charbonneau. However, from the time they were living in Amherstburg he began attending fewer AA and Brentwood meetings and within eight years had stopped going completely, feeling he could now rely on himself. He had made it.

"Talk about a mistake. Relying on self is the biggest problem with alcoholics. Self-centeredness is the beast and I was in full flight. In some ways it was as though I had learned nothing."

Many of Tait's cases during the period of the 1980s and 1990s remain some of the highest profile in the city's history. His defence of Joe Cuffaro, a member of Montreal's money laundering family and one of five men charged in a heroin trafficking ring in Essex County, made national headlines. In a sting operation, Windsor police had wiretapped conversations between Cuffaro and his uncle who owned a body shop about thirty miles east of Windsor. During the operation they dug up jade rocks buried on a farm owned by the uncle and found a stash of heroin they estimated to be worth more than $500 million. Its destination was New York. Cuffaro and three other men were arrested and charged.

The Justice Department alleged Cuffaro, 30, the son of reputed mobster Giuseppe Cuffaro, was the mastermind of the operation but Tait successfully presented a case that showed his identity as the mastermind could not be proved from wiretaps presented in court. Investigators could identify the uncle but not the caller but said they were certain it was Cuffaro because the men talked about Cuffaro's family, his twins and named his wife. In court, Tait argued that the tapes should not be admissible. The judge ruled that if someone has a reasonable thought of being wrongly intercepted it would be admissible. The uncle did not have that expectation.

Tait countered that the person at the other end of the conversation didn't have that expectation and all the mentions of his wife and twins were made by the uncle, with the person at the other end agreeing. He argued if that evidence was accepted and you knocked that out of the evidence, the Crown had nothing – everything they had was coming from the uncle. The next ploy was to get the other three men to plead out, allowing Cuffaro to walk.

"I had all of the accused and Cuffaro sit in a room together behind closed doors and asked them to make a deal about pleading guilty. The reason I got them all together with Joe was to deliver the obvious message that he was the leader and they will be in deep shit when he gets out. After about five hours Joe comes out, winks at me. We go back into the courtroom."

The Crown agreed that if the other men pleaded guilty he would stay the charges against Cuffaro. The men agreed and Cuffaro stepped down from the prisoner's box a free man. Three of the men, who were defended by other lawyers, were convicted and sent to prison for eighteen years and a fourth man was given a -year jail term. Tait's client was so grateful he and his wife took Tait and Johanna, Tait's partner Bobby DiPietro and an office secretary on a vacation to Tahiti. He also bought Tait and Johanna Cartier pens – silver for Tait, gold for Johanna – which they still have tucked away in a drawer.

This was the kind of courtroom drama Tait lived for – getting off on the intrigue, using his sharp wits and knowledge of the law to be successful; and the risk taking – knowing there was always a chance if one of his clients was unhappy with a trial outcome he could end up like a Montreal lawyer who was shot full of bullets. But it brought him notoriety, attention, respect and accolades – at least in the daylight hours. He would go to bed on a high. WOW! He was king of the world, operating at high levels of legal dramatics. He would wake up in a cold sweat, terrified and full of fear of failure, fear of being exposed, fearful that people would find out he wasn't really that good. Only the next fix in court would banish the debilitating thoughts and let him prove his worth another time. The truth of the matter was he was really good, but the truth of the matter was he never believed it, so he had to have more. On the outside, everyone saw a guy who had it all together but inside he was the antithesis of the brash, confident arrogance he exuded.

It wasn't difficult to feed his "more" addiction. The guilty always came looking for him. Another case that brought him international attention came in 1990 when teenager Raymond Laroche was convicted of beating his infant son to death, tying him up in a plastic bag and tossing his small body in the Detroit River. Tait defended Laroche, basking in the glaring spotlight of foreign media, particularly the Detroit media, whose stories were filled with comments from the highly quotable lawyer. Laroche was jailed for manslaughter and served his entire ten-year sentence. (He died in September, 2013.)

In 1995 Tait had three major cases that yet again made international headlines.

He defended NHL star Ed Jovanovski who was charged with sexually assaulting a woman he met while playing with the Windsor Spitfires. The case caused a media frenzy and Tait played it like a maestro. He called the media to a press conference where he was going to release the name of the woman accusing Jovanovski of the assault. Women's groups were enraged. The charges against Jovanovski and two other Spitfires were dropped.

Tait caused yet another media uproar when he defended a Leamington teacher also accused of sexual assault. He made it clear he intended to use counselling records of the woman Nick Carosella was accused of assaulting in his defence in court. This outrage prompted the Sexual Assault Treatment Centre to shred all of the woman's confidential records to avoid them being used at the trial. Carosella's case ended up before the Supreme Court of Canada, which upheld a lower court ruling to stay the charges against Tait's client.

Perhaps one of his most notorious cases was that of Windsor plastic surgeon Keith Caughell who was charged with drugging and sexually assaulting women in his clinic. To the public's astonishment and disgust, Tait's defence gets the criminal charges against Caughell withdrawn but he was later suspended by the College of Physicians and Surgeons of Ontario. Those years and all those cases Tait remembers as the greatest of his career and it astounds him still. He was billing a million plus a year and living a life most only dream of.

"I used to shake my head because I couldn't believe it. This little fuck head from New Brunswick so full of fear could actually gain the notoriety and reputation that I had. People were afraid of me. If they didn't respect me they were scared of me and they always came calling when they were in trouble."

Tait recounts an encounter with a staff sergeant from the RCMP during his defence of a member of the Mafia. Worthen Spence pulled him aside one day in court and asked, "How do you sleep when you represent scum like this?"

"Like a fucking baby," Tait retorted.

Just six months later the phone rang in Tait's home at 6 a.m. O'Reilly put down his coffee cup and picked it up.

"Who's calling?" demanded O'Reilly. He called Tait and told him Worthen Spence from the RCMP was on the line.

"I need you," said Spence.

"Here he was, asking me to defend him. He was charged with fraud. I defended him and he pled out. They had him cold turkey. He was the head man and should have gone to jail but they allowed him to resign."

Spence, a thirty-year veteran who was named commander of the forty-six local RCMP officers in Windsor in 1990, was charged with defrauding the RCMP of $10,500 through credit card use and expense accounts. He had been allowed to resign, repaid the money and was put on one-year probation. About why his client committed the crime Tait told the court, "There is no explanation. He can't explain it. No one can explain it."

Tait worked hard to create the persona of Don Tait as a man in charge of his own life and destiny, a legal ace to be reckoned with and bon vivant. Even though he had stopped going to Brentwood meetings and AA, he continued to visit Charbonneau and served several more years on the Board of Directors. Despite the success of his practice and stable home life, Tait's nemesis with the pitchfork was never far away. But to keep him at bay Tait overworked and overachieved.

"I had it all under control. But what I was doing was substituting wealth and acquiring things for the alcohol I was no longer consuming. I loved it all, but each success would only last for a while. I became used to the power and once the feeling of success started to wear off I'd need another fix. The cases kept coming and I worked hard to make sure I got that fix. I had not surrendered anything."

Montello could not have been happier to see his young friend healthy and successful. From their first meeting in 1971 he said he knew the brash young rookie lawyer would become a force to be reckoned with. He was also proud of Tait because of his generosity.

"He helped many, many young lawyers who were getting started. He even paid some of their academic fees. If you needed help and asked Don, he never turned you down. But he did it quietly and didn't ask for any big hoopla about it. He was just simply generous. I knew from the outset that Don was going to be successful. He was so impressive to watch in a courtroom."

But despite leading what most saw as a charmed life, and while he forced himself to always present a cock of the walk confidence, there were rare moments when he let his guard down. Years earlier, in 1988, I was covering many court cases for CBC Radio and often sat in on his trials. All the media would be at a Tait trial because they so often involved larger than life criminals and Tait's performances made great coverage.

During one particular case the media watched in fascination as Tait destroyed a Crown witness and no one did it better than Tait. He could be utterly ruthless and would not hesitate to shred the dignity and confidence of a witness if he thought it would free his client. That behaviour wasn't a surprise. It was a Tait trademark and few left the witness box unscathed.

What did come as a surprise in the courtroom that fall day was the brief glimpse I had of Tait's insecurities and was convinced it was done on such a subconscious level he never expected anyone to see what he had revealed.

As he always did during a brief recess in court proceedings, Tait, confident and pumped, swaggered over to talk to the media gathered at the wooden railing that separated spectators from the judge, lawyers, jury and the accused. He came to boast confidently about the previous hours of testimony, his defence and cross examination; but this was different. Following a particularly brutal grilling of a witness, the judge had called a recess to allow the woman to compose herself. Tait wanted to know if he had been too hard on her. It was a rhetorical question that did not expect an answer.

"I know that witness hates me. I know she does. She hates me. I can see it in her eyes, but I was just doing my job. It's my job," Tait said with consternation. No one spoke. The Crown called him away and with his head at an arrogant tilt, he lithely strutted across the room oozing confidence. The reporters looked at one another and shrugged. It was just Tait. But what they had just witnessed was a brief, significant chink in his armour. Behind Tait's tough-talking, I-don't-give-a-damn-about-anything attitude there appeared to be a strangely insecure man.

Three days after Tait had inadvertently let his guard down, he stood like a peacock on the steps of the courthouse, basking in the success of freeing a client, preening in his trademark black Armani suit and performing for the media. Little did I know that strange day in the court room was to be an omen for how our lives would intersect many years later.

During the early years following his release from Brentwood his relationship with Johanna appeared to be on solid footing. Tait, the notorious womanizer, says he was faithful to his wife. They were "hot" together and lived like royalty. He showered her with gifts of clothing and jewellery and she wanted for nothing. It all seemed invincible.

112

"In those days I could see a lot of women would be more than willing to get together with me but I really only wanted Johanna."

Then, a seemingly harmless, innocent event was to set off a chain reaction that Tait says changed their lives forever, and not for the better. Many years later he would admit that, because of his reaction to everything that happened, everything that followed was completely his fault. One of Johanna's sisters was divorced and needed a job. Johanna asked if Tait would hire her in the office to give her some experience. He did.

"I didn't care. I was making lots of money and it was for Johanna. Of course I'd do it. It was no big deal. I had sent her parents to Holland because I knew how much her family meant to her. So, I told the office manager to help her out. I was enthralled that she asked me because it showed she was depending on me to help her family."

But after two or three months Johanna told Tait there was trouble at the office and the manager and employees were complaining about her sister. It seems she was selling Avon products over the phone and not doing any work to help out the other staff. Johanna asked Tait to deal with it.

"I didn't care what she was doing but I didn't want trouble so I asked her to do it discretely so that the rest of the staff didn't get upset. But I said it's not any business of the staff. It's my business. I brought her in, there was never an ugly word spoken. I told her I understood her dilemma, just go someplace that was private to make calls. She said 'OK' and to me that was the end of it."

The first inkling Tait says he had that all was not well was the first Sunday Johanna's parents didn't come to dinner as they had done for years. Tait could hear snippets of furtive phone conversations between Johanna and family members.

"One day I heard Johanna say, 'Don wouldn't say that' and I

wondered what was going on. Well, it turns out that the sister told her parents I had ripped her over the coals and told her if she wanted to make money she should tie a mattress to her back and go out on Wyandotte Street. They ostracized her and I was proud of her for standing up for me. Because Johanna told them I wouldn't say something like that they stopped talking to her. But one Sunday they turned up again and everything seemed ok."

Tait said he didn't think any more about the incident. But it wasn't to be the end of it.

"One day Johanna said 'You know Don I've been thinking. I know you - you probably did say something to my sister.' I couldn't believe what I was hearing. I know she did not believe her. It was so obvious to me and I couldn't believe how dishonest she was being about it. To me this was a betrayal. And I don't take well to feeling betrayed."

Tait's reaction was volcanic. He was outraged and rattled by what he saw as the ultimate betrayal and went to talk to Charbonneau who suggested he and Johanna separate until the issue was dealt with. They didn't.

"We fought about this for a year. Everything blew up between us. I used to tell her that it wasn't that she disbelieved me, I knew she didn't, but it was the fact she was pretending to disbelieve me. It was a betrayal I could not get over. I could have handled it if she had actually believed I had done that, but I knew she didn't believe it. That to me was a total rejection – that her family was more important than me and my life was about getting approval. I should have moved out but I stayed and began fucking around on her. I felt we had no relationship left. We were both responsible but because of her lie everything went to shit between us. It changed everything and nothing was ever the same again. That sounds stupid now, but it was how I felt at the time. It wasn't a very adult or sane reaction."

Johanna, on the other hand, could see their life changing when she realized Don wasn't attending AA meetings and had no interest in devoting time to recovery. "That was the real downfall of everything. It was starting to happen then and there. It's part of the alcoholism. And no matter what else happened, things started changing because of that but Don couldn't see it."

Tait says because he no longer felt he had a relationship with Johanna he began a merry-go-round of women and there was never a shortage. The first was a secretary who "looked cute" and Tait kept her in an apartment on Ouellette Avenue for six or seven months. Johanna says the woman later sent her a note telling her she was involved with both Tait and his partner. She even supplied hotel receipts indicating where they had gone for sex. She said Tait split with her when she decided to go to nursing school and began dating a cop. His behaviour was stupid and wrong, Tait has said many times in the past several years, and today wishes he had dealt with the crisis in his marriage in a more mature and ethical fashion.

"My response to it was I was married but having affairs. I shouldn't have done that. I should have listened to Father Paul and separated. I should have looked at why Johanna felt she had to side with her family and to understand that. To me it was a betrayal of me and it was all about me, so my reaction was to start having affairs. It wasn't her sister who destroyed our relationship, it was my reaction. It goes back to that fat boy who was never good enough. This to me was rejection and I couldn't handle rejection. It wasn't about sex. It was about getting the approval I felt I wasn't getting at home. I needed that approval. It was my survival."

In the summer of 1992 Tait and Johanna got into a fight that turned physical. They had been at Johanna's parents' home to celebrate her birthday. Tait was angry the sister was there and the argument that started in the car on the way home intensified when they got in the house. Johanna says Tait grabbed her and ripped her blouse. "He pushed me on the floor and had his hands around my neck and left marks."

Tait again called Charbonneau who advised him to do the right thing and separate. But by this time Johanna had put up with enough of Tait's behaviour and infidelity. She had contacted a lawyer in Toronto and prepared to leave. She also hired a private detective who told her about the secretary. Johanna left and moved in to a house Tait had put a down payment on for her in the Riverside area of the city. Before she moved out Johanna was driving a 500 Mercedes SL which Tait had leased, while he drove a Porsche. He gave her their black Mercedes four-door passenger car and provided her with a monthly allowance of $8,000.

"He was downsizing because of all the money he owed keeping apartments for three other women," Johanna recalls unhappily. She believes the incident with her sister is just Tait's way of justifying his affairs. Tait vehemently disagrees and says while he takes full responsibility for his behaviour and lays no blame, without the incident there is no telling what might have happened and feels it was possible they would have stayed together. But the rift that started then continues to plague them both. With Johanna gone, Tait needed another drug to fill his craving for approval and nowhere could he find it more successfully than with other women.

"I had a lot of women after that I can tell you. So many I can hardly remember or believe it. But it wasn't that I was a sex addict. Far from it. I craved approval. It was a huge hole in me and the more I got the more I needed. I knew I could get that approval from women."

In his quest to find a woman to share his life he began to notice a nubile young woman who worked in his office. She had long dark hair and made no secret of her attraction to Windsor's celebrity defence attorney. One afternoon hey were driving back to the office following a luncheon event she reached across and let her left hand evoke a volcanic response. He was fifty and she was twenty-two.

Despite admonitions from his colleagues the two became inseparable. They travelled to Jamaica and Antigua, France, Italy and New Orleans and many other destinations in Europe, Canada and the U.S. They would fly to Florida for a weekend or take Tait's boat to the town of Tobermory in Northern Ontario, then fly back and forth for weekends. He bought her a 4.5-carat diamond ring, they shopped in Paris and Detroit's Somerset Mall buying clothes and accessories by designers such as Gucci. It was "only the best, all the way," Tait recalls. She moved in to the house on Riverside Drive.

"I was happy. Everything was going my way. Money. Notoriety. We both got certified as divers and twice rented a yacht in the British Virgin Islands where we would spend days diving, on the beach and idyllic nights together. We were really having a great time. I wasn't drinking but I started smoking grass with her in Jamaica where we once rented a hacienda. There were rolled joints in every room."

When he turned fifty Tait jokingly commented that no one had a party to celebrate the milestone. But just before his fifth-first birthday a friend on the Miami police force called to say he was coming to Windsor and invited Tait to a polygraph seminar he was giving. He explained he wouldn't have time to get together other than to talk at the event. Tait agreed to attend. When Tait walked into the Caboto Club conference room Tina Turner's song "You're the Best" was blaring over a loud speaker and a roar of "Happy Birthday" erupted from the masses gathered in the room. He realized his American friend was in on the biggest surprise party of his life. The room was filled with hundreds of members of the legal profession at all levels, police officers and senior officials, members of the media, politicians and clients. Those who couldn't attend sent telegrams of congratulations.

While he and young Tami Brewster were having a swinging time, the May-December aspect of their relationship was eating at Tait's insecurities. He counted all the ways things were working well. His daughters and his granddaughter

Courtney got along very well with her – partly because of her personality and no doubt in some respect because she was closer to their own ages. Tait was delighted that, like Johanna, she also loved his German shepherds.

They were together for a period of three years but during much of that time Tait kept waiting for the axe to fall on the affair. He believed as he aged she would lose interest and there was the matter of his having had a vasectomy. He lived in fear she would want a younger man and have a family of her own. However much she tried to reassure him, it wasn't enough to convince him. For Tait it would be rejection, something he knew he had to prevent at all costs.

"For an addict there is nothing more devastating than rejection. There is no doubt that my decision to give Tami up was based on abject fear of being rejected. I couldn't let that happen. I also thought about the fact that she would be only thirty-eight to my sixty-eight and how difficult that might be."

As his insecurity grew his reaction was to start letting other women come into his life, a sure-fire possibility of driving her away.

"She was a child physically but emotionally she was mature. She really loved me and forgave me over and over until she couldn't take any more. I rejected her because I was afraid she would reject me. It had absolutely nothing to do with her, it was all about me and the way I dealt with things. You see it was always all about me."

Then, in January 1994 he first saw the woman who would forever change the course of the rest of his life, who would set him on a path to a short-lived happiness followed by destruction and, strangely, ultimate redemption. No mean feat for a slim, dark haired, emotionally fragile young woman who for the most part had no idea of the real role she was playing in Tait's world.

Tait had heard about Sandra Martin from colleagues who told him one of the married lawyers was having an affair with her and had moved her in to an apartment near the court house. One Sunday afternoon when Tait was driving into the country on his way to Colasanti's Greenhouses, a local tourist attraction, he saw the lawyer and Martin heading back to Windsor in a bright red Ferrari convertible with the top down.

The second sighting was about two to three years later when that relationship had ended and Martin had married. She was in a restaurant across the street from Tait's office with her husband, sister and sister's fiancée. Tait was having dinner with several colleagues and when Martin and her sister walked past his table on their way to the bathroom Tait gave them a concentrated scrutiny, thinking Martin was "strikingly beautiful" but nothing more.

Tait was also still living with Tami. In late1994 Martin's aunt, who ran a successful women's clothing store on Erie Street, called Tait for advice. She said Martin had told her she was being abused by her husband from whom she had separated and asked if Tait would speak with her. Tait called Martin but after an hour-long conversation advised that the alleged assault was so minor it would never get to court and suggested if anything happened again Martin should call police. He told her he would be happy to have her drop by the office if she wanted to talk or they could meet for coffee.

Martin called several days later and said she would be more interested in going to dinner than having coffee. Tait said fine. They met at his office around 7 p.m. and drove in his Mercedes 600 SL to one of Tait's favourite restaurant in Detroit – the Golden Mushroom -- where they spent about four hours.

"I wasn't drinking but I ordered a bottle of good champagne for her and she was animated and talkative. She pretended she didn't know who I was but I knew that wasn't true. I didn't say anything because I thought it was her way of showing me she didn't care about my status or that I had money. She was feeling no pain when we left the restaurant and for some reason decided she didn't want to go home. She checked into a downtown hotel and wanted me to come in but I had Tami at home and refused. But it was clear that she wanted to spend the night together."

Several days later she phoned and asked Tait to meet her in the parking lot of the Lido restaurant where they sat and talked for about an hour. Then, a few days later asked Tait to pick her up at the Chatham Street Bar and Grill in downtown Windsor. She said she wanted him to come into the restaurant to get her. Tait thought this was odd, but parked and went inside where he saw the lawyer with whom Martin had an affair, dining with his wife. Martin was nowhere to be seen. Tait asked the Maître d' if a Sandra Martin was waiting for him. He replied she had gone to the bathroom. Tait nodded to the lawyer and his wife and soon saw Martin come up from the basement area, making a show of ensuring the lawyer saw her and could see she was leaving with Tait.

"Then I understood what that was all about. I didn't say anything to her. We just went to dinner and back to her place. There as a lot of kissing going on but no sex. Another time we decided to get a room at the Ponchartrain Hotel in Detroit. I arranged the best champagne, Beluga caviar and a great meal. Again, lots of necking but no sex."

Despite Martin's earlier attempt to get Tait into her bed, she put sex off-bounds and this continued for several months. It has to be remembered that Tait still lived with Brewster but was able to get away with being gone at odd hours because he often saw clients at all times of the day or night. After one evening of heavy petting at Martin's house a frustrated Tait snapped.

"I said 'look, what the fuck are you playing at. I'm not a game player. You were the one who wanted sex, now you're playing this game. Call me when you're interested.' I drove away and

120

she called me on the cell. I went back and that's when the affair started."

While the relationship now included sex, it was not an exclusive relationship since Brewster was still in Tait's home. Martin had also been seeing a goaltender with the NHL. That didn't bother Tait in the least. On one occasion the goalie called Martin at the Amherstburg police station where she worked to invite her to a hockey game at Joe Louis Arena in Detroit. Before the end of the evening she called Tait and said the evening was going badly and asked him to pick her up.

"I picked her up outside the Joe Louis and took her home. There was nothing committed here. I thought she was fun but she had serious mood swings and I never knew what to expect. I woke up one morning and went to the bathroom around six or seven and she was sitting in her car across the street watching the house. She later said she was just waiting to see who came out and was waiting for me. I had a lot of questions about her and as time went on there was something about her that made me feel great but cautious. She often seemed emotionally irrational and it concerned me at times."

During this time Tait was not only cheating on Brewster with Martin, he was also seeing a local TV anchor who had been interviewing him because of the controversial Carosella case. The gossiping media began referring to Tait as a "coke head," but not without the familiar ring of respect always afforded one of their most quotable courtroom heroes. The relationship was short lived and soon fizzled. Martin began dropping by Tait's office.

"She was always kissing me and laughing and as time went on I got hooked. I would take her to her aunt's store and buy her lots of clothes. The sex was getting wilder and I was spending more and more time with her. Then, in my mind I was beginning to see her becoming the woman who would take the place of Tami. Who would fill that void in me. Who would prevent me from being rejected."

121

Besides allowing him to avoid rejection, being caught with Martin would also give him a coward's way out of the relationship with Brewster. Such was the irony of Tait's life - while he would spend many hours getting under the skin and into the head space of his clients, he spent no time looking inward. His way of dealing with his personal life was mostly reactive, never trying to deal with, or come to terms with, the demons from his youth. Perhaps in some mental recess he knew such introspection would demand an analysis he was not willing to risk. He dealt with emotional adversity in the only way he knew which was to take the kind of action that ensured he inflicted the least harm on himself. He began taking Martin to more public events, letting everyone see them as a couple.

One of those events was the retirement dinner for the Town of Amherstburg's chief of police and it was that evening he decided he had found the answer to all his insecurities. On his way to pick Martin up, Tait stopped at his car dealership and swapped the BMW for a Ferrari. He insisted that she drive it to the party.

"As I watched her doing the Macarena on the dance floor that night, she looked happy and bubbly and really having a good time. It suddenly struck me, as clear as a bell. I had everything - notoriety, money, big expensive cars, a yacht, everything except a relationship, and I was still reeling from what I saw as a betrayal by Johanna. Now, this woman was going to be the answer to everything. This makes it all real. This is what I really need to fulfil me. And at that point I put on her the biggest demand possible - you are my salvation I was saying. That is now your responsibility. You will make me happy. You will be the icing on the cake and everything will be complete and wonderful. It had absolutely nothing to do with what I could do for her, but what I could do for her so that she could give me what I needed."

Tait began spending more time with Martin than with Brewster and the absurdity of it all was that both women's families lived on the same street. Brewster often stayed with her mother and on those nights Tait would have Martin spend the night at the house on Riverside Drive. It was inevitable that the two would eventually meet in confrontation. Brewster knew Tait was lying to her and one day followed his Ferrari to Martin's home where she saw them together. She flung Tait's 4.5-carat back at him, went home, packed and moved out. But there was another confrontation yet to come. One evening, when Martin was staying over at the house on Riverside Drive, she walked into the living room naked.

While that scene was playing out in the living room, Brewster was climbing the locked iron gates into the property. Hearing someone coming in the door Tait put Martin in a nearby closet. Brewster had come for the diamond ring. As they stood arguing in the middle of the living room, Brewster went to the cupboard where she knew Tait kept the ring. As she was going to open the door out stepped the naked Martin. Before Tait had time to react the two women began a catfight that ended up out on the driveway.

It was spectacular entertainment for neighbours in apartment buildings overlooking the Tait compound. Brewster, hurt and humiliated, eventually left, but she was not about to give up on winning Tait back. Attempting to reconcile, she took him on a visit to Chicago, hoping to convince him that she loved him far too much to ever leave and that she did not care about his vasectomy. She would prefer to have him to having children. While Tait wanted to believe her, the frightened ego that feared rejection would not let him. And so, they parted.

"When she finally decided she'd had enough of me, that was it, she had enough. There was no room for me after that. She wanted absolutely nothing to do with me. It went from one extreme to the other. Who could blame her?"

With Brewster no longer in the picture Tait concentrated on his stormy relationship with Martin. She and her small daughter became fixtures in Tait's home and he had one of the bedrooms decorated for a little girl. For the most part Martin was living up to Tait's expectations but he soon came to realize there was no way on earth she could fix everything inside him – and she had her own demons.

"She was mentally fragile and when she would be going through her nightmare it would become my nightmare. I began to see that when she was in a depression the thing that would take her out of it was marijuana so we started using it all the time. It was a rollercoaster. When she was firing on all cylinders she was magnificent. She was loving, kind and funny and we got along well. Then she would start going nuts and end up in hospital."

Their first Christmas together Tait threw a big New Year's Eve party and invited many of Martin's family members. He remembers it as a great evening. While her father was slow to warm up to him, Martin's grandmother and Tait became fast friends. Tait says because of their volatile relationship Martin moved out of the Riverside house many times but was always moving back. She sold her house and moved in, then moved out again. Whether she stayed or left depended on her mood swings which ranged from mania to depression. Because she enjoyed smoking weed, Tait introduced her to cocaine. He suspected she didn't know much about the white powder she was consuming, but he said she enjoyed the high and they were soon freebasing. It probably didn't help that she was also taking prescription medications for what she said were mental health issues.

"I have never had any doubt that Sandra is a wonderful human being but I also suspected she had some kind of serious mental health problems before I came on the scene, and she told me she was under the care of a psychiatrist. I knew how to make her feel good with the drugs and alcohol so that she could then make me feel good. And that's what this was all about – making me feel good."

While their bad times were quite grim, Tait recalls they did have some very good times. One lasting memory Tait says was a New Year's Eve which they spent alone. Yet, even then, it was as though they were playing out the scene of a play.

"It was a magical night. We had a dinner that included Beluga Caviar and champagne and the best cocaine you could buy. We were sitting in the living room watching through the big, rounded window as a big boat all decorated with Christmas lights kept going up and down the Detroit River. It was just the two of us, in this room like nothing and no one else existed in the world. But there was a huge piece of reality missing."

The media, always on the lookout for stories or information about Tait, were fascinated by his relationship with Martin. One day there was great merriment among the news media gathered for another Tait trial when Martin arrived with a friend to watch Tait perform. Dressed like a runway model, she sat in the front seat and whenever Tait delivered a particularly rousing bit of oratory she would gleefully, but soundlessly applaud. It was difficult for reporters to concentrate on the court proceedings when they were fascinated by the antics of Tait's girlfriend.

In hindsight, it is difficult to speculate on how Tait's life might have unfolded had it not been for two small discs in his upper spine. Would the relationship with Martin have ended in disaster anyway? Would Tait have continued sobriety and maintained his expensive lifestyle? Or, would the shaky foundation of that sobriety have eventually crumbled and ultimately brought Tait to his knees. All moot now in the light of the approaching disaster.

THE OLD BAILEY – Silencing the orator

LOOKING GOOD IN ARMANI took work and Tait worked hard at it, hitting the gym every day to pump iron and work the cardio machines. In the winter of 1997 he began having problems with his left tricep muscle, so much so he couldn't lift the smallest weight. An MRI in London, Ontario showed two deteriorated discs in the upper area of the spine were causing the problem and by summer he was in constant and excruciating pain.

His doctors gave him only one choice – he had to have surgery. The specialist explained the surgery would involve fusing the two deteriorated discs in the upper neck. She would also be cutting through the front of Tait's throat in order to repair the discs on the left side of his vocal chords. It all sounded simple and his fear was somewhat alleviated by the confidence of the surgeon.

The surgery repaired the offending discs. However, there was a side effect the doctor had not mentioned – the procedure prevented his vocal chords from opening and closing and left him with no voice. Hope, and reassurances, that this was a temporary side effect of the surgery dimmed when even two weeks later he could barely squeak out a word and his doctor admitted there was no guarantee he would ever again speak above a whisper.

Many people probably would not see this as a fatal catastrophe but for Tait it was a death knell to his career. Even though friends and colleagues pointed out that there was more to law than the performance in a court room, Tait was inconsolable. For him, there was nothing more to the law than his performance, his ability to use his oratorical skills to browbeat a witness and win over a jury. He could see nothing

126

but a bleak future, the end of him, and his emotional turmoil was profound.

"I lost something when I lost my voice. I was like a musician without hands. It was probably the most traumatic experience of my life. More than being a man, a husband or a father, I identified myself as a lawyer. It was the essence of who I was and it had been taken away from me. I was left with nothing. Nothing but desolation."

It was a depressing period and he began spending many hours sulking in front of the television. One day while watching events in England surrounding the death of Princess Diana, Tait decided a few days in London might help lift his spirits and lighten his depression.

Not wanting to travel alone he decided to ask Brewster, who had just returned from Greece, if she would accompany him. Tait drove to her house and knocked on the door, holding his breath. They talked for several hours in her bedroom but in the end, she wouldn't be persuaded and refused to go to London. She said she couldn't do it knowing she would end up getting hurt again. She was also seeing a therapist to help deal with the emotional torment of the breakup. On his way out of the house Tait met her mother who immediately started screaming at him for the heartbreak he had heaped on her young daughter. Tait kept apologizing but she wasn't relenting and her scornful condemnations followed him to his car. He drove away and called Martin who immediately agreed to go with him.

END OF SOBRIETY AND BEGINNING OF THE END

THEY ARRIVED IN ENGLAND on a typically cool, misty morning in September and checked into the Ritz hotel in central London. After freshening up they took a taxi to visit some of the older areas of the city. Martin soon tired and they returned to the hotel but Tait was restless and not wanting to lie around decided to go for a walk.

He went to Fleet Street and then, almost subconsciously, began walking in the direction of the Old Bailey. This was his sixth visit to London and third to the crucible of the western world's Common Law – the Central Criminal Court of England and Wales. Walking past the venerable edifice this time, however, was different. Standing there, his gaze shifting between St. Paul's Cathedral and the building that represented his raison d'etre, he fought back tears.

"I stood there thinking if I never get my voice back it's all over for me. Everything I've worked for will be gone. Without that everything goes. I may never talk again and that means never addressing a jury again. This is my whole identity and without it who am I? I am nothing. It was like I was dying."

Now, even more depressed, Tait returned to the hotel where he found Martin still sleeping. He left the room and went downstairs to one of the hotel bars. A waiter passing with a tray of beers asked what he wanted to drink. Tait said a coke. He finished the drink and when the waiter walked past him again with another tray of beer Tait looked up and said, "I'll have one of those." In that moment he ended 18 years of sobriety and started the beginning of the end of his life as he had known it. There would be no going back. There would be better days, but a dark tsunami had been spurred.

"It was a total mental blank spot. There was no thought and I don't know what made me do it but my alcoholic obsession kicked in immediately. The moment that glass hit my lips, it was over. Later that night at dinner, when Sandra went to the washroom, I ordered a double scotch and drank it before she returned. I had no idea of just how devastating those drinks would be to the rest of my life."

THANK GOD FOR PIGS

WHILE TAIT WAS FALLING apart in England, in Windsor his presence was sorely missed in the courtroom. Crown Denis Harrison postponed many of Tait's cases, waiting for news his voice had returned. Gossip had him getting his voice back, other gossip had it never coming back.

Tait came home from England "feeling useless." He was angry and depressed and scared about what was to become of him. His vast ego that depended on being a celebrity lawyer, the big shot of the courtroom, was in freefall. He listened to no one because only he knew what was best for him and that was being the great Don Tait. Lawyer. Then, one afternoon he received an unexpected call from Brewster who told him she had heard about a new procedure being performed in Detroit that might help restore his voice. He called Henry Ford Hospital and made an appointment. Driving across the Ambassador Bridge to Detroit his battered ego was wriggling itself out of its black hole and he began thinking of how powerful he would feel stepping back in the courtroom. Everyone would be watching. The very thought almost makes him giddy.

At the hospital doctors tell him the procedure is risky but Tait felt he had nothing to lose. His voice was gone and he was willing to take any chance - risky or otherwise - if there was even the smallest hope he would speak again. The process involved injecting pig fat into the damaged left vocal cord to re-inflate it. And it worked. "It was an awful procedure. I was awake through the whole thing but it was worth it. I felt reborn."

Again, as they always did when there was a Tait story to be told, the media came calling. They wanted to interview the newsmaker, wanted to know every detail of what had happened to him, what the surgery was like, what it felt like to have his voice back and how he was feeling about being back on top. Tait preened and gave them all his best quotes. He revelled in the attention and congratulatory handshakes. He was making news. No one thought to ask if he was still off the booze and drugs.

Within days he was back in court. His booming oratory restored, he defended two members of Quebec's Rock Machine motorcycle club charged with drug trafficking and weapons possession in Tilbury, a town about thirty minutes east of Windsor. Because of the nature of the clients it became a highly publicized case and Tait basked in the attention. His face was on newspaper pages and in nightly TV and radio newscasts. The highly quotable Tait was the talk of the city. His ego was where he wanted it to be. Fully in charge. It was also being fuelled by alcohol.

Tait was drinking but he was winning and that's what mattered. He gave absolutely no thought to the possibility, or the certainty, that there would be a day of reckoning, that travelling this path would not end well for him. But this was now and he was defending clients in one high profile case after another. On April 15, 1997 a jury found Tait's client Frank Hupalo not guilty of murder. This was a case watched in fascination by the public and the media.

Hupalo, then a twenty-seven-year-old university student, was sitting on a bench outside a store front on Windsor's main drag with his girlfriend Sarah Lawn. They were talking about getting married while waiting for another couple they were meeting for dinner. They noticed three youths who appeared to be urinating on the wall of the travel agency partially owned by Lawn. Hupalo and Lawn yelled at them to stop.

The three became angry, crossed the street and attacked Hupalo. He pulled a knife he used for opening wine bottles from his back pocket and told Ali Cetin, 19, to back off. Cetin lunged at Hupalo twice and both times the knife plunged into his chest.

"I fought for my life. I didn't want anyone to get hurt. I wanted them to go away. They wouldn't go away," Hupalo told the jury. Tait produced photographs of Hupalo's swollen face and bloodied nose. He also produced evidence of the criminal histories of Cetin and his friends and pointed out contradictions in their statements to police. When he turned to the jury he pulled every emotional string in the book to convince them that Hupalo could be every single one of them. It was a convincing argument.

"I believe that the jury put themselves in the position of Mr. Hupalo and said, 'if that was happening to me, I would have done exactly the very same thing he did,'" Tait told reporters after the verdict. He said Hupalo spoke for average citizens when he told reporters "You can't take anything for granted. You drop a dime and that could be the end of it. Live each day like it's your last. It could all be taken away."

It was a case that resonated in the community for many months and one Tait was particularly proud of winning.

"It's a case like that that makes you realize how important it is to be the best you can be, to do the best for your client because if you don't it could mean an innocent person being punished. In this case it could have been a clean-cut kid with no criminal record."

Just a few months later he began the defence of two Windsor cops charged with assaulting and forcibly confining a LaSalle teenager they believed had broken into the personal vehicle of one of the cops. Tait's defence saw the cops acquitted but he and associate Robert DiPietro had to fight for their $180,000 fee because the police board insisted the two officers were outside their Windsor jurisdiction without permission. Tait reminded the board the officers had actually informed the police dispatcher they were outside city limits and thus the board's argument did not stand up. Tait got his money.

Tait was again running on a winner's high and he couldn't get enough of the publicity. But trying to keep up appearances and maintaining the workload required to keep winning was causing cracks in his armour. Those watching who did not know him well thought he had it all together. His close friends and associates, however, could tell something was amiss, and were waiting for the proverbial shoe to fall. As Tait recalled..."I felt like I was twenty-nine again. I felt like king of the castle. I was top notch. I was winning. My ego was intact. Everything was going my way. The problem was I forgot I was a drunk."

Tait and Martin flew to New Brunswick early in 1998 to a family wedding. Tait introduced her to his relatives and they toured around the places where he lived including visiting the UNB campus and the graveyard where his parents were buried. There wasn't an angry moment between them.

"We had some wonderful periods of time together, often for several months when she was normal and we got along really well. But I was drinking again and all bets were off."

Tait was feeling unstoppable. Invincible. But his success was tainted with the smell of booze and constant cocaine use. His relationship with Martin became more chaotic as she stumbled in and out of psychiatric wards, her mental stability compromised by the cocaine use. Dealers were in and out of the house and Tait was spiralling into a worse abyss than the one he had visited twenty years earlier. He was so out of control himself he would even smuggle bottles of vodka into Martin in the psychiatric ward.

He was knocking back more than a pint of vodka a day. He denied he was drinking, vehemently lying even to his closest colleagues and friends, but they had seen this before and there was no mistaking the tell-tale signs – Tait turning up in court drunk or hung over or not turning up. Tait off his game.

Martin begged him to call Charbonneau to get help. The suggestion made Tait angry because there was no way he was going to admit he was on the skids again. As it did almost twenty years before, intervention eventually came in the face of Brentwood's Charbonneau who in recent years had not been seeing much of Tait. This lack of contact was a warning sign, Charbonneau said, that Tait, an alcoholic, had become "too full of himself."

"We were good friends, but Don had forgotten what he was and that's a fatal flaw for a drunk. I knew it was only a matter of time before he got into trouble again," Charbonneau said, displaying a sad resignation combined with anger and frustration. "Here was a guy who had gone down this road before and knew the pitfalls. But when the ego is in charge there is only one direction this can lead and that's straight down. Another problem is that he never dealt with the insecurities he carried around since childhood. He might be a high-flying lawyer but he's ruled by a sad little boy inside him."

One Sunday night at around 9 p.m. Tait started drinking at home, alone, just him and his forty ouncer of vodka. At first his vodka on the rocks tasted "like guilt" but it was "an easy way to take away the pain." Tait may have been soaked in booze but he had enough sober moments to know he was on the permanent downslide of the rollercoaster that was his life. Those lucid moments made him more depressed so he drank more.

On Monday morning, when he should have been in court, Tait, dressed in filthy sweats, sporting a three-day beard and reeking of booze, was lying in a stupor on the living room sofa. Barely able to focus, he awoke to his "worst nightmare" - the craggy, angry visage of Charbonneau. He was there yet again in an attempt to pull his hard-living, now pathetic friend back from another volcanic spiral. Charbonneau took Tait to his home and stayed with him during the rest of that day and into the night as he battled the DTs. Hardly leaving his side, Charbonneau kept him there until he was well enough to go home, warning him that he had better come to AA meetings at

Brentwood.

"He did not lecture me. It was pure unadulterated love from that man. He did everything he humanly could to help save me from me. So, I went to a meeting."

In Brentwood, the icon of criminal law stood before several hundred residents of the rehab and declared: "I'm just like all of you. I'm not special, just gifted in certain areas. Most of my success happened by accident and was the result of people helping me. It's OK to make mistakes. I just hope you don't make the same stupid mistakes I've made. The most important thing you can do is accept help. We can't do this ourselves. Once I admitted I needed people, things changed for me. I became a better person because of it."

Laudable words but mostly lying bullshit because even though Tait may have somewhat believed what he was saying at the time, he was far from getting his life together. After drying out he left Brentwood and boasted to everyone who asked that he was back and all was well again. But, while Charbonneau was devoted to helping Tait stay on a sober path, he was never one to pull his punches and made no bones about his expectations for Tait after his second release from Brentwood.

"He is a bad dude. The lying and deceit about his drinking will do him in. This fall was harder. He had no pride to lose the first time because he'd been drinking for so long. This time he's built up a lot of respect. He's not special. He's a good lawyer, many say great, but no way is he a special drunk. There's a good possibility he will fall off the wagon again. I'd say it's absolutely certain he will. He has a constant fight on his hands and he had better be honest with himself. Unfortunately, I'm not hopeful."

Despite his harsh criticism, Charbonneau talked about Tait with warmth, caring and worry. While he was not the only one concerned about Tait, his closest friends did not want to admit he was in freefall. His ever-loyal friend Montello defended him

135

and admiringly called Tait "one of the leading criminal lawyers in Canada," and admits he has always admired his unabashed love of the good life.

"He likes to be well dressed, live in lavish homes, drive lavish cars and scuba dive, but he also works extremely hard. He always did. He is a colourful character with a good many years of success ahead of him."

It was wishful thinking. Tait was dry for about two weeks. During October and November 1998 the police were constantly called to Tait's home. On November 12, according to police records, two officers were assigned to check out a case involving a woman who had been picked up by ambulance attendants at a Mac's Milk convenience store on Strabane Avenue in Windsor, not far from Tait's house. They first interviewed the woman, Sandra Martin, in the emergency department at Metropolitan Hospital and was told by her "No. I do not want to talk to the police."

They noted she "had redness to the left side of her cheek, her eyes were red and glassy and she had a strong odour of an alcoholic beverage on her breath. Her speech was slightly slurred and she was whispering at times, and crying."

They then drove to Tait's home where they interviewed O'Reilly and Tait. Tait explained that for the past several weeks Martin had been asking him to help her stop drinking. He also told them she was "very jealous" and because he was worried about her had taken her to Chatham with him earlier in the day where he was representing a client. After dropping her back home around noon Tait went to his office, returning home around 5:15 p.m. Martin's daughter and Tait's two grandchildren were in the house.

"I went upstairs to take a shower...Sandra came upstairs and started shouting at me about my ex-girlfriend. I told her not to make a fool of herself in front of the kids. Sandra ran downstairs. I heard a smash and came downstairs. She was still screaming about Tami. I told her she's done this too many times and she was causing problems with the neighbours. She went to the front door. I tried to go to her. My feet slipped and I fell in the foyer. She ran out the front door and out the gate...I saw her fall. Then she got up and ran. By this time Sandra was completely intoxicated. I was worried about her hurting herself because she's had psychiatric problems before. I sent Bill to check on her...she was saying I assaulted her. I do not assault Sandra. I do not touch her. I never laid a hand on her. I have tried to help this woman because I really care about her."

Tait also told police that a month previously, after a fight, Martin went to stay at her parent's home when they were away in Spain. While drunk, she fell downstairs bruising her eye and nose. She told her sister Tait had assaulted her. Once she was sober she wrote a statement admitting she'd fallen and that Tait had not assaulted her and didn't cause her injuries. Concluding his statement to the officers Tait said: "I am a very tough guy in court. I'll cross examine the shit out of them. I'll embarrass them. But I would never hurt a woman or a child."

In his recounting of events that day, O'Reilly said he put on his coat and followed Martin. He was worried because he knew she had been drinking vodka and "darn near drank forty ounces." O'Reilly said he had not been drinking because he didn't drink. "I didn't see any marks on Sandra's face. She looked fine other than it looked like she had been crying."

The partying and lunacy never stopped in Tait's Riverside home. One evening when O'Reilly and Martin were snorting cocaine O'Reilly insisted that Robbie Peters, who lived with Tait and did odd jobs around the property, had insulted him. He left the house and returned with a gun. Sitting in the living room he pointed the gun at Peters, intending to shoot him in the head. Tait wacked O'Reilly's hand, causing the gun to point downwards, shooting him in the leg instead. Not wanting to get police involved, Tait called a former client who was a medical doctor and surgeon who had operating room equipment in his office and headed there with Peters yelping and bleeding in the car. The medic stitched up the bullet hole.

On June 25, 1999 Tait was invited to deliver a speech at Montello's retirement party and was assigned a seat at the head table with the guest of honour and other legal dignitaries. He invited Martin but explained that she, and the partners of all the speakers, could not sit at the head table. This made her very upset and she was still upset when they arrived at the event. She was sent into a further tailspin when she saw the lawyer she was with prior to her relationship with Tait, at the event with his wife.

After his speech – which to the surprise of many, he delivered in a relatively sober state – Tait noticed Martin was missing. He discovered she had left the hall and driven away in his car. At the end of the evening he hitched a ride with a colleague and arrived home to find the tall, wrought iron gates in front of his house locked. He had no key so he climbed over the gate and up the narrow, winding steel staircase to the upper balcony where he knew the door to his office would not be locked.

Once inside, his anger erupted and he and Martin and a "hellava fight" that would put alley cats to shame. But as was not unusual in their relationship, they made up the next day. Tait invited her to accompany him to Goderich on the shores of Lake Huron where he would be defending a man on an impaired driving charge on Monday.

To prepare for the trip Tait bought cocaine from his dealer and picked up a bottle of Vodka. They set out from Windsor at 10 a.m. in Tait's Mercedes 600 SL and on the drive consumed most of the vodka and shared some of the cocaine. They reached the Village of Bayfield at 2:30 p.m., checked in at the Little Inn and went to a nearby bar where they continued to drink. They left the bar to eat at a restaurant close to the hotel. Both were strung out and emotionally charged. Tait became impatient, calling Martin names and swearing because she was taking too long to order. There was more drinking during the meal and both were visibly intoxicated when they

138

staggered out.

They returned to the Inn at around 4 p.m., checked into room thirty-six and got into the remains of the cocaine. At 6 p.m. they called room service and ordered a bottle of champagne. Tait called again between 6:30 p.m. and 7 p.m. asking for a room service menu and the staff member who brought them the menu was to later testify in court that he noticed the empty champagne and vodka bottles. A requested cheese plate arrived at 7:15 p.m. and Martin answered the door in a towel. A short time later when the main course was delivered the waiter could hear Tait yell at Martin to get the door.

"We are not getting along," Martin told the waiter. "We're fighting."

"If you need anything, I can help," he replied.

"She knows not to ask for any help," Tait quipped as Martin thanked the waiter.

When the same staff member returned with the bill, Martin again answered the door in a towel. Tait, who was in bed, signed the bill. The waiter pointedly told Martin to call if she needed anything. After dinner, Tait and Martin began arguing over the events that took place the previous evening at Montello's retirement dinner. At around 9:45 p.m. the fighting escalated to a pitch only possible when two people are drunk and stoned.

Out of control, Tait slapped Martin across the face with the palm of his hand. She fell against the sink, struck her nose and broke it. Her nose began bleeding profusely and she started screaming at the top of her lungs that she was "being killed." Tait, realizing this would bring hotel staff and likely the police, told her to stop. He pushed her into a chair, put his hands around her throat and her mouth to try and make her shut up.

"Stop. Somebody help me," she yelled out. "My God. He is killing me."

A guest in the next room called hotel staff who called police. Martin asked staff members who came to the room to get Tait away from her. All the sheets were off the bed and they were stained with blood and there were bloody handprints on the mattress. Martin was taken to an office and Tait stayed in the room where police found him drunk with "red-rimmed eyes and a flushed, dirty face." He stumbled as they walked him from the room. He asked police why Martin was trying to ruin him.

Tait spent Sunday night and Monday morning behind bars. In the morning, suffering the humiliation of wearing prison-issue paper pyjamas and paper slippers, he was taken to court – where he should have been acting as a lawyer – in a paddy wagon with a group of prisoners arrested overnight. He was allowed bail and cooled his heels waiting for O'Reilly to arrive to get him out of jail. O'Reilly drove home in Tait's Mercedes 4 x 4 with Tait following in the Mercedes SL 600. Two officers with the Ontario Provincial Police drove Martin back to Windsor where she went to stay with a friend.

As part of his bail conditions Tait was not to consume alcohol or drugs, not to associate with Martin and to continue to reside at his Windsor residence. Just three days later, however, Tait and Martin were in his home sharing a stash of cocaine and having sex. The now sober Martin did not want to proceed with the charge and did not want to appear in court. What she does want is to continue the relationship with Tait and ignoring the court order, constantly called him on the phone.

"She sometimes called 60 times a day. One day she was calling me, and then when I left court she started following me in her car, cutting me off. I had to call the cops."

His stormy relationship with Martin continued and the notes she often left for Tait at his home reflected her state of mind. When she appeared to be more in control her handwriting was an elegant cursive style, but when she was mentally stressed she reverted to a backward slanted style of printing. The two styles were so disparate they appeared to have been written by two completely different people.

In July, 1998 in a letter to Tait she began with a cursive style...

I know you are under a lot of pressure. We both are. My nerves are so, so bad. I keep getting these awful panic attacks. I'm so afraid for my future and my daughter's. I need to stabilize where she lives. As she continues the cursive turns to the loose, juvenile, printing style as she expresses a need for help to rent or buy a place to live.

If you are willing to spend $9,000 in rent can we not use this for a down payment on a town house? And then I could afford the monthly mortgage payments. Please let me know a.s.a.p. (I believe this makes much more sense).

Yes, I cannot wait to start the job! I need to do something with myself besides cry and worry all day. Please provide me with the details a.s.a.p.

Don, I know last evening you said you were going to keep dragging this trial on. Where does that leave us? I cannot put my life on hold again. And I cannot start a life of sneaking around to Detroit – again. My mind cannot handle it.

In early July Tait called Windsor police to complain about the phone calls. Police officers who went to Tait's home filed a report stating that Tait explained he had been arrested on assault charges and a condition of his release was an order of non-association with Martin.

Tait reports to us that Martin is continually calling him and relaying messages to him. Martin has reportedly left notes and a letter for him. (In Tait's possession). Tait's concern was that this contact by Martin could be construed as being instigated by him and result in a breach charge being laid.

While we were at the residence the phone rang (1348 hrs). Tait answers the phone and indicates that the caller was Martin. I spoke to the caller who identified herself as Sandra Martin. She acknowledged that she knew Tait had been released from custody with a condition not to communicate with her. I informed Martin that she should not be calling Tait as it could compromise his release if thought to be instigated or continued by him.

Tait expresses concern over Martin's state of mind. Tait reported that he has heard through independent sources that the OPP keep interviewing Martin on several topics related to Tait (not only the alleged assault, but any drugs or guns in Tait's possession). Tait is concerned that Martin is in a frail state of mind (psychological problems) that could be worsened by additional stress.

Such was their obsessive relationship and because she now had no place to live, Tait paid $12,000 in advance for rent on a home in the swanky Southwood Lakes subdivision for Martin. He also ignored the bail conditions and they began planning to get married and have a honeymoon in Bali. There was nothing normal about their relationship and neither was in a fit state of mind to make a sane or realistic judgement about anything they were doing. They were both in desperate need of professional help – two pitiful people totally out of control who were each other's worst nightmares.

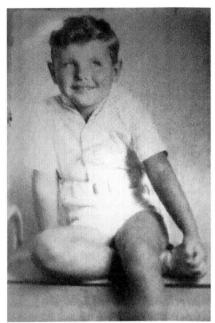

Tait as a young boy

Tait as a leaner teenager and two years before his first drink

Melanie and Barbara

A young Tait in Windsor

Tait in his office and at home in his heyday

Tait with his parents

Two of their several homes

Tait with his beloved German shepherds and on his boat

On the day he wed Johanna

Melanie, Tait, Johanna and Barbara

Johanna with their dogs

Tait walking in the Plaza Coutura

'Si, Señõr Don'

Card dealers, bartenders form Tait's circle of friends

PM set to name election team

Chretien hopes to silence critics

By JOAN BRYDEN
OTTAWA

Prime Minister Jean Chretien is hoping to use next week's national Liberal convention to quell leadership speculation, unite the troops and put the governing party on a war footing for an election next year.

A regular at the gambling tables

Gregarious on double vodkas

With the author in Costa Rica

Crying over his fate during dinner in Costa Rica

Tait at home when he arrived in Africa

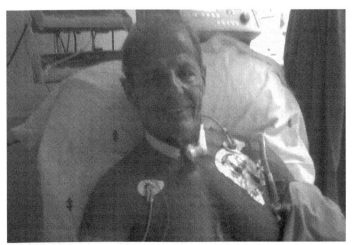

Tait in hospital following his heart attack

Cedars in Dududu

Township of Dududu

Tait with Cedars counselling group

Johanna teaching classes at Cedars

156

Tait on his last visit to Windsor with the author

Visiting Andre Retinger (left) in South Africa

Keith Wilkes

Caleb

Kingsley Ball "Sarge"

Proud grandfather with Jack

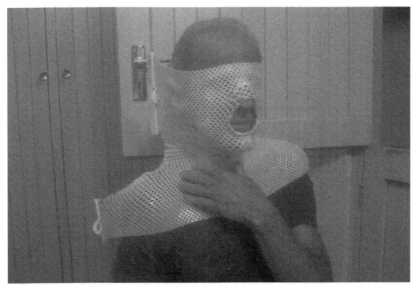

Tait preparing for radiation bombardment to treat throat cancer

The agony of radiation pain

Tait in a counselling group despite suffering the pain of radiation aftermath. He refuses to miss a day at Cedars

Tait listening in pain at Cedars

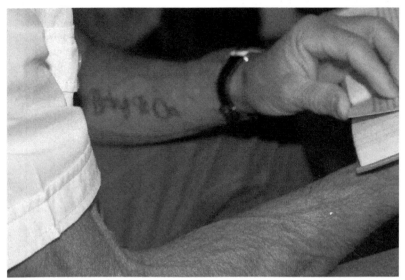
Tait's mantra Bring It On

Tait and Johanna in Africa

Tait after receiving his QC designation

ON THE RUN

TAIT HAD NOW BEEN DRINKING and doing cocaine for more than two years. His drunkenness was keeping him from appearing in court and his practice was deteriorating. His client roster had dropped off by more than sixty per cent. He was using cocaine three to four times a week. He always had access to the heavy duty uncut "good stuff," and even though he protested to colleagues he was doing OK, his constant state of inebriation was impossible to hide. He was freebasing cocaine and his house was always filled with "wackos" and drug dealers.

Canada's taxman was after him for almost a million in back taxes. He spent months trying to negotiate a payment plan. He sold his boat and told the chief tax collector in the city he would sell his home and everything he owned. He would declare bankruptcy, he said, whatever it took to satisfy the debt but he needed time and asked to be allowed to pay in instalments.

But, like others before him, Tait discovered the local tax hound was not interested in helping any poor wretch drowning in financial despair. In contemptuous arrogance he told Tait "All or nothing. I'm not interested in payments." It was baffling to Tait that he would rather risk the government getting nothing than working out a plan with him.

"That guy running the show in Windsor at the time hated me and wouldn't agree to anything. He wanted it all. Right now. He was an ego-driven weasel-type bureaucrat who knew he could wield a hammer and deliver a fatal blow to one of the city's 'hot shots.' It was a power he was savouring the day he smiled and told me 'I want it all. No deal. All of it.' He prevented the CRA from getting any of its money."

164

Tait didn't have the money and it was clear to anyone taking even a cursory look at his life, there was not ever going to be the big income generation of previous years. Had the chief tax collector been less vindictive and smart enough, and perhaps less greedy, he would have agreed to Tait's liquidation plan. Tait was already in freefall and the worst was yet to come.

"I kept getting crazier. I couldn't draw a sober breath, I was charged with domestic assault and I knew I would not be able to cope with the court stuff that was coming up. I was addicted to Sandra, coke and alcohol. I couldn't see a way out of it all. I knew I had two choices. Kill myself or run."

He started with the first option.

One Tuesday morning O'Reilly heard Tait's car running for an unusually long time in the garage and looked inside but couldn't see Tait. As he entered the garage the smell from the exhaust told him exactly what is happening. He ran, opened the back door and pulled a drunken Tait from the car – determined that this would not be the day his troubled friend would die. Tait, bloated, his legs wobbling because of the alcoholic nerve damage that was developing, now decides if suicide was not going to be an option, he would run. He called an old cop friend, Bill Delaney, who owned a home in Costa Rica and told him he had decided Costa Rica was where he was going to live out the rest of his life.

"I had this insane fantasy I would buy a shack on the beach, let my hair grow long and grey and drink and do coke for the next couple of years which was all I felt I had left. I would ease up on drinking from time to time and in my state of mind I imagined that everything, all the bad shit, would go away."

To prepare for his exit from Windsor, he had O'Reilly take his three luxury cars - a gold Mercedes 600 SL 2-seater, Mercedes 320 4 x 4 and a $100,000 Jaguar - to the parking lot of Overseas Motors in the early hours of the morning before the dealership opened, and leave them on the lot. As soon as the banks opened he cashed in his $250,000 retirement fund and visited his jeweller at Joseph Anthony to sell his Rolex. He counted out $8,000. He then instructed O'Reilly to sell as much of the furniture as he can and send him the money. He called his daughters, told them what he was planning and gave Barbara his two beloved German shepherds – Sadie and Jessie. Within days his watch was bought by one of his legal partners, something that once bothered him, but no longer, having realized that it had nothing to do with him personally.

"When he has visited me I noticed he didn't wear the watch. One of our mutual friends suggested he return the watch as a gesture of friendship but that hasn't happened and I don't think it will. But that's OK. It is what it is."

Tait was in turmoil. Leaving Windsor after twenty-nine years evoked a mixture of relief and fear. He knew he was not just running away from his problems, family and friends. He was also absconding from the law, the tax man and his clients and for that there would be a day of reckoning.

"The hardest decision was leaving my family. Next, was knowing that I was leaving my clients in the lurch. I feel very badly about that. I always will. Some of them will never forgive me and will always hate me for it and I understand why they would."

On Tuesday morning, January 25, 2000 Tait packed a small suitcase with scuba gear, deciding it would be important for his plan to live like a hermit on a Costa Rican beach. With only the clothes on his back, he had O'Reilly drive him to Metro airport in Detroit where he boarded an American Airlines flight to San Jose, via Miami. Tait was drunk. So drunk, he left his passport on the plane and had to stay in Miami three days in order to sober up and persuade a Canadian Consulate clerk to give him a replacement.

He began drinking as soon as he had a passport in hand and a rebooked flight to San Jose. By the time the plane landed Tait was almost incoherently intoxicated. The cabbie who drove him from the airport realized he had an easy target and relieved Tait of all but $50,000 of the $250,000 he was carrying, his Amex Gold card and his wallet. He dumped Tait in front of a small hotel where he checked in and, even in a drunken stupor, he was frightened enough to barricade himself inside the room, in case the cabby came back. The following day he checked in to La Gran Via hotel.

"I was in a state of insanity, delusionally insane. I didn't have enough money left for that shanty on the beach but I was just as determined to drink until I died. There was a small grocery store and liquor store next door to the hotel so I would send someone from the hotel to get me some food and booze. I often stayed in my small room with the TV on and drinking until I passed out."

As Tait was settling in to what he believes are the final days of his life, in Windsor people are beginning to ask, "Where's Don Tait?"

O'Reilly began selling some of his best furniture - $30,000 of it to a local wealthy businessman living in a stone mansion on Riverside Drive. But the money never reached Tait. His daughter Melanie was living with O'Reilly and before he could send the money to Costa Rica she left and the money disappeared with her. He was convinced she or her boyfriend took the money.

"O'Reilly found her and her boyfriend at the time in a local motel. He wanted to kill the boyfriend and called me to ask if I wanted him dead. I said not to kill him so instead he pistol-whipped the guy and never spoke to Melanie again."

LATE NIGHTS

WHILE I WAS IMMERSED in journalism pursuits made possible by the stories I had written about Tait's plight in Costa Rica, reality had become his most unkind friend. An exile with no purpose, tortured by demons real and perceived, Tait was self-destructing. He began calling me when there is no one else he could reach at the end of a phone. The calls usually came around 2 a.m. and sometimes lasted for up to three or four hours. My phone bills skyrocketed. But there was an odd bond I seem to have developed with this pathetic self-destroyer and felt compelled to continue listening.

He had inadvertently brought me accolades, so I sit in my home office in pyjamas with a mug of tea, listening and taking notes while he talked. His rants were often incoherent, punctuated by bouts of crying. It was sometimes heart breaking to listen to but then I would remind myself his pain is self-inflicted.

In one particular call at 3 a.m. on a Wednesday morning, he eagerly wanted advice about his decision to sneak into Florida by boat. He had talked to "some guy" with a dubious quality boat who would take him to the U.S. under cover of darkness. Once there, he planned to sneak over the border into Canada. After that, he had no plans. He just wanted to be home, whatever the consequence. The conversation was surreal. He didn't start with "Hi," but launched into the beginning of a teary tirade.

"I feel shitty. I'm lonely and I don't know what to do. I hate to feel sorry for myself. I hate self-pity. I tried to kill myself last night. Put a bag over my head and neck. Then didn't have the balls to do it."

"What do you want to do?"

168

"Fix my life. I miss the kids. I've let people down." Then he cries.

"Have you gone to AA?"

"No, but I'm going. I'm going to learn some Spanish."

"When?"

"As soon as I can arrange it."

"How are your legs?"

"Bad. I can't walk far. It's hard to get around. I want to come back to Windsor but cops everywhere are looking for me. I don't want to end up in jail. Maybe that's where I should be. In Jail. Wouldn't that make the headlines? The once great Don Tait in jail. People who hate me would love it. I don't sleep much. I'm exhausted but it's hard to sleep. I'm sorry to keep calling but I need to talk. I don't know why I'm talking to you. I really don't know you that well. I trust you. I never meant to hurt anyone, especially not Sandra. We were drunk when all that bad shit happened. I did hit her and I broke her nose. I didn't mean to. She was coming after me with a bottle and I pushed her into the sink. I didn't mean to hurt her. Not anyone. Honest to God, I never meant to hurt anyone. How the hell did things go so wrong? I wish my mother was alive.

She'd help me get over this." Then more crying. He continues.

"I still love that girl. You can't change your heart. This is a fucking sick love story."

"How much are you drinking?"

"I'm cutting back. I'm going to get off it. I talked to a guy about getting a boat to the U.S."

"You what?"

"I met a guy who said he could get me into the U.S. by boat. It wouldn't cost much. We'd have to walk through a bit of forest

169

but he said it wouldn't be too bad. I'm looking into it."

"Who is this 'guy?'"

"I don't know – I met him in the casino and told him about my problems with the police and getting back to the U.S. and Canada and he said he could get a boat to take me to Cuba and then to Florida."

"What kind of a boat?"

"Not sure. Something with a motor."

"Have you thought about how dangerous this is?"

"He said he's good with a boat. Knows what he's doing."

"Have you thought about it when you're sober? This is really dangerous and it's a long way, thousands of miles. And you're not well. You can't walk. You certainly can't walk through a forest. And you don't even know if you can trust this guy. You can't do this. Don't you agree to anything." I could tell he wasn't listening to anything I was saying, just waiting for me to stop talking.

"I can't take this anymore. It's really bad. I'm useless. I'm no good to anyone. Not even me. I can't even have sex for fuck sake. That word doesn't apply," he says laughing piteously. "I used to be able to do it for hours. Now nothing. I'm useless. It's useless. None of this would happen if mom was still alive. She'd get me fixed up. I can't even kill myself successfully."

"You sound exhausted. Why don't you try to sleep?"

"You're tired. Sorry. I'm keeping you up," he becomes solicitous.

"It's OK but you should get some sleep. But listen to me. Don't you go off in any boat with someone you don't know. Promise me."

"I'll let you know. Good night."

170

"Tait, promise me you won't do this."

He had hung up.

Such conversations would continue until either Tait exhausted himself or I began falling asleep. Hanging up the telephone there was always the thought the next call could be from someone telling me Tait was dead. It was like watching someone running headlong into a train.

When he was conscious he was full of bravura. At one point he considered getting involved in a sketchy business with a disgraced Windsor doctor and a strip club owner. They wanted Tait to be a conduit for young girls to staff the stages of the local strip club. At first he thought it might be "interesting" but soon realized it was a ludicrous venture for him to get involved in on many levels. He eventually told the pair "I can't do it. Even if I wanted to I can't get out of bed most days and I can't stay sober."

The following week, near the end of March, Tait was drinking in his hotel bar. The manager became worried because the friendly, likeable Gringo appeared more than drunk. He looked and behaved as though he was on death's door. He was sweating and losing consciousness. Montero called an ambulance and had Tait taken to ER.

Diagnosing severe alcoholism they sent him to the psychiatric ward. The staff could speak little English and Tait no Spanish, but he continually impressed on them that he was a "big shot." After a week of treatment they discovered Tait couldn't pay the hospital bill and armed guards were brought in to make sure he didn't leave without paying. O'Reilly flew down to pay his bill and take him back to the hotel. He was destructively drinking again within twenty-four hours.

KINDLY HOOKER

MANY NIGHTS TAIT FOUND solace in a friendly prostitute. She would lie on top of the bed covers with him and hold his tired body, providing a comfort he knows is hollow. He'd often think about having sex but no amount of coaxing could bring life to his penis – a raw reminder of the toll alcohol has taken on his once overactive libido. Many nights he cries after those efforts, adding to the misery that surrounds his existence.

The friendly prostitute, Maria, is a twenty-year-old Spanish girl. She lies close to him, gently massaging his swollen, sweaty face. She feels sad for the strange, likeable foreigner. She has an impression that he was once someone important and wonders what caused him to become such a pathetic, beaten man. She doesn't mind giving him comfort. It's somewhat of a relief not to have to perform.

During those moments, lying next to a beautiful woman, he can smell the shampoo in her long black hair and imagines what he'd like to be able to do. There was a time when this scene would have led to a night of raucous sex. Now, an empty shell of the man he used to be, he lies inert, grateful for the darkness of sleep. His days and nights begin to blur. He can't remember what it feels like to be sober and coherent. Most times he can't remember what it felt like to be a hot shot, expensive lawyer. The future looks dimmer by the day and the uncertainty begins to scare him. Tait's good buddy O'Reilly tries to visit as often as he can but knows it's just a matter of time before Tait will have to be rescued. Or, he would be despatched to bring him home in a shroud.

The Outlaw Enforcer with no compunction about shooting a perceived enemy between the eyes, had a soft spot for Tait that made him a protector to be reckoned with, but he also knew Tait would have to hit bottom before there was anything he could do to help save him. If indeed he could be saved.

SUICIDE AND WAKE UP CALL #1

DEPRESSIVE DAY FOLLOWS depressive night. Jack Daniels and Vodka continue to be Tait's constant companions. They are his saviours and his executioners. He yearns for home. More importantly, he yearns to be a human being free from emotional and physical torture but can't get sober for long enough to be able to figure out how to get there.

In Windsor, cards and letters began pouring in to The Windsor Star from people who wished Tait well and from people who wanted his head on a platter. People were calling media outlets with "Tait" sightings in bars and convenience stores. One wintry afternoon lawyer Gary Klein was walking away from Windsor's Provincial Court Building and waved to a young police officer he recognized. The officer slowly rolled his cruiser up to Klein, opened the window and asked if everything was "OK."

Klein said that it was. The officer asked Klein where he was going, to which Klein answered, "Back to work." The officer opened his door, got out and started telling Klein everything was "OK" and "cool," speaking as though Klein had just escaped from a mental institution. Placing his hands-on Klein's shoulders, he began saying "You're Don…you're…Oh no! You're Gary Klein!"

Tips about Tait and what was happening to him came in to the newsroom daily, some with a grain of truth others wild speculations, not unlike Elvis sightings. "Tait is living in a motel on Ten Mile Road in Detroit." "He's living with a biker gang." At one local eatery – Bubi's Awesome Eats– owner Buddy Miloyevich posted a sign on his electronic bulletin board offering Tait free burgers for a year.

174

In Costa Rica Tait is amused to hear he was in a category with Elvis. He was a legend. But in the cloying heat of his hotel room, the walls are shrinking and Tait does not feel like a legend.

He concluded that he and everyone he loves would be better off if he disappeared from the face of the earth. Suicide was something he'd tried in Canada and Detroit but was stopped by O'Reilly and he had considered it weeks earlier in his hotel room but couldn't complete it. This time, on a particularly depressing Friday night he made up his mind. This time, he was determined to kill himself. And O'Reilly was more than two thousand miles away.

After a day of drinking, he opened and guzzled a bottle of vodka and, on the verge of passing out, he pulled a plastic bag down over his head, closed it tightly around his neck and lay on the floor. His hope was that the plastic would do its job as he slipped into an alcoholic coma. But Don Tait was not going to be allowed to die on a filthy carpet in a cheap hotel in Costa Rica's capital. Perhaps there would yet be a reckoning and a path to redemption.

He woke up in the morning. Alive. "Fuck. I can't even kill myself." But it would not be his last attempt to take his miserable life. That would come several weeks later when a similar attempt left him stunned and dazed and close to death. In the early hours of the morning - or late night - Tait, drunk to near unconsciousness, tried to asphyxiate himself again with a plastic laundry bag. He pulled the bag over his head, tried to tie it snugly but was too drunk. Later, he pissed the bed and while trying to get up he fell hard, striking the glass coffee table with his swollen legs, cutting his wrist and hitting his head on the floor.

Lying there, unable to get up and with blood oozing from his arms, he knew this time could be the end. He was out of money and there was no will to live left in his heart. With what he hoped would be his dying breath he cried out "Help me, please. Make it stop. Make it stop. Please, Please."

Totally and absolutely beaten down, he pleaded with a higher power to put him out of his misery. But he wasn't sure if he wanted to be saved from death or helped to it. Tait didn't know it then, but he had grasped the first rung on his ladder to redemption. However, that was yet a long way off and there would be much more suffering and humiliations to come before this tortured soul found peace.

Worried that her sad gringo friend just might try to kill himself because of his rapid descent into depression and despair, Maria made a point of dropping in on Tait fairly frequently. That morning she let herself into his room and seeing him lying on the floor bleeding and unconscious, thought he was dead. She ran to him, shook him and he stirred. She called her mother who came and helped move Tait from the floor to his bed. Anna, an overweight, greying, 45-year-old whose face had weathered many storms, cleaned his wounds and kept watch with her daughter while Tait slept in a fitful stupor.

In Spanish, she told her daughter they must persuade the half dead gringo to go back to his country. He is going to die and he should be home, she said. Maria suggested they might be able to get him help. Her mother told her to take a good look... how did she think they could help someone who was so far gone. He should go home, she said again. Maria stared down at the pitiful man on the bed and agreed.

When Tait awoke, they told him he must go home. Too sick and worn down to argue, Tait agreed. He was down to his last $12. Maria asked for his return ticket to Detroit and called America Airlines, explaining the ticket holder needed serious medical help and asked them to change the date so that he could get to Canada as soon as possible. They agreed and found him a seat on a Detroit-bound flight later that evening.

She and her mother cleaned him up and got him dressed in his grey suit – still his only suit. She helped the barely functioning Tait into a taxi and accompanied him to the airport. Once there, she and her mother took him to the American Airlines departure gate in a wheelchair and stayed until his flight was called. He had no luggage because there was nothing he owned worth taking with him.

Then, pressing his one-way ticket to Detroit into his swollen, shaking hands they said goodbye, knowing they would never again see the tortured soul they'd learned to care about. Maria watched as Tait feebly rolled to the departure area, wondering if he would live long enough to get home. She truly hoped so. Tait had no plan beyond getting on the plane and had no idea what he would do when he eventually arrived in Canada. All he could think of was that he was probably going to die and now wanted to die in Windsor.

The plane landed in Miami and Tait was wheeled through the airport by an attendant. It was later learned that although Tait's name had been red flagged and noted while the plane was in flight, he was not stopped by immigration officers. Once out of immigration he planned to call his old buddy Moe Parent to let him know he was in Miami, but decided against it and asked to be taken to the connecting flight for Detroit.

Tait has little memory of his last days in San Jose. Alcohol had caused severe nerve damage and much of his time in the country has been obliterated from his conscious mind.

TAIT'S RETURN- Ignominy of Defeat

ON THE PLANE RIDE back to Detroit Tait drifted in and out of consciousness. Conscious, he would order more alcohol. He couldn't get comfortable. He was sweating. His bulky, swollen and painful body was cramped in his seat and even moments of alcohol-induced sleep offered little relief. He spent most of the trip drunkenly telling the well dressed and elegant woman sitting next to him his sordid life story. She sat wide-eyed, disgusted and fascinated by the pathetic, smelly drooler burbling incoherently about his non-believable life.

Once on the ground he asked the air attendant to order a wheelchair and a worker wheeled him to the pickup area. He phoned O'Reilly to let him know he needed a ride to Windsor. O'Reilly sent a fellow biker to pick Tait. O'Reilly's buddy brought Tait a baseball cap in a lame attempt to disguise his identity. However, the immigration officer on duty didn't bother asking for identification from the passenger and Tait's facial features were so bloated and deformed he would have been unrecognizable to his own mother. The plan was to take Tait to Tilbury, a small community about an hour east of Windsor and set him up in a trailer in the buddy's back yard. They had not reckoned on the severity of Tait's condition, but they were soon to find out.

"I was a nightmare for them. I was in the DTs, hallucinating, I pissed my pants. I pissed on his couch. I was yelling and screaming. It was a total nightmare."

After two nights dealing with Tait's behaviour, the buddy called O'Reilly and told him there was no way he could have Tait in his house and it wasn't safe to let him stay in the trailer by himself. O'Reilly drove to Tilbury and took Tait back to his apartment on Ouellette Avenue in Windsor. Tait's condition and behaviour deteriorated. He was completely

178

uncontrollable and was screaming about the strange things he was seeing in his hallucinations. O'Reilly was worried a neighbour might call the cops and he would get arrested for hiding a felon. More importantly, he was also worried that Tait was dying.

Despairing how to handle the increasingly difficult situation, he bundled Tait into his car and took him to the Airport Motel, a small one-storey cinder block building on the outskirts of the city. After a day and night, he was convinced Tait was very likely soon going to die and called Montello. After hearing O'Reilly describe Tait's condition, Montello called Tait's former partner Andy Bradie. Montello and Bradie decided the best course of action was to get Tait to hospital. Montello called O'Reilly and told him to get Tait to the ER at Hotel-Dieu Grace Hospital. O'Reilly told Tait he was taking him somewhere more secure and where there would be "lots of booze."

It was a struggle but O'Reilly managed to get Tait in the car and headed for the downtown. As he turned into the hospital's ER area, Tait asked "Where the fuck you going man?" O'Reilly said he had taken a wrong turn and pulled up to the doors where it said, "No parking." A commissionaire came over to the car asking if they needed help. O'Reilly said he had a very sick man and could he get a wheelchair. Once Tait was in the wheelchair, O'Reilly pulled a baseball cap over his head, wheeled him inside the doors of the ER and told him to "Wait here. Someone's coming." Then he left.

Sitting in ER, Tait was a caricature with the baseball cap perched on his bloated head. People were staring and it was getting uncomfortable so he managed to wheel himself outside the doors. As he rolled out, he looked up and saw Bradie walking towards him. Bradie got him out of the chair and into his car. Tait was freaked because all he could see was the face of a werewolf – Bradie's beard and moustache were feeding Tait's DT hallucinations.

"Fuck Andy, you're scaring me."

179

Bradie told Tait he had spoken to a doctor and was taking him to get help at Windsor Regional Hospital. Bradie looked at his old friend. The GQ lawyer was sweaty, filthy and stinking. The DTs were so severe Tait asked Bradie to stop somewhere to get booze in him to calm him down. The liquor stores were closed so he drove to the home of one of the assistant crown attorneys and brought Tait out a water glass full of vodka. He guzzled it down like it was water. It would be Tait's last drink. By the time they drove the 15 minutes to the hospital, Tait was semi-conscious. Bradie got Tait in a wheelchair and rolled him into ER. Once hospital staff realized who their patient was they called the cops, got him into a bed and pulled the curtains.

Tait briefly regained consciousness and out of puffy, swollen eyes, recognized a sergeant he once defended in court but he is incapable of speech. His eyelids are practically swollen shut and he appears dead.

"How is he doc?" the cop asked a doctor who appeared inside the curtain.

"I don't think he's going to make it. He's pretty far gone. I just don't know."

Hearing his response Tait is relieved. He remembers thinking "It's all over. I know it's over. Shit, I should already be dead." He also remembers being angry he was still alive. Through a tiny slit in one eyelid he sees the cop peering at him with tears in his eyes. Tait fades to black. It is May 30, just over four months since he fled to Costa Rica.

The next time he opened his eyes he was in a private area of the Intensive Care Unit. The warrant for his arrest had been executed overnight and he was now remanded in the custody of the provincial jail. There were three prison guards assigned to him and his hands and feet were shackled to his hospital bed.

"Government regulations require a person to be physically

restrained so they restrained me. It must have been quite a cost to taxpayers because I had two full time guards around the clock. It was sure a lot of overtime. It was a bit of overkill because I was barely conscious and I couldn't have gone anywhere even if I wanted to try. My legs were shot."

Tait says most of the three weeks he spent at Windsor Regional Hospital are a blur, mainly because doctors were keeping him heavily sedated and medicated as they tried to save his life.

Montello, anxious to see his former prodigy and friend, walked in to his room and winced at seeing him shackled to the bed, even though he well understands the legal reasons why. But when he moved closer and could see his face, he felt sick. If he had not been told that it was Don Tait lying in the bed he would never have recognized him.

"He was a mess. He was bloated and swollen. Unrecognizable. He looked nothing like Don. It was shocking to see him lying there in that condition. I couldn't see how he would survive. I was really and truly afraid this was the end of him. It all seemed so sad that this was the kind of terrible end for a great guy, a great lawyer."

Johanna, also worried Tait was dying, visited often during his stay in hospital. No matter how often she told herself she should stay away from him, he pulled at her like a magnet.

"This was exactly what I feared would happen to him. When I first saw him I didn't think he would come out of it. I think everyone thought it was just a matter of time. I felt really bad for him, seeing him in that condition."

Several weeks after he was admitted Tait learned that Barbara was also in the hospital, on the maternity floor giving birth to twins. The day she walked into his room was an emotional time for both of them.

"I knew things were bad for dad and I hoped hearing about the twins would give him something to feel good about. I wanted to cry seeing him in the shape he was in. I couldn't believe he was still alive to be honest. I was glad he was alive but couldn't imagine what his life was going to be like if he survived and got through it all."

While Tait was receiving medical treatment, word was leaking out that he was in a Windsor hospital in bad shape. No media pressure could persuade hospital officials to give out any information on their notorious patient. Montello would only admit Tait was "nearly dead but expected to live." Broadcast and print media were in a frenzy to get more and camped outside the hospital. After more than three weeks in the acute care hospital, Tait's physical health was stabilized and doctors decided to transfer him to the psychiatric unit at the Prince Road campus where he was remanded for another three months. He was still a prisoner and the law demanded he continue to be shackled with guards assigned to keep him under surveillance day and night; and because of his notoriety he was placed in a private room.

The unit, where patients were taken for short term observation, consisted of a large square room with a nursing station, square tables and chairs and could be converted into a lounge, meeting room and dining hall. Patients' rooms are positioned around the perimeter of the room. It was, as Tait describes those months, "Surreal. Total unreality."

Arising at 7 a.m. he would line up with other patients to get his meds - a "heavy duty" combination of Valium-type sedatives, anti-depressants, medications for blood pressure and narcotics to prevent seizures. Breakfast was followed by long periods of sitting around that would be broken only by visits three to four times a week from a psychiatrist, twice weekly visits from a psychologist and regular discussions with a psychiatric nurse. Much of Tait's consultations included talking about suicidal thoughts and his depression. He also spent time in the gym - a basketball auditorium-type room where he used the treadmill to strengthen his deteriorating leg muscles. They were no longer the size of large tree trunks but the cerebellum ataxia - alcoholic nerve damage - had taken a toll on them and he has since been told that only lifelong exercise would keep him walking, albeit with a stilted gait. He also spent hours walking the hospital's long connecting tunnels. For those walks the guards, with whom he was quite friendly, would often remove his leg irons and walk with him. At night they would get in golf carts and race down the corridors. Some days he did laundry.

On June 12, 2000, Tait signed an undertaking with the Law Society of Upper Canada not to engage in the practice of law, and agreed that the undertaking would remain in effect until the following conditions were met:

a) the completion of any and all investigations by the Law Society;

b) the completion of the hearing of any conduct, capacity, professional competency or non-compliance proceedings arising from those investigations; and

c) the Law Society is provided with a medical report from a psychiatrist or psychologist satisfactory to the Secretary of the Law Society that the Member is fit to carry on the practice of law.

It was not unexpected and Tait began to feel the lid slowly closing on his law career. As it always was in the case of Tait and his life, the gossip mill was in full roar. Rumours were rampant in the hospital and throughout the city that the mafia was either going to attempt to free him or kill him. Those rumours made his guards somewhat jumpy and the state of their jangled nerves was evident one afternoon when they were all sitting around the lounge watching television.

"There was a loud bang that sounded somewhat like a gunshot. It was just a noise and none of the patients paid any attention to it. But both of the prison guards hit the floor. They were so hypersensitive. It was amazing how fast they were on that floor."

When required, he made appearances in court via a video link and he knew there was still to be a day of reckoning before a judge in a court of law. Tait's psychological state was precarious and alcohol had caused such serious nerve damage, doctors were not certain how many cognitive skills would be permanently damaged.

"One day a psychologist gave me a wooden puzzle the size of a serving tray. She handed me the five pieces which depicted the side view of an elephant and told me to put them together. I couldn't do it and it took me a very long time to figure out how those five big pieces fit together. Then she gave me a newspaper and asked me to read it out loud. I could read the first line but when I got to the second line I had forgotten what I read on the first line and would have to re-read it. I just could not remember what I read in that first line."

In addition to his physical ill health, Tait struggled with the psychological humiliation of what was happening to him.

"I was living in what was for me an unreal world. I'm back in Windsor, the place I ran away from because I didn't want to face what I knew I'd have to face which was the reality of what happened in Goderich with Sandra. It was all like a nightmare dream and didn't seem totally real. I was drugged on medications, in leg irons 24/7 and here I was, the once great Don Tait, almost on public display walking around a psych unit in shackles with two prison guards. I had no money. Nothing. One day Bill O'Reilly brought me a pair of shoes. I still have those shoes."

Tait had few visitors during his hospitalization. O'Reilly came three or four times every week, Johanna once a week, Montello would show up occasionally and Bradie would come to discuss Tait's case because he was dealing with court details.

REHAB #3

ON AUGUST 2, 2000, Tait was remanded to the addiction division of the Homewood Health Centre in Guelph, Ontario, about three hours east of Windsor. To be sent to Homewood, Tait had to be released on bail because he was still a prisoner of the court. He was taken from the psychiatric unit in a prisoner transfer van to the police station and courthouse in downtown Windsor. The media was waiting as the van approached the building.

Getting a good shot of Tait was difficult because the prisoner drop- off area was in the basement of the police station. Photographers and videographers chased the van right up to the closing of the underground garage door and pointed their cameras through the row of windows, capturing anything that might give them a shot of their target.

As Tait stepped out of the van that morning to twenty cops were there to welcome him. Seeing him, they all applauded.

"It was amazing. They all came up to me to shake my hand and were telling me they wish I was back and wishing me good luck. I knew them all and had represented many of them. It was very emotional and brought tears to my eyes."

In court, Tait entered a plea of guilty in respect of five counts involving breaches of the criminal code. Those included: Assault causing bodily harm; Assault with a weapon; Failing to attend court on Feb. 21, 2000; Failing to attend court Jan. 25, 2000 and Breach of Recognizance on Feb. 11, 2000. This breach related to the fact that following the assault on his fiancée in June 1999, Tait was required to "reside at 3442 Riverside Drive East in Windsor, and to refrain from associating or communicating directly or indirectly with

Sandra Martin and to abstain absolutely from the consumption of alcohol and non-medically prescribed drugs."

Tait breached those conditions when he ran off to Costa Rica on Feb. 11, 2000. Bradie advised the court that "agreement had been reached on a Statement of Facts in relation to the matters." Tait was granted bail by the Honourable Mr. Justice Michael O'Dea and remanded without guards to Homewood. His buddy O'Reilly drove him to the centre. Tait was admitted into Homewood's detox unit for the first week and shared a semi private hospital-type room with a cop from Toronto who was in "really bad shape." Within the week the cop died from complications caused by his addictions. His bed was taken by a young man in his twenties.

Once doctors were satisfied that Tait's medical condition was sufficiently stable they moved him from the detox unit into the main rehab centre where he was weaned off all his medications. This would be the first time in more than a year he was to experience some sense of reality and it was a shock to his system.

"Up until this time, my brain was soaked in alcohol and drugs. It was fried. Now, I had some degree of reality, but I was still in a state of denial. I told myself this is temporary. I had the idea that I was going to come back and while I didn't know how, I was going to get it all back. I was also thinking about how I would get even with people, how I could do nasty business on them. It was a continued, ridiculous insanity."

Tait was assigned to the care of Dr. Graeme Cunningham, the Scottish sixty-seven-year-old director of the addiction division who has worked with the world-renowned centre for more than twenty years. He was one of five doctors in the section. All of whom, including Cunningham, are recovering alcoholics. Cunningham is a no nonsense, straight-talking counsellor who opines that SOBER stands for "Son of a Bitch Everything is Real."

Tait's mornings started at 7 a.m. He would get coffee from a vending machine, have a cigarette and head to the gym where everyone in the program would be working out with assistance from a trainer. The sessions started with everyone walking around the gym to the blaring beat of "500 Miles." Tait would also take long walks down several flights of stairs and around the grounds.

After showering there was breakfast and meetings. Tait and seven to ten other patients would meet with the doctor, a social worker and a nurse. The centre is pro AA and patients would read from AA literature. That would be followed by a coffee break and a meeting of all seventy to eighty patients in the program.

After lunch his small group would meet and be given assignments - writing life stories or given various handouts to be completed. They would also watch educational videos. At 5 p.m. they were allowed personal time. Once a week a counsellor from AA came to the centre and at least two to three evenings per week Tait often walked to AA meetings out in the community.

While Tait lived in close proximity with Homewood's residents, especially those in his group, he did not form lasting relationships. Rehab was a means to an end, an end he was convinced would lead him back to the life he once knew. The one thing he was certain of was his need to be sober and to stay that way. There were no magical, out of body life changing experiences as reported by many who attend rehab and write about it. This was only the harsh reality of getting sober.

Despite the occasional bravado he would return like a phoenix, Tait was living in a very bleak and dark place. This wasn't surprising given the fact that everything bad about him and his life had been exposed for the world to see and gloat over or feel badly about. His mind was filled with the experience of being shackled to a hospital bed and guarded by cops, referred to a psychiatrist, of realizing everyone now

187

knew for certain what he had feared all his life – they knew he was no good, he was totally useless and not worthy of anyone's time. He had an overwhelming feeling of being totally and absolutely alone. In rehab he mostly had no thought of getting well, only that he wanted to die.

Tait's road to redemption was to be one of many twists and turns, punctuated with yet more heart break and disappointment. But there was a seminal, almost spiritual event that helped Tait's recovery and it had nothing to do with rehab but everything to do with the extraordinary bond recovering addicts have for one of their own.

One evening, Tait heard a loudspeaker announcement asking him to come to the reception area. There he was told two Windsor cops were waiting for him. His first thought was that they were there to hit him with more charges and arrest him. He walked in to the waiting room and noted they were not in uniform and had big smiles when they saw him. The three sat outside in a private area of the garden and talked about everything except alcoholism, rehab and getting well. Peter and Mike told funny cop stories and regaled Tait with the latest rumours circulating about him. The conversation was about nothing serious and it made Tait laugh for most of their hour- long visit.

They told him when he got out he was to make sure he contacted them. They were cops Tait had defended on alcohol-related charges, got acquitted and then in to AA. One told Tait "I owe you a lot Don and I want to help you now any way I can." As Tait watched the two men walk away that evening he burst into tears. They had no idea that their visit had an immeasurable impact on him that was probably far more profound than anything he'd experienced in rehab. Those two cops also had no idea that their true generosity of spirit and the love they showed for that broken human would be the catalyst that would one day lead him to help countless others like themselves, thousands of miles away in a remote part of Africa.

"Looking back at it now, what was happening was something most people wouldn't understand. We all knew we were drunks, there was no judgement of any kind and them driving that distance, spending money on gas, showed me how they had changed over the years from being self-centred to loving people, giving unconditional love. They did it because they loved me as I was, at that moment."

Tait didn't quite understand what was happening to him but what he was absolutely sure about is that he wanted more of that feeling.

"Back in my room I thought about what those guys had done. They travelled three hours in each direction to say hello, not to lecture or berate me, not to ask for details about what happened to me and didn't tell me I had better get to AA. They just visited with me. For that hour with them I was in the moment. I forgot about me. I felt so good because I felt loved. I felt God. When they left I was back into it again but that one little visit really did start to change everything. I started to understand I didn't have to be anything other than me. It was the beginning of the end of my addiction and of learning I didn't need cars, sex, women and money, everything I had spent my life getting off on. And, it fuelled a passion to get out the message, to get it across to just one person, or more, that it's okay to be exactly who you are. I was finally beginning to learn that God loves me just the way I am."

Tait remained in the intensive patient hospital program from August 4 until September 21, 2000. In his report, Cunningham said Tait was compliant with all his treatment and had gradually developed insight into his personal recovery needs.

"There was a suspected mood disorder that had presented with severe depression and suicidal ideation. This disappeared as abstinence continued. His elevated blood pressure noted on admission to Windsor hospital also settled with continuing abstinence from alcohol."

Tait was released from Homewood in late September and by court order, enrolled in Homewood's nine-month continuing care program. He travelled to Guelph to meet with Cunningham weekly – from 4 p.m. to 6 p.m. until his incarceration in early 2001. He also started attending AA meetings in various small towns around Essex County. He contacted Peter the cop who would pick him up and take him to the meetings.

"I felt like the prodigal son being welcomed back without judgement, no condemnation, no one special, just smiles and hugs and welcome. I also got that feeling I'd had when Peter and Mike came to see me. I got that feeling from others at those meetings as well. I liked the feeling so much I began going to ten meetings a week and that added up to a thousand meetings over the next two years."

In the beginning, Tait was going to AA meetings because when he was there he believed people really cared about him. He knew that O'Reilly and Montello cared, but what he now felt at AA was different, in a way that it had never been before.

"I now know that we needed each other. It's a give and take thing. I had been around the program but I had to have that experience...those two people, self-centred alcoholics, not being self-centred. God worked through them and everything changed after that visit."

Tait met regularly with his sponsor Peter who never hesitated in reminding Tait he was just another drunk. Once, as Tait was driving them back from an AA meeting they were cut off by a driver in a hurry and Tait became furious, beginning to swear and vent about the "fucking stupid idiot cutting me off." Peter suggested he take it easy and told him firstly, the driver had no idea Tait was in a hurry, and secondly, the driver had "no idea how important you used to be." It may have been unconditional love, but it was certainly also tough love.

Also by court order, Tait was not allowed inside Windsor city limits. Fortunately for him, Montello lived on a secluded, wooded acreage in Essex County and offered him temporary refuge. Sitting at a big wooden table in the large dining room of his log-built home surrounded by large trees, where Tait sought some semblance of peace, Montello pours two glasses of his home made red wine and talks about his friend.

"He was a broken man who was going through another bad period in his life. The worst. He is like a son and of course I would do whatever I could to help him through all this. He is brilliant, absolutely amazing in court. He was one of the best in the country in my opinion. But he couldn't stay sober. He did for a long period but once he went back to the bottle it was like the beginning of the end. There was no hesitation on my part that I would have him stay with me until he got on his feet. He is like a son and I would do anything to help him."

Tait had made a disability claim to his insurance company, however, the company wasn't paying and even after many frustrating phone calls they were giving him only an occasional cheque for a couple of thousand dollars.

"Frank took care of me. I ate and slept a lot and we did a lot of talking. His wife had died the year before and he was really distraught, so it worked for both of us. It was certainly essential for me. He gave me access to a vehicle and even though I couldn't go into Windsor, I could drive around anywhere in Ontario."

He wanted to get a vehicle and in a casual conversation mentioned it to a patient (an anaesthetist) he met at Homewood who was getting rid of his Jeep Cherokee. He told Tait he could take over the last four months of his lease payments. Tait agreed. At least he would be mobile and not relying on Montello to drive him around.

"Frank was convinced I should prepare for my eventual Law Society hearing into whether I could continue to practice law and that should be my whole mentality."

But Tait was doing the calculations. The best he expected from the Law Society was a two-year suspension. Those years, plus the two he had already been away from the law meant he would be at least 62 years old when he resumed his career. He also had that million-dollar tax debt hanging over him and a bill close to $400,000 from the Law Society.

"This whole thing was a friggin' nightmare. I had no drugs to help me out. I'd lost everything. I was almost fifty-eight-years-old. An old man with no fire left in his belly."

A CONVICT IN ORANGE AND WAKE UP CALL #2

AS FALL TURNED TO WINTER, Tait began to mentally prepare for his January court appearance. Having already pled guilty to the charges against him, this would be a sentencing hearing. On Monday, Jan. 5, 2001, he appeared once again before Judge O'Dea. Dr. Cunningham appeared and spoke on his behalf, as did some of the most well noted and well-known lawyers in the province of Ontario. After hearing the evidence and submissions of counsel, as well as a brief statement from Tait, O'Dea told Tait he was sending him to jail.

"Considering all the aggravating circumstances, a sentence in the range of nine months would be appropriate. Taking into consideration the mitigating circumstances, the pleas entered, as well as the fact that this is his first offence and Mr. Tait's contribution to the community in the past, I would reduce the sentence to seven months. And with the time spent at the various hospitals in Windsor, I would credit a further four months of pre-disposition custody. I would give no credit for the time spent at Homewood.

In all, I will impose a sentence of incarceration of three months. On the assault causing bodily harm, one month. On the assault with a weapon, once month consecutive. On the charge of breach of a recognizance on February 11, 2000, by failing to abstain and seek treatment, one-month consecutive. On the charge of breaching a recognizance between January 16th and January 25th, 2000, by failing to report to attend court in Goderich, one month concurrent. You will be prohibited from owning or possessing any weapon described in s.110 of the Criminal Code for a period of ten years from this date. You will also be the subject matter of a Probation Order for a period of two years commencing upon your release from custody, which will be subject to the these terms:

First, you will keep the peace and be of good behaviour.

Second, you will report within two working days of the day of your release to a Probation Officer in the City of Windsor and as frequently after that as your Probation Officer may dictate appropriate.

Thirdly, you will reside where directed from time to time in writing by your Probation Officer.

Next, you will notify your Probation Officer forthwith of any change in your address.

Next, you will not communicate or associate, directly or indirectly with Sandra Martin, unless in context with counselling related to your recovery and rehabilitation.

Next, you will abstain absolutely from the consumption of or possessing, any alcoholic beverage.

Next, you will abstain absolutely from the consumption of or possessing, any non- prescribed medication.

Next, you will attend Alcoholics Anonymous on a daily basis.

Next, you will continue with the treatment plan put into place by Dr. Cunningham, or his designate, and you will be amenable with its practices and teaching and you will use all efforts to apply same to your daily routine.

And finally, you will remain within the province of Ontario, unless written permission to leave is granted by your Probation Officer."

Each pronouncement was a blow to his ego. Words he had often heard aimed at his clients were now focused on him. When the judge had finished reading the terms of Tait's Probation Order, he was taken from the courthouse, placed in the transfer van and taken to the lockup on Windsor's west end.

In jail, Tait donned an orange, prison-issue jumpsuit and became a convict. The jail was overcrowded with three to a cell and prisoners slept on mattresses on the floor. There was no privacy and they used a toilet in the corridor, all subjected to the sounds and smells that came with it.

Because of Tait's reputation, everyone in the cell block knew who he was and kept asking him for legal advice. His notoriety eventually became a problem and prison officials discussed sending him to a facility in Ottawa, the nation's capital. Tait wanted to stay in Windsor and was relieved when a second solution was proposed. He was moved into an old execution holding cell that consisted of a very large room with bars across the middle. It was private, had a single bed, toilet and TV and Tait could reach a pay phone just outside the bars. The executioner's ring was still on the ceiling outside his cell and he could see the stairwell where hapless prisoners would swing to their deaths.

On his own he did a lot of reading, sleeping and just sitting around. Prisoners in county jails did not have to work or take part in activities that are expected in provincial and federal facilities. At night the guards would visit, bringing him Tim Hortons coffee and to "shoot the shit." The celebrity in the holding cell was also not subject to routine searches the way other prisoners were. Tossing the cells, which included strip searches, were one way guards could attempt to keep contraband – mainly drugs - out of the jail. When word got around that Tait was getting special treatment an order was issued that he and his cell were to be searched. The older guards who knew and befriended Tait refused to carry out the search so three young guys Tait had never met were sent to do it.

"Excuse me. You're here to see Mr. Tait?" The prison guard had finally returned.

"Yes."

"He's on his way out."

"OK. Thanks."

This was the first time I was seeing Tait up close since saying goodbye to him in Costa Rica. Stories about his return, rehab and incarceration had been written by the Star's court reporter. At first, I felt left out of the story I had been so invested in, but I also had a sense of relief not having to deal with it and Tait. Yet, here I was, about to see him. The fit and trim Tait who walked into the room and sat down on the opposite side of the glass partition was a stick man compared to the bloated frame he inhabited a year earlier.

"You're looking a lot better - certainly thinner," I said, not feigning surprise.

"Yeah. There's a bit of a difference."

"What's it like here?"

"Well, I've had to shit in the corridor with a bunch of guys watching and I've had to bend over to be searched."

"How did you feel about that?"

"How'd you think I felt? It was extremely humiliating but one major thing came out of it. I was fuming that I was being treated like a common criminal and boy I was mad. I wasn't a criminal, I was a criminal lawyer. I shouldn't be treated like a common criminal. Then, it suddenly struck me 'yeah, I should be treated like a criminal because that's what I am.' I had this idea I was someone special and I'm not. Those thoughts made me start to have insight into the cowardly things I'd done and that I was dealing with a piece of shit - me."

"Your legs bothering you? You look as though you're finding it hard to walk."

"The doctors say the nerve damage from the alcoholism has caused a lot of damage and it will probably never get any better. I just have to keep them moving or they'll seize up. If I'd gotten treatment earlier my legs would have been saved. All I needed were Vitamin B shots."

"That's too bad. Happy belated birthday. It was on the 11th. right?"

"Yeah. I'll remember my 58th birthday that's for sure. I read all the stories you wrote about me."

"Yeah? And?" I didn't know what to expect here.

"Some of my friends were not happy to have people from across the country reading all that stuff. But it was all true. My enemies didn't care. They probably would have written a lot worse."

He laughs, that old Tait laugh with mirthful eyes and a crinkling of crow's feet.

"The letters to the Star have been interesting," I tell him.

"Some people love me and some hate me. That's fine. Some people have good reason to hate me.

I've pissed a lot of people off and caused people a lot of pain. You weren't in court."

"I was working at the National Post in Toronto."

"Oh yeah, you pissed Frank off."

"Yeah, well that's another story. He really pissed me off. What happens when you get out?"

"Don't know yet - I still have to deal with the Law Society. I'll be staying with Frank for a while. Here's a laugh for you - there's some publication that did a survey asking people to rate people and things they think are the best - you know, best dentist, family doc, best supermarket - well, here I am sitting in jail and they rated me 'best lawyer.' Isn't that weird."

We laugh heartily. "Think you'll do the 90 days?"

"I'll probably get time off for good behaviour."

"I really am glad to see you looking so well. By the way - do you remember the telephone calls you made to me late at night?"

"It's a blur. I know I talked to you but haven't got a damn clue what I might have said. Was I nuts?"

"Yeah. Pretty much. I'll tell you about it sometime. I'm still paying the bills. Well, I have to be going. Look after yourself." We laugh.

"Thanks for coming. Maybe I'll talk to you sometime."

"Sure. Take care of yourself. "He's staring at me.

"Sure."

"Good luck."

I walked out of the small room, glancing back as he turned the corner, almost dragging his legs along. He'd weathered another storm. But with Tait you knew there would probably be more to come. I wondered if I would ever see or hear from him again.

On Saturday, January 20, Tait watched the inauguration of George W. Bush on his jail cell TV. He had just received news that with one month off for good behaviour, he would be

198

released on parole February 4. He would be allowed to travel freely into Windsor but was still forbidden to have contact with his former girlfriend and not allowed to consume alcohol. He had served sixty of his ninety days.

HOMELESS AND HOPELESS

JOHANNA PICKED TAIT UP at the jail just after midnight. As a concession to the lawyer he was released at midnight so that he would not have to wait another entire day for processing. She drove him to her house and later that day they drove the 30 kilometres to Montello's home. There, his old friend again urged Tait to begin preparing for the Law Society hearing and maintained his opinion that Tait should not have gone to jail.

"I just didn't think that was necessary. I don't believe he should have been in jail and I did and do believe he could have gone back to practicing law. He still had it in him," Montello said even years after Tait's decision to give up on the law.

Tait continued to attend seven to ten AA meetings every week and also made the 292 kilometre drive each week to Homewood for a counselling session. Tait may have been free from his jailers but he was held captive by the jailer with the biggest key - himself. As the Law Society hearing approached, Tait was examining his chances of ever going back to what he had before his nightmare began.

"I kept asking myself where the fuck this was all going. If they gave me a two-year suspension I'd be sixty before I could even get started again. If I go back Canada Revenue Agency will confiscate almost every single buck I make. They are continually calling Frank's place and it will take at a minimum five to seven years before I even start to make any money."

He was finding it difficult to concentrate. He was frustrated and depressed and again often thought about suicide as an easier option. During those early weeks at Montello's few of his old friends and colleagues came to visit. One colleague who had been a very close friend and who bought Tait's Rolex only days after he hocked it at a local jewellery store, came only once. Tait noticed he didn't have a watch on and surmised that he didn't want him to see it. That also angered and hurt him. Tait also spent a great deal of time with Charbonneau who was never one to sweet talk and always reminded Tait he was a drunk who had to work hard to get his life together.

"He is a good man and a good friend. But I wasn't going to lie to him. He had a hard struggle ahead of him and there was no one going to be able to fix him. He had to want to do that for himself. I've never been one to beat around the bush and Don never expected me to. He knew he could always come to me but he also had to learn to stand on his own two feet as a sober man."

Tait divided his time between Montello's home and Johanna's. The ever-present Johanna who never seems to abandon Tait. His most consistent visitor and supporter was his old friend O'Reilly. When he didn't come out to Montello's Tait would go to his apartment on Ouellette Avenue in Windsor where they played Gin Rummy for hours. Tait says it was disheartening at first that the only loyal friend he had, besides Montello, was a hardened criminal biker. He became resentful.

"I kept telling myself 'look at the shit I've done for everyone over the years. Now they don't want to come near me.' That hurt and resentment was driving me nuts. My life was finished and the resentment was building inside me. I was thriving on blame and resentment and it was a miracle I didn't drink."

Tait says what saved him was AA.

"When I went to those meetings it was the only time I got relief. Just being there felt good and Bill often came with me. I always had a feeling of belonging when I was there with people I understood."

Cunningham was pleased with Tait's progress. In statements to the court, he wrote:

"While in jail, abstinence was maintained and I saw him again after his jail sentence on the 23rd of May 2001. A significant statement was made to me on that visit by Mr. Tait that he felt that 'his brain was working now.' By this he meant that his concentration had improved, his attention span was back to normal and he didn't feel unusually stressed or pressured by trying to concentrate or read simple material. This was a significant improvement. Over the fall months, both his treatment team and I myself had been concerned for significant cognitive blunting as a result of his severe alcoholism. I was impressed that by the summer of 2001, cognitive blunting appeared to have disappeared."

The last time Cunningham saw Tait was on March 14, 2002 when he wrote...

"While alcohol dependency is a progressive and ultimately fatal illness, recovery from severe alcohol dependency as witnessed in Mr. Tait is a progressive experience of improvement. Mr. Tait is a completely different human being now than he was in September 2000, when he completed our intensive hospital treatment phase. There is no doubt in my mind that this man could return to the practice of law or any other employment without limitation at this time with the proviso that he must never again distance himself from his 12-Step fellowship, keep regular attendance at a minimum of five meetings of Alcoholics Anonymous per week and that he continue a relationship with his sponsor."

Then came the inevitable day of reckoning. One April morning, dressed in a short sleeve button shirt, black shorts, white socks and running shoes, he paced on the back porch. Anger bubbling to the surface, he clenched a fist and screamed to the surrounding forest where leaves were appearing on the acres of ash, elm, oak and black walnut trees.

"I'll be back you fucking bastards. Just you wait. I'll be back." The echo that came back to him in the deafening silence hit with volcanic force. The reality of it all whispered loudly that he was never coming back. Never.

"I was broken. I had no energy left. I was done. I had no home of any kind. Everything was all gone. I was mooching off a guy, people were afraid of me because they didn't know how to approach me and didn't know what to say to me. How do you talk to a guy who fucked up so badly? The guy who bought my watch didn't do anything wrong. I had to come to grips with it - I sold the thing and even though he did not do everything he promised, I was the one who left him with a load of shit to take care of. I was the villain here."

Tait was also painfully aware of the research that shows people who relapse after long term sobriety - like his nineteen years - hardly ever get well. Experts say it is too hard to deal with the years that have gone. Based on everything he had learned, he knew his long-term chances of survival were slim.

"This was one of the great moments in my life. For the first time in my life I had to look at me. Everything – all the trappings, all the women, the so-called fame – all gone. Now, I had to look at who I really am. Whatever I used to be was finished. In reality, all of that wasn't who I was so everything I believed to be essential to self and success had to be removed before I realized who I was. This was a major moment, a realization I wouldn't be back. It was all over, forever. My whole life was about getting and getting off but life is not a journey to get, or get off, it is a journey to who you are. Everything I thought was important and thought I couldn't survive without was gone. I tried to hang on to them because it was hanging on to my life but the only way forward is to let it all go."

Tait believed, again, he had two options – suicide or move on.

"In the bleakness and blackness of that moment I realized I would never again be that person I was. I didn't have it in me. I didn't have the desire in me to do it again and even if I did I knew it would end in disaster. All of those successes didn't work for me. Because it's never an outside job, it's inside. It's not the world that needed to change, it was me. I was on the run from everything close to being attached to me because to be who I was would mean being a lawyer and I just couldn't. I was staring down a process of annihilation and accepting the annihilation. I wanted love so badly but I was so wrapped up in myself I couldn't really love anyone. I had been self-obsessed and self-centered. Now I had nothing. I owned nothing."

Tait needed money to start over, no matter what he would be doing as a job and feared that the chances of getting an insurance settlement were slim.

"They say 'You get $20,000 a month if you are unable to practice law,' but the doctor at Homewood says he believes I am fit to practice, that everything is good, I'm not disabled. But I can't practice because the Law Society says I can't and I don't believe I should. In the moral sense of it all, I am not fit to practice. The reality of it is that at 60, a clean and sober drunk, the only thing I can resign myself to is a mediocre job, like being a greeter at Wal-Mart. Everything was coming back to me that day and I knew there was no one to blame. Just me. There was nowhere to go and that's a lonely place to be. It is hopeless and there's no one to blame but me."

And, he asks himself, where the hell do you go when everything you've worked for is gone and everyone you thought you knew have pretty much abandoned you? Mostly with good reason. Truly believing himself unworthy to attempt a comeback in the profession he had so disgraced, Tait decides it's time to disappear again.

In the months following his incarceration Tait would often spend many hours sitting in leather easy chairs at Chapters bookstore in the local mall, drinking Starbucks coffee and reading. One afternoon while browsing the shelves, he spotted a magazine with an enticing name - Exotic Places to Retire. It featured a story about Costa Rica and having little memory of his time there, he bought it. He thought he might give it another try now that he was sober and needed to get out of town again.

There was also an article in the magazine about South Africa. Cheap. Tropical. English speaking. He bought the magazine and went home to read more. Africa. It became more intriguing the more he thought about it. He asked his probation officer for permission to leave the country for a short vacation. He agreed. But there was the matter of his probation which still had 18 months to run. The probation officer told him if Martin would write a letter saying she was not afraid of him, he was confident a judge would agree to revoke the balance of the probation. Tait thought this might be difficult. However, Martin agreed and Bradie took her letter to a judge who had the probation cancelled.

AFRICA and the rest of the story

IN LATE JANUARY 2002 Tait bought a ticket to South Africa to check it out. Little did he know it would be the beginning of what is likely to be his final chapter. He wasn't sure where he wanted to live so he started in Cape Town, one of the most interesting and enticing cities on the African continent. Since he was expecting, or at least hoping, Johanna would join him, he decided a one bedroom flat he looked at would be too small so he drove to Cape Francis and looked at various places along the drive there and back.

Deciding against living in Cape Town, he flew to Durban, a seaport and third largest city in South Africa. Located on the eastern coast on the Indian Ocean, it is the economic centre of KwaZulu-Natal. After a week checking out the city and surrounding towns, he found the perfect spot to call home in a middle-class neighbourhood located less than forty miles south of Durban in a town called Scottburg. He pulled up to the bungalow on a hillside that overlooks the Indian Ocean and knew it was where he wanted to be. It had the perfect climate and the beach was close.

On his return to Windsor Tait consulted with Johanna about the house and they decided it would be a good place to live. His friends, none believing he was serious about leaving the country, were urging him to begin preparing for the Law Society hearing that was due in late May. Montello was adamant that Tait's talents should not be denied. He had many long conversations with him about an eventual return to practicing law and impressed on him his absolute belief that his friend was "...better than I ever was." But that was not how Tait saw it.

"I told him that isn't true and that I could never be half the man he is. Just look at me. There's a lot not to be proud of but

Frank on the other hand had a successful career and had retired with integrity."

Tait's friends and advisors were all much more confident in his comeback than he was because in his heart Tait knew the jig was up for him. His decision to leave Canada, he believed, was the absolute right decision on many levels. On May 15, 2002, two weeks before his scheduled hearing before the Law Society of Upper Canada, Tait sat down at Montello's computer to write his letter of resignation. The letter is a deep expression of remorse and regret.

"My name is Donald H. Tait and I have been a barrister and solicitor and a member of the Law Society of Upper Canada since 1971. I am also a recovering alcoholic. The former describes what I did for a living and the latter describes what I must do to live.

Let me start off by saying that I truly loved this profession and for the greater part of my career I was steadfastly faithful to its principles and practised it to the best of my abilities. For that I was rewarded in ways that only a fellow colleague who practised in the criminal courts could fully comprehend. During those years I loved the community in which I lived. And I loved my family and those very special people who I call my friends.

A desperate and lonely man who committed suicide while suffering the ravages of chronic alcoholism left these words in a note - "The faceless one came again and this time stole my heart away." Alcoholism, the faceless one, stole my heart, my ability to love and in the final stages, my very dignity as a human being. I have embarrassed my profession, betrayed the solemn trust bestowed upon me by my clients and injured deeply those unfortunate enough to have loved me.

Yes, I could stand before you and plead that I was a sick man and this terrible transformation was a brief aberration from what was otherwise a stellar career. I can ask for your forgiveness and in fact I do, but that divine gift given to human beings does not excuse or justify what I did or what I became.

For that I am responsible and for that I stand accountable.

I am told that in recovery the day will come when I will not regret the past and not wish to shut the door on it. That day has not yet arrived. Shame and guilt still rear their ugly presence and I believe until I am able to forgive myself totally and without reservation that I cannot be the effective advocate that this profession demands. I am aware that Dr. Cunningham has indicated in his opinion that I am ready to re-enter the practice of law. His opinion is based on my mental and physical recovery from the effects of extreme alcohol addiction.

However, this opinion does not take into account that I would feel inhibited in my attack of a witness or in forceful argument with a judge. To use the vernacular, I feel like 'damaged goods.' In addition to these two debilitating emotions, I would also have to deal with the pressures of re-establishing a practice while at the same time facing a financial debt which seems insurmountable at the present time. However, I do believe that one day I will be freed from these two debilitating emotions and will be able to face the consequences of my acts in a responsible and dignified way.

Someone once said that making a living and making a life are not the same thing. Before I can honestly say that I am ready to ask that I be allowed to re-enter this profession I must first make a life that is worthwhile so that my heart and dignity have been completely restored. Until then, a re-entry into this profession would be premature. It would truly be putting the cart before the horse.

So, it is with great regret and deep sadness that I tender to you my resignation as a member of the Law Society of Upper Canada and I hope that you will accept it in the spirit that it is offered.

I am admonished that my recovery from this disease requires, in fact demands, that I be honest and fearless from the very start. Half measures will avail me nothing. I have searched deep within me and I feel that resigning is the honest and proper thing to do. But it is not done fearlessly. By doing this, there is a

208

gnawing fear that I may have closed forever any chance that I can ever again be an active and contributing member of this profession. This is definitely not my purpose and I can only pray that it will not have that effect.

Let me close by offering my sincere and deepest apology and regret to all who have been injured by me either directly or indirectly. No words can ever express how truly sorry I really am. To those who have loved me and gave me the gift of hope, I will be forever grateful. It is through your support and kindness that I derived the desire to live and the courage to change."

On May 15, Tait left Montello's with three suitcases and drove to Johanna's house where he met Johanna and O'Reilly. With a sense of deja vu, Tait was running away, but this time there would be no one coming after him. This time he was flying from a Canadian airport – Pearson in Toronto. There he said goodbye to O'Reilly and Johanna, whom he expected to join him within months. He couldn't look back. Wounded but hopeful, he could only look ahead.

Tait flew directly to Johannesburg, changed planes and flew to Durban. In Scottburg he checked in to the Cuttysark Hotel, stayed one night and moved to the Blue Marlin Hotel, which had been booked for him by Johanna. In the following two weeks he bought furniture, a fridge, stove and everything he needed to set up a new home. On May 30 he moved in. It was a special anniversary - his second year sober.

"I was pretty excited but it didn't seem real. I really didn't know what I was getting into. This was a new culture and I really did not know how this was all going to play out. But I figured this was it. I knew my daughters and Frank thought what I was doing was insane and that I should return to Windsor. Peter, my sponsor in AA, told me if South Africa doesn't work out take responsibility for it failing and don't feel guilty about the decision." Tait said he carefully assessed what his life would be like if he did return and it wasn't pretty.

"I would face at least a two-year suspension from the Law

Society and what would I do during that time? And how would I pay back the Society and Revenue Canada? I don't know how I stayed sober in those two years since coming back from Costa Rica. I was manipulating and lying and playing games in order to get myself to Africa. I knew there was no way I could continue to live in Canada. I would have failed. I'd want to get my name as a big shot back and the money, but I would have to deal with Revenue Canada and the women thing. But I'd just had enough. Father Paul understood. He had the ability to see that I could never try successfully to get back what I had. And he didn't think I should."

Tait also knew that the odds of him staying on a sober path would be a challenge because only a miniscule number of people who relapse, after long years of sobriety, remain sober. He would have to carve out a very different life if he wanted to survive and some instinct was telling him his chances were better in Africa than they would be in Windsor, Ontario, where expectations and temptations could pull him over the edge in a nano second.

Two weeks later, while Tait was settling into his home in Africa, the Law Society of Upper Canada held a hearing to determine his fate. There, all his dirty laundry was aired before the august body whose principles he swore to uphold. Had he been there it would have filled him with shame and was a day etched in the minds of those who attended.

Yet, although the evidence read at the hearing was devastating and damning, there was a surfeit of support for Tait. Dozens of letters were submitted from across the province of Ontario and Detroit. They included senior lawyers, police officers and detectives, high school teachers, members of the RCMP and Windsor's then mayor Mike Hurst who is also a lawyer. Letters came from reporters - one who wrote, "Just as Wayne Gretzky was born to play hockey, Don Tait was meant to be a lawyer." Testimonies also came from recovering alcoholics in positions of power in the business world who had been helped by Tait and from Crown

Attorneys.

Michigan's leading forensic pathologist Werner Spitz wrote "I have thanked Don Tait in the third edition of my textbook "Medicolegal Investigation of Death, 1993 for his advice and input to the book and I refer to him on page 774 as the eminent Donald H. Tait, Q.C. and indeed eminent he is in every regard."

Sandra Pupatello, a former minister in the Ontario government, then Deputy Leader of the Official Opposition, offered this: "His passion to defend his clients is the stuff of legend...those who watch his practice consider him to be one of our nation's best advocates."

The Law Society decision was to allow Tait to resign, keeping the door open in case he changed his mind sometime in the future and wanted to return to the practice of law. To this day, Tait becomes emotional when reading the warmth contained in the letters from so diverse a group of people. He still believes the decision to resign was the best for him and the Society.

But while moved by the passionate defence of him by so many of those he respects, he is also acutely aware that there are still many who would be just as happy to see his neck on the chopping block. Those jealous of the elevated status he enjoyed, did not lament his meteoric fall from grace. Others were angry he did not pay back money he owed the Law Society and for them forgiveness would come only if they were to see that debt repaid. Don Tait had a polarizing effect on many people. There are those who love him, those who feel badly for him and some who would be happy to never see him again.

Insurance consultant John Comisso had Tait referred to him by the late Canadian politician Shaughnessy Cohen.

"I was nervous because I would be dealing with one of the best criminal lawyers in the country and I was afraid to screw up.

But the man who sat in my office that day was charming and joked a lot. He is a great character and there are so few in the world who are truly great characters."

Comisso and Tait became good friends and it's a friendship Comisso values. Like many who are intimately acquainted with Tait, he has his own stories to add to the legend.

"One day Don was in family court and the judge was surprised to see him so he asks, 'To what do I owe this pleasure to have Don Tait in family court?' and Tait answered, "Your Honour, it's all about the money."

But while Tait may quip in that way about money and made no secret that he liked to earn big bucks and spend them, Comisso, who always refers to Tait as "King," echoes many who knew about his generosity.

"There were so many young lawyers he helped financially and career-wise but he never talked about it. Then there was one time when one of my clients who was very poor needed a lawyer. I asked Don if he would represent her and send me the bill. He did, but I never saw a bill. Don isn't the kind of guy who brags about the things he does for people. If I was fundraising for any charity I was involved with all I had to say was 'Hey King, I'm trying to raise money...' and I wouldn't get my sentence finished before he asked, 'How much?' and that was the end of it.

"Another time I went to see him and the secretary told me to 'go on in.' When I walked in to his office he was sitting there with his eyes closed and rubbing his head. I waited for a few minutes and asked 'King, what's up?' He said, 'I just got back from court and I couldn't prevent my client from going to jail.' It made him feel terrible that he didn't get the guy off. He had a big heart. It wasn't all dollars and cents to him."

There were also many amusing stories.

"Don's big German shepherds had an air-conditioned house in the yard but he would often have them upstairs in his bedroom. One day I asked him why and he said, 'Well John, with the characters I deal with, you never know...' There was another time when several members of the mob were in court in Windsor and he was defending one of them. They paid him a big chunk of money and I asked him "King, what if you lose?' and he said 'Comisso, that is not an option.' Well, he got his client off but his client's friends all went to jail."

Comisso used to hope that Tait would one day return to Windsor. But when he asked Tait when he would be back, if he was coming back, was disappointed to hear Tait's definitive answer "No. Never again."

"You know, so many people didn't really know him. There was just this image that they knew. But if you sat with him one on one and got to really know him he would often let you see the real Don."

One of the young lawyers who says she owes her career to Tait is Helen Conway. As a law student she often watched in awe as Tait conducted cross examinations on witnesses.

"I was there one day when he was defending a client on an impaired driving charge. It was like something out of a movie. He was the Perry Mason of his time. I knew I wanted to be a criminal lawyer because of him."

In September 1991, needing an articling job, Conway met Tait, who was clearly in a hurry, as he was walking into court.

"Excuse me Mr. Tait. I'm Helen Conway. And I'm looking for an articling position."

"What are you doing now?"

"I'm working at ..."

"Send me your resume."

Conway met Tait in his office for an interview a few days later and began telling him how well she had done in law school, mentioning her A-standing.

"I don't give a fuck about your grades," Tait told her. "I want to see if you can stand on your feet."

Tait didn't offer her a position immediately, that came after she had been offered work by another law firm in the city.

"The year working with Don and Andie Brady was the most stressful, amazing year of my life. I won my first trial, a traffic offence, but I felt so incompetent and mentioned it to Don. He said 'You are. You are incompetent. It took me five years to get comfortable in the courtroom.' He was trying to toughen me up and that year working in their office gave me the confidence to start my own law practice. The pressure he put on himself to be the perfect lawyer - and he was – well, how does any human being handle that? He was so smart. I've studied in the U.S. and I've never watched anyone with that kind of gift. He had the brilliance and advocacy skills that, in my opinion, rivalled those of Eddie Greenspan. He was unique. One of a kind."

Tait was still creeping in to conversations in Canada and causing people to speculate on where he was, what he was doing and how soon it would be before he went down in flames again. In Africa, Tait was telling himself he was carving out a new life, but in many ways he was still walking the delusional tightrope – wanting to find a better life, yet feeling the pull to get himself together and go back to "show everyone" he still had the Don Tait mojo working.

SOUTH AFRICA - REHAB

IN SEPTEMBER 2002, a woman named Julia walked into a small church hall in Umkomaas, a short drive from Scottburg. She was looking for a group meeting of Alcoholics Anonymous. Julia, an ex-pat Brit, had been a raging alcoholic in her younger years and was forever recovering from relapses.

That evening she saw four men sitting around a table drinking tea. They greeted her affably and she asked if this was an AA meeting and could they read the AA preamble. Their response somewhat baffled her.

"Umm...well, we just usually sit and chat about cars..."

She thought OK, cars. Welcome to AA South Africa style. Julia was mildly amused by one man who regarded her, smiling and with a curious apologetic amusement. She thought he looked as much out of place as she was feeling. After the meeting, such as it was, she was introduced to the man who gaily told her about the millions he had lost through alcoholism and women and cars (more cars she thought). She found him to be highly articulate, well mannered, smartly turned out carrying a "leather man bag," interesting and a "tad demented." His name was Don Tait, from Canada. And so, their journey of friendship began.

Between September 2002 and March 2003, Julia and her partner Keith purchased "The Cedars" and painstakingly began to rebuild and transform the old sugar baron mansion into a unique rehabilitation centre. She occasionally saw Tait at meetings but with working seven days a week on the house, she never took much time to chat with him. This made her feel somewhat guilty at the time because she thought that as "ex pats" they should probably all stick together but was not entirely sure why she thought that. Once the house was ready they started holding meetings there and one Saturday Tait arrived with an attractive Indian woman. They sat holding hands throughout the meeting which Julia thought was "a bit grim and not good form" as far as she was concerned. The relationship was short-lived and she suspected it was probably because the woman wanted a commitment Tait was not willing to give and, in Julia's opinion, the woman was a "wee bit neurotic."

Julia also reflected at the time that the more she saw of Tait the more she believed he was a "deeply troubled" man. Despite their differences, Tait and Julia and Keith began to develop a mutual respect. Julia says she was beginning to somewhat understand the complexities that drove Tait to the point of self-destruction.

"Don had spent his life organizing and creating the props he desperately needed in order to create some sense of 'self.' Through sheer hard work and undoubted ability he gained the prestige, the notoriety, the money, women and so forth. In Africa, all of this had been stripped away. He was a man without an identity, a man without a face. Don could no longer be defined as a 'prestigious lawyer' as he simply was not. His previous life meant little to the people here with whom he now associated. And he was alone amidst it all. Don was really left with...Don. As we talked it was clear that he lived solely in the past. Full of bitterness and resentment for old 'slights' and perceived betrayals, regrets and 'if onlys' mixed with dollops of guilt and shame. The result was quite a mess and one I was frankly unwilling to even attempt to help with. Yet, within it all I found a man with great humour, intelligence and strength. And, unfortunately for him, the residue of a vast ego."

Still unfocused and unsure of where this new life was taking him, Tait turned his attention to making himself strong. He developed a workout routine that started with an hour on a stationary bike in his house from 4 a.m. to 5 a.m., followed by two hours at the local gym. There he also began making friends, which wasn't difficult, according to Kingsley Ball "Sarge."

"I was manager of Total Gym when he started coming. I could tell he wasn't from South Africa because of his accent. He was with Vincent, the man who looks after his gardens. We started talking and just clicked. He started telling me about the beautiful, glamorous blonde (Johanna) who was going to be coming to join him. I loved talking to him and when I learned about his incredible experiences I thought 'There should be a movie about this man.'"

Sarge, 80, also said he was astounded by Tait's strength, being able to lift ninety-pound flat dumbbells – which not even the much younger men in the gym were able to do at the time. And that was praise indeed from Sarge who had run the 89 km/56 mile Comrade's Marathon twenty-five times and was no slouch himself. The Comrade is the world's largest and oldest ultramarathon.

Tait's gregarious personality attracted notice in the gym and he talked to everyone. He was also generous with his time and never hesitated to give workout tips to anyone who was receptive, and most were. His ego that used to always need attention was still seeking it, though he wasn't totally aware of it at the time. He still lived with the fantasy of going back and proving he still "had it" and one day would be able to "show them all."

One of the people who welcomed Tait's attention was Ravi Govender, a Warrant Officer with the Crime Intelligence Unit of the Scottburg police department. Govender, 38, was born in Umkomaas and descended from a line of ancestors who had emigrated from India more than a hundred years ago. As a very young boy and man he lived through the last years of South African apartheid.

"As a white guy he was different from anyone I had encountered. He sees no colour. He sees only the person. I was

217

surprised to see that he always brings Vincent, his Zulu gardener, to work out with him and he treats him like he would treat any white friend. He is an inspiration and always there to encourage you to do more and better. He's the kind of friend who is always positive and is always supportive. In those early days if we booked to work out for one hour we would talk twenty minutes. If I didn't show up for a few days because I got a bit lazy, when he saw me he would say 'I expected to see you in the obits.' He has a very unique way about him."

While working out and attending AA meetings were his main preoccupations while he plotted his potential return to Canada, Tait's life was about to take yet another dramatic turn. The next step on his journey was to be a catastrophic game changer and the real beginning of a spiritual life.

READY TO DIE – Bring it on

PAIN SWEPT ALONG the left side of his jaw like a pesky hot ant. Ignoring it Tait took a deep breath, stooped, grabbed the 250-pound weight and lifted it off the floor. Breathing out, he replaced it and repeated the exercise a second and third time. The hot ant was insistent. What seemed to be a vicious toothache was now spreading down into his left arm and embracing his chest in a vice grip. The hot ant on his face had become a blistering volcano.

He tried to think what could have led to this pain. The day had started like any other Monday morning. At 4 a.m. he hauled on work-out shorts and headed down the hall to the spare bedroom which houses his stationery bike. He pedalled for an hour, fed the dogs and had a bowl of cereal. He woke the guy who had spent the night in another spare room – a South African who was two months into sobriety and had been doing Step five of his rehab program the previous night. Grabbing his gym bag, he called Vincent and the three of them set out to pump iron. He felt fine. Now this. It suddenly occurred to him what the problem might be. He turned to his house guest who was working out next to him.

"I think I'll go home and phone an ambulance. I think I'm having a heart attack."

Now the pain was so intense he could hardly concentrate. Sarge, sensing something was not right with Tait, came over to ask, "What's happening to you?" Sarge could see that his friend was "going blue in the face" and suggested he get to hospital. Tait, instead, decided to go home and call his doctor. His house guest drove him the twenty kilometres home and once there a very worried Tait called the ER at Kingsway Hospital.

219

He was told to get to ER immediately and to have someone drive him. They get back in his car and drive at breakneck speed to the Kingsway.

During the twenty-minute drive (reduced from the usual forty minutes because of the speed they were doing) there is no relief from the punishing agony ripping his heart apart. To dull his senses and hopefully the pain, Tait lights a cigarette, taking long inhaled draws as it shakes in his trembling fingers. The minutes seem very long.

As the car screeched to a halt at the ER door, doctors and nurses pulled the thin, now feeble Tait from the passenger seat and loaded him on a gurney. As he sucked back a final, long drag they took his half-smoked cigarette and ground it into the concrete. In ER doctors gave him an anti-coagulant to prevent blood clotting and did an external assessment. They soon realized he urgently required an angioplasty for them to get an inside look at his cardiac arteries. For that, they told him, the best place was St. Augustine Hospital in Durban where they specialized in cardiac care. At 1 p.m. he is in the angioplasty unit and can feel EKG leads being stuck to various parts of his chest with a cold jelly. A thin catheter was inserted into his groin and an attempt made to access his arteries.

Through a pain haze he is able to hear disjointed bits of conversation. He hears "My God, they're totally plugged. All five of them." Tait recalls that in those moments it was as though life started to move in slow motion. He no longer thought about what was happening to his body on the table. What did become very real was the realization he was probably dying.

"Lying there, and knowing I was dying, I felt absolutely fucking powerless. And I was angry."

Those were thoughts swirling in his head as he was taken to the intensive care unit. There, the cardiac surgeon explained he needed immediate surgery but it could not be done until the following day because of the earlier injection of the blood thinning medication. It would be too risky due to the possibility of him bleeding to death on the operating table. The surgeon kindly but bluntly explained to Tait that his chances of survival, because of the severity of the blockages and the beating his body had taken because of his alcoholism, are in a very low percentage. He recommended that Tait speak with a psychologist who counsels people who are dealing with a life and death diagnosis. He left, allowing Tait time to absorb everything he has said.

In his room alone, Tait thinks about having developed a rudimentary idea of the existence of God and is momentarily filled with irrational fury and anger that God does not care about him. He must not, he rationalizes, because why else would he have kept him alive for more than two years after Costa Rica, "through those two gruesome years," giving him hope only to fell him with this catastrophic heart attack.

But, as he is lying there, his tanned body a contrast to the white sheets, feeling punished and resentful and consumed by negativity and anger and condemnations, an unusual peace sweeps over him and begins to dispel the blackness eating at him. He is suddenly filled with a total and absolute surrender. He stops struggling and fighting. Whatever is going to happen will happen and he realizes it doesn't matter to him if he lives or dies.

He grieves for what he has left undone and unsaid. In many ways he has been fooling himself. He realizes his surrender was half-assed, on his terms, and in this moment of clarity the fog lifts. The previous two years flash quickly past. He sees himself for what he truly is – a broken man who has not let go of the past; an angry, bitter man whose ego thinks he can "show them all."

Now, he is dying, alone, in a foreign land. He has so much left undone and it all seems so unfair. He had convinced himself that the only reason he had survived up until now was because God had "big plans" for him, big plans that had not yet materialized. He silently cries "What kind of fucking God are you?"

From somewhere comes a voice admonishing him "Who do you think you are? What kind of man are you? You're not so special. Why shouldn't you die? Why shouldn't you die? Why shouldn't you die?" Why shouldn't he indeed die? It had finally sunk in that he truly is not special, that there is no reason in the world why he should not have suffered, why he should not die. He has been pretending to believe this and mouthing the words, but he now knows he's been lying to himself. It is the most humbling moment of his life. He closed his eyes and surrendered.

"God forgive me. I am not special. Whatever I am about to experience God, bring it on." As the thought enters his mind, the muscles in his entire body begin to relax and he feels a sense of well-being seep into him. He knows, then, he has finally come to that spiritual awakening he'd only previously glimpsed for a brief moment in Costa Rica during one of his suicide attempts. In that moment it does not matter whether he lives or dies. It is totally out of his hands. There is no choice left to him. He believes he is in good hands.

"It was the start of my surrender to something more powerful than me. I was powerless. I knew I was in God's hands. They felt like very good hands and knowing death was closing in on me was not bad news."

He is filled with a peace he has never imagined and only later would wonder if it truly was spiritual, morphine-induced, or both. His pain lessens and he lets go, surrendering to the peace. It is so profound a surrender its physical effects are noticed by attending doctors and nurses.

"They told me they had never seen a patient so close to dying who looked so content. It was baffling to them but I had reached an extraordinary place. I didn't care about anything. Nothing else mattered but this moment. No fear. No worry. No more pain. There was just this feeling of my commitment to

God and asking Him to 'Bring it on' even if it is the last day of my life."

A cardiac surgeon entered his room to explain and describe in detail the sawing open of his breastbone, stopping the heart and doing major repairs on all of his arteries. Tait smiles and quips to the confused surgeon "At least people in Windsor will know I really do have a heart."

"You're in good spirits."

"I'm ready for anything. Bring it on." Tait is smiling and relaxed.

"You could die. You understand the risks?"

"Absolutely. Bring it on."

Even though it appears his patient does not need the advice, he told Tait there are professionals in the hospital who are available should he want "to talk."

"Thanks doc."

The following morning at 8 a.m. he is wheeled into the operating room where the anaesthetist is waiting for him. The doctor is taken aback by the blissed-out patient who says he is content whichever way this goes. He could live or die. Either is perfectly acceptable. As the anaesthetic needle enters his vein and the warm liquid begins coursing through his blood system, it all begins to fade to black. His last thought is for the extraordinary road that led him to this moment, where the life inside his chest is stilled and whatever God is, he had experienced it.

That extraordinary feeling lasted for more than twenty-four hours after surgery but he remembered it and knew he had glimpsed the feeling of absolute freedom.

"I didn't believe in God and if I had not experienced AA I would not have understood what was happening to me. When I heard those words 'My God, they're all totally blocked' I truly believed it was all over and it just didn't matter."

CEDARS – A new beginning

ABOUT A MONTH AFTER her visit to Tait's home, Julia received a telephone call from a man in AA who had been staying with Tait for a few days. He told her about Tait's heart attack and subsequent multiple artery bypass surgery and explained he was in critical condition.

"I felt quite overwhelmed. It was not as if Keith and I were particularly close to him at that time but the idea of a man lying in hospital with no family, no one who loved him, thousands of miles from anything familiar, was quite dreadful. So, whether he liked it or not, I decided we needed to be a temporary surrogate family."

Julia loathed hospitals. She was always irrationally afraid people would take the moment she was there at their bedside to die. Despite that she took a bunch of flowers and cards from AA well-wishers and went to see Tait.

"He was frail, shaky and physically tangibly diminished by the trauma he had just experienced. Yet, there was something different, a gentleness in his eyes, a sense of peace. The cynic in me reflected upon the amazing temporary spiritual power of morphine, although I honestly could see this was different."

After the usual pleasantries of how are you etc. Julia touched his arm.

"It's going to be alright you know."

"You think so?"

"Yes. I think so."

In that moment, Julia said they forged a significant trust.

"We became friends. We understood each other."

No matter how much she begged and tried to persuade him, Tait refused to allow Julia to contact Johanna or his daughters. He wanted to make sure he was going to live before telling anyone. She worried about how unpleasant it would be if he died and she had not allowed them "one last conversation" while he was in hospital. He eventually agreed to call. Because of his previous behaviour, and with good reason, he thought Johanna would be sceptical about his heart attack story. To convince her he photographed his surgical scar replete with stitches and sent it to her as evidence. Johanna saw this as Tait's insecurity, not her own, but she agreed to visit.

Tait was released from hospital on Sunday, five days following his open-heart surgery. He had made a remarkable recovery. His doctor sent him home with admonitions to "take things slowly" for several months to allow his body to heal. Tait hears and agrees. But he is now on a mission. He has been given yet another chance at life and he doesn't intend to waste this one.

Anxious to get his body strong again, and whether the doctors think it's a good idea or not, he headed to the gym Monday morning. He couldn't drive the car so he figured out a plan that would have him sitting in the driver's seat operating the clutch and gas and changing gears, while Vincent, his Zulu friend who does not have a driver's licence, sat in the passenger seat, took the wheel and steered.

The regulars, knowing Tait had undergone cardiac surgery a week earlier, had their chins drop when he walked in to the gym. They were surprised and relieved and Tait was certainly the last person Sarge expected to see that morning.

"He looked OK. I couldn't believe it. We all greeted him and when he got on the bike, we told him to take it easy. But when I looked, about forty-five minutes later, he was still on the bike. He also began doing weights but he started slowly and it took about a month, then he was back just like before. This is a very remarkable man and we are so lucky to have him here in South Africa."

Govender also couldn't believe his eyes when he saw Tait stroll into the gym so soon after his heart attack. He was astounded because his father had suffered a heart attack and it took him many years to get back on his feet. Govender says his father "fell into the sea," and in fact, never fully recovered his pre-attack stamina. "It was like Don never had a heart attack. He is so strong mentally and physically. He is extremely focused and was right back helping us train, supporting and encouraging us."

However, although he was back training in a usual fashion, his gym buddies noticed a change in his overall demeanour. Tait was no longer coming in exhibiting his usual gregarious personality. He was more reserved and quiet. Sarge saw the change immediately.

"It was very noticeable. He was more self-contained and quiet. He was definitely a changed person and seemed to draw more inward. He didn't seem to want to attract attention to himself the way he used to, and it was clear to me that something had happened to him during the time he was in hospital, something more than just the heart attack."

Sarge was delighted to have Tait back in the gym and pleased to see how excited he was that Johanna was coming to visit. Sarge said Tait and Johanna remind him of the Hollywood couple Humphrey Bogart and Lauren Bacall, describing them as "a good pair together." He considers them both friends and is constantly worried about Tait's health. To help regain his strength Tait had Vincent walk up and down their steep driveway with him every morning. The incline of the driveway is a challenge at the best of times but Tait was undeterred and saw it as a means to hastening his return to normal.

Shortly after his discharge from hospital, in May 2003, Tait agreed to volunteer at Cedars, the rehab centre started by Julia and Keith. He began a daily study group based on the

Basic Text of Alcoholics Anonymous, which he truly believes is the only way addicts can conquer and learn to live with their life-long affliction. Julia devised a detailed program for him to teach the Big Book Studies which she estimates Tait followed for all of two weeks, ultimately putting his own stamp on its delivery. His is a no nonsense, no BS type of counsellor.

"I've done everything they've done and more and I tell them you can't bullshit a bullshitter

Don't even think about lying because I'll see through it and don't waste your time in the program because you'll get nothing from it if you are not willing to just surrender and come clean."

In the weeks and months that followed his surgery, Tait, Julia and Keith formed an "unshakeable" bond forged by their collective "recovery." Julia said she knew Tait was lonely and lived a solitary existence, kept company by his Alsatian "Tager," his father's nickname. The puppy was beautiful, says Julia, but basically an uncontrollable nightmare. While Tait insisted he was "just a puppy," the puppy eventually had to attend Puppy Boot Camp to be trained – with not much success. Somehow, the unmanageable puppy grew into a fine adult dog.

Johanna arrived for a brief visit to determine if she could see herself making the huge geographical change to South Africa and, once again, throwing her lot in with Tait. She would be taking a monumental risk. After several weeks she returned to Canada in a "terrible dilemma." She sold her house, ready to leave for Africa, then changed her mind and bought another one. Tait said he wasn't aware of her change of heart and assumed she was still coming to live with him. Julia corresponded frequently, encouraging Johanna to take a leap of faith and return permanently.

After more soul searching, Johanna returned to Africa but their road to relationship renewal was indeed not to be smooth sailing. Their old grievances were simmering below

228

the surface and getting in the way of an open and honest friendship. They set up home together, along with their four dogs. She was surprised to find O'Reilly living in the house with Tait and fear ran down her spine. But, to her delight, she discovered an older, more mellow O'Reilly with whom she developed a respectful relationship. They went to church together on Sundays and despite his devotion to Tait, O'Reilly told her "If Don gives you any trouble I'll straighten him around."

Only weeks after Johanna arrived this new, sensitive O'Reilly, told her "I think I should move across the road, into a place of my own." He didn't say that he recognized the fact they should be alone, but Johanna and Tait knew he understood the importance of them living by themselves. One day, not many months after she arrived, she was having coffee with O'Reilly when he told her he thought he should be going home. "I really need to go back," he told her, and it was clear he felt there was some urgency in his returning to Windsor.

On the night before he was to fly home O'Reilly confided that he was "nervous" and had a "funny feeling the plane was going to crash and he was going to die." He said he was "really scared." His words were to be prophetic. Only hours after flying into Detroit, arriving in Windsor and speaking to his daughter, with whom he had very little contact over most of her life, he died of a sudden heart attack. Tait was grief stricken.

The next few years for Tait and Johanna would be a challenge but their fates seemed to dictate that despite all the ups and down of their relationship, they ultimately stay together. In South Africa, it is patently evident Tait had truly found a home - physically and spiritually. It gives him solace when he needs it and it is where he also spends countless hours counselling dozens of Cedars alumni as their sponsor. His sponsorship roster is longer than most people would carry but Tait finds it impossible to turn anyone down. The brown leather couch in Tait's TV room had become an iconic roosting spot for men

229

and women at various stages on their journey to sobriety and spirituality.

Tait's own journey is nurtured by his constant reading of books on spirituality, addictions and redemption, his growing understanding of himself and a belief in what life should really be about. He spends many hours dissecting his life to find out why he became the person who was Don Tait, the lawyer. The growing awareness of self is often painful as he slowly faces up to who he was and what he has done to the lives of others. It takes considerable soul searching to be able to not only admit negative aspects of his life, but to also then allow himself to accept that he wasn't all bad, that not all of his life was ego driven, that the kind things he did for people came from a good place in his heart.

But, make no mistake about it, this isn't an easy road for Tait to be travelling. He works hard at trying to figure it all out and often wonders why he is still alive, why he has been spared the grave so many times. The only conclusion that makes sense to him is his belief that he was supposed to experience life the way he did, to experience its catastrophic depths and to end up in a rehab in a sugarcane field in Dududu, South Africa, to use that experience to help others find their own roads to redemption.

"I don't see things the same way. I wish I had done things differently in my life but I didn't and I don't regret the past. I can't. I have asked forgiveness from all those I hurt and some forgive me, some never will, some might one day. But that is not for me to judge and I respect however they decide to react to me now. One thing I know for sure is that I have absolutely no doubt that it is the choices you make that create your own reality. We are all a mass of potential but it all depends on our choices and decisions. We can all say that our experience of life was perfect, based on the choices we make. Life is letting go of attaching yourself to something and asking yourself 'what is the purpose of this?' For me to exist I had to find a union with God. The solution is in me and surrendering is a journey of the soul. You surrender yourself to the experience. I look at life as a journey of experiences. Being able to accept that, I believe, truly makes life more enjoyable.

The message is not a dramatic, huge thing. It's a process of experiences. We are all here for the experience. All of our experiences are what we need to get to the stage where we realize and understand that life is not the problem. We are the problem. Life is not my problem. I am my problem and how I deal with every experience in that life.

I was constantly looking for what made me happy and I never found it. When I used (drugs and alcohol) I felt okay, there was magic in me. There was nothing real about it and I continued the struggle when I wasn't using. But sobriety is when you face reality and look in the mirror at who you really are every day. Then, you don't struggle. You surrender and you live by the Steps. It doesn't mean you can stop working on yourself because that's an everyday job for the rest of your life. The payoff it that it doesn't just feel good, it feels better. You have to deal with life on life's terms. There are no mistakes in life. Life doesn't need to change, I need to change and having had a spiritual awakening, I know I am changing."

While many people had suggested to Tait that his life would "make great reading," he was never interested in exposing his life to more people than those who already knew all its sordid details. However, one afternoon when he was watching the Oprah Winfrey TV show he heard an interview by a fellow who had written a book about being in rehab. Tait grew more furious by the minute as he listened to what he believed to be "absolute bullshit that could actually hurt people trying to recover from addictions." He thought long and hard about what he had heard and decided that perhaps it was time, that maybe he could help people by letting them hear his story of survival. Several months later he looked up a phone number and picked up the phone.

Half a world away I ran upstairs to answer the incessant ring of my phone.

231

"Hello."

"Hi. It's Tait."

"Tait?" "Tait who?"

"How many do you know?"

"Don!"

"When you were leaving Costa Rica you said if I ever wanted to have a biography written you'd be interested. Are you?"

"I guess. Sure. Why now?"

Tait explained how angry he had been by the "lies" he heard from the author on the Winfrey show.

"Lots of people will listen to that jack ass and really believe he was telling the truth. It's all a bunch of lies and will do more harm than any good. I can't believe he is passing this off as the truth, but there was Oprah buying it hook, line and sinker. People need to know the real truth about addictions and what it takes to live in recovery. I'd like you to write that story. I don't need any more notoriety. But I believe if people understand how I was able to create a better life in recovery it will give them hope. What it won't do is fill their heads with a bunch of lies and bullshit."

Tait talked at length about what he had been doing in Africa and the changes in his life. His growing spirituality and success with clients in the rehab at Cedars had given him confidence that his philosophy on addiction recovery and the methods to get there actually work. He was seeing it in the men and women working their way to better lives because of their treatment at Cedars. At the end of a multi hour conversation it was decided. Work was to start on the book the following Sunday and conversations would follow every Sunday after that until the Tait tale was concluded. However, there was an admonishment.

"But, I want you to make sure that you tell the truth. Don't whitewash any of the things I did in my life. People need to know the good and the bad. They need to know that if I can find a better life there is hope for them. I want to stress that they can find a better life that does not have to be the grandiose promise of becoming the CEO of a company or the next billionaire. That kind of fiction happens to one in a million addicts and when people don't achieve that they feel like failures. That kind of future might be in the cards for the very few, but what I and the team at Cedars offer is a way to conquer the addictions in order to live better lives, which can then bring success. This is what I am devoting my life to because I know it works. I have seen it work. The best evidence is me."

Tait's reaction to the Winfrey interview proved to be insightful. Not many months later the author of A Million Little Pieces confessed that what he had written was less than the truth. In fact, it was total fabrication.

SOUTH AFRICA

March 2009

AS THE SOUTH AFRICAN AIRLINES jet was on its final approach to Durban International airport I wondered aloud to my husband "I wonder what this Tait is going to be like?"

We had been talking on the phone for several years and I had pages of notes from those conversations that I would be using in the writing of this book. However, we both agreed that without coming to see what his life was like and to witness the work he was doing at Cedars it would be impossible to fully understand it.

So, here I was – about to see Tait for the first time since my visit to him in the Windsor jail. I was anxious to see if Tait and Cedars would be what I was expecting based on our conversations or if everything he had been telling me over the years was nothing more than Tait aggrandizing himself and inflating the benefits of what he was doing at the rehab.

After collecting our baggage and walking out into the waiting area I was as surprised by Tait's appearance as I was when I saw him walking towards me all those years ago in Costa Rica; albeit for a very different reason. This Tait was tanned, healthy and fit, the antithesis of the Costa Rican Tait and certainly much healthier looking than the convict. He and Johanna were welcoming and Tait was an engaging raconteur during the drive through Durban and to a dinner at a restaurant in the city's casino before heading to their home in Scottburg.

We spent several days close to home recovering from jet lag and doing a great deal of talking. It was clear to me that Tait was indeed a more spiritual person than I had observed him to be in his previous life. The Tait of old would hardly have acknowledged the possibility that there was more to life than the accumulation of wealth and power, let alone have it seep into his conversation as a matter of course, without guile or artifice.

I soon realized that the man at the other end of the phone for the past several years wasn't bullshitting. He believed in the spirituality he'd found and he was walking the talk. I was looking forward to seeing how the people he was counselling at Cedars responded to him. I was going to Dududu at the end of the week to sit in on his group meetings.

"We admitted we were powerless over alcohol--that our lives had become unmanageable." - AA Step One

AS THE BLISTERING AFRICAN sun raises the temperature in the main meeting room at The Cedars rehab centre, about a dozen men and women take a seat on hard chairs in a semicircle around the man they call their "guru." It's a moniker Tait finds uncomfortable and unwarranted.

The former grand sitting room is now a large, square, bare, empty space relieved by the tall, wide windows that allow in light. They are a motley group of men and women who represent a wide swath of the social spectrum. Having hit the wall of no return, these desperate addicts have washed up at The Cedars hoping to find help to beat their addictions and stay alive. They walk into the room with varying degrees of enthusiasm.

A man accused of murder but who has not yet gone to trial sits down next to a rich businessman whose alcohol-fuelled lifestyle has lost him his business and his family. Next to him is a twenty-something lesbian from Durban's slums. Alcohol, drugs and prostitution helped her deal with a myriad of problems related to her sexual orientation. Fearing her frail body wouldn't take much more abuse, she allowed a social worker to drive her to Cedars. She is in a conversation with a middle-aged physician whose drug and alcohol addictions over many years have seen him booted from the profession. She hopes to get off the streets and he hopes Cedars will be his redemption and that he will one day be able to return to some form of delivering medical care.

Chatting with the young son of a rich businessman is the forty-five-year-old wife of a millionaire landowner.

The rest of the group includes a medical specialist, several unskilled, unemployed men and women in their twenties and thirties and a group of middle class professionals. In the normal course of life most of them would probably not have much to say to each other. Cedars, however, is a great leveller and they all have one unifier - they are all down and out addicts who have lost control over their lives.

The Cedars, once a symbol of the splendour of rich sugar barons, is now a utilitarian rehab of last resort in a cane field in Dududu, South Africa, where the chances of addicts learning survival skills are better than most. There's no putting on airs here, no elitism. This is just a group of good people from across life's social strata with bad habits that have derailed careers, ruined relationships and put futures in jeopardy. They joke with each other and Tait with a familiarity only those who spend extended periods in a living hell can know and understand.

The bone doc – a middle aged man who does not have the confident air of a surgical specialist – leans forward in his chair. His drug proclivities once led to his kidnapping by a bunch of Nigerian drug lords running a drug trade. He was rescued in a commando-style raid by Keystone Cop-counselors from Cedars and is now desperate to kick his habit, get back to sobriety and doctoring.   He is welcomed back to the group by his addict comrades; their warmth an apparent balm to his desperation.

As is part of the treatment pattern at sobriety meetings, members share their personal stories in an effort to unburden their anguish and gain some measure of solace. Some in the group that morning tell chilling stories about their descent into personal hells brought about by drug and alcohol addictions; others give an update on the progress they've made since the last meeting while several have to admit they've fallen prey yet again to the addiction siren. They deliver progress stories with hope and optimism. Regression stories are filled with sadness, but oddly enough, not despair. The varied but familiar tales are filled with sordid and squalid descriptions of volcanic descents into the soul-destroying hell of addiction and the long slow road they are all travelling – they hope – to redemption of body and soul.

Each life recanted creates a surreal expectation not always matched by the teller. The clean-cut businessman in well-pressed dress pants, shirt and tie is getting sober before presenting himself before a court on a murder charge. He is accused of a vicious, frenzied stabbing of which he has no recollection.

A twenty-something woman with dark hair tightly pulled back from her face is clearly anxious to share her progress. Her thin, shaking fingers are tightly laced in her lap. She lifts her head. Her very large brown eyes fill with tears as she describes her ascent from an alcohol and drug-filled life of prostituting herself for a fix, alienation from her family and abject hopelessness to almost a year of sobriety. Her lower lip trembles. An unbidden tear travels along her overlarge nose and is caught with the lizard-like flick of her tongue. It is apparent she finds it almost too painful to speak the most positive words she has been able to utter in almost a decade.

"My parents are becoming almost proud of me, now. I'm doing great. I couldn't have done it without you. You really understand," she says to the leader sitting in front of them.

All eyes refocus.

Don Tait nods. His broad, darkly tanned smile accentuates the deep creases in his face that tell their own tales. His lean body looks comfortable, clad in a black T-shirt and shorts and running shoes. His closely cropped grey hair gives him a no-nonsense air. He is their addiction counsellor and these are some of the sweetest moments of his day - sitting in this room, using his experience and listening skills to help them drag themselves back from the abyss.

They listen to him because he is one of them. They know his story. They know how his addictions caused him to blow his lucrative, respected position as a leading criminal lawyer and lose everything he owned – even doing jail time - before his escape to Africa and finding his personal road to redemption. He has been beaten down a number of times, but little does he know that for him there is still horror yet to come. Today, he is giving fellow addicts some of the wisdom he has gleaned from his endless fight with life.

They wait. He looks around at them.

"Do you know how fortunate you are to be an alcoholic?"

They stare back. Not sure where this is going. Nothing about being an alcoholic or drug addict feels "fortunate."

Tait continues.

"The addict is looking for happiness. We've been on a quest looking for the truth, but never realized it. People say the addict is a coward but we were constantly fighting - against the odds. Some of you will continue the battle until you get the experience you need to have. Suffering comes before sobriety. The greatest shock is knowing I know nothing. Step one, if done right, is absolutely devastating and makes everything very, very clear...I have a progressive, fatal disease and no human power can relieve me of it. I am hopeless. Denial is your enemy. You tell yourself I know I can stop. If I don't pick up a drink my family and my life will be saved and we'll live happily ever after. That's the lie. That's the problem. We can't stop. The disease is not being able to stop. Addicts are told 'Self knowledge is the key.' The idea that self knowledge is the solution is a big fat lie and it has to be smashed. If you say, 'I am at a stage in my life where I know I am hopeless' it can be the greatest catalyst but you have to go there first. You have to plead 'Tell me what to do, please. Anything.' Well, guess what happens. You will get well. And what prevents us from getting well? We believe the lie! We deny what this disease is.

The nature of this disease is denial and we believe the lie that's killing us. There is no room for self and God. The ego edges God out. The key to freedom is to recognize we are absolutely powerless. Admitting that opens the door from hopeless to joyousness and freedom. The road to that freedom comes with you saying to yourself 'I am alcoholic and I can't stop killing myself. I need a power greater than me and even if I don't believe it, I am prepared to do whatever it takes because I must find some reason for living from a power greater than I am or I will die.' Scott Peck was convinced that God created alcoholics so they could create AA as a solution for all of us. There is fear in admitting you are powerless, admitting you have to depend on something you can't see. Each day when you get out of bed get on your knees and pray."

The group sits transfixed. Riveted. Absorbing Tait's every word.

"We have been given an overwhelming thirst for the truth and we find it in that moment when we are up to our necks in pig shit. We cry out 'Help me!' The light comes in and we open our lives to love. In that moment we are loveable. We cease pushing love away and the Father is there with open arms welcoming us home. Grace is a gift. That moment you welcome it. When your arms are full how can you receive anything. This is a program for every single human being. We, as alcoholics, are at the front line. Many are called but few answer. For those who reach out and receive it, who become loveable...we become loving. The most selfish group of people around become more giving. Cease fighting, ask and do as you are told. When this happens the first thing you'll want to do is to give it to someone else. When I came out of jail after one year of sobriety the Law Society hearings were coming up and I was staying with a friend who was giving me food and cigarettes. I was angry. I wanted it all back, everything I had lost. I was 57 years old and it was all gone. I stood on his porch one day and I screamed 'I'll be back you fucking bastards. I'll be back.' The echo that came back told me "You won't be back." It was devastating. I knew it was all over. The truth is devastating. I wouldn't change one thing about my past because all my experiences gave me ... this. I know now there is a God. God is life...everything that is good about life."

Tait stands. They all stand, form a circle and clasp hands, reciting the Serenity Prayer.

JOHANNA – Taking another chance on Tait

ALTHOUGH THEY'VE NOT BEEN easy, the years since her first split from Tait have also been kind to Johanna, particularly in the looks department. Heading out to the gym in Scottburg with her blonde hair pulled up in a ponytail, wearing shorts, a t-shirt and running shoes, she looks decades younger than her age.

While she had every right to despise him, the love she had always felt for Tait continued to be more powerful. And, despite the risks a second time around, when he asked her to come to Africa to live, she decided to "see what happens." She wanted it to work out this time. Wanted to understand him and have him understand her. She wanted something better but it was not going to be an easy journey...yet again. It was certainly not going to be an easy decision to give the relationship another try. Her friends were worried but hoped this time would be different.

"I came here hesitantly because he was trying to get me to come but I found out that before he left he was seeing Sandra and it seemed nothing had changed. It took me about a year to make the decision to visit him. I was expecting a call from him the week before he had his heart attack in March but didn't hear from him. He called the following week and sounded terrible. I asked him what was wrong and he told me he had a heart attack. He sent me a photo to show me his surgery scar in case I didn't believe him. That was his insecurity, not mine."

Johanna was working and had a life in Windsor and even after a week visiting Tait in Africa she still wasn't sure she wanted to disrupt the life she had made for herself and start again with him. It caused sleepless nights and days of angst but after many long-distance conversations, she decided to make the move in December 2003. When she first arrived Tait was working three mornings a week and they had time to spend together to work on their fragile relationship. As Cedars became busier he began working five days a week, leaving the house at 7 a.m. and returning late into the evening. That left them only weekends for any meaningful togetherness. However, even that time was filled with constant interruptions with people calling him and coming to their home for counselling.

"I was always supportive of Don's work and I supported his work at Cedars and his work with the people there. But here we were, trying to get this relationship together and it was almost impossible to find any time to be together."

Tait's daughters came to visit and during one stay, Melanie spent time in Cedars, where she met a young man who fathered her son. Tait's granddaughter also visited and Johanna was always happy to see the young women. In the summer of 2010, however, Johanna overheard a conversation that led her to suspect that Tait was seeing a client for whom he was a sponsor, for reasons other than counselling. The woman and her ex-husband spent many hours at Tait and Johanna's home talking with Tait. The woman also often came alone. The relationship that needed a lot of attention began to go sour and Johanna had a foreboding that was all too familiar.

"I sometimes felt ganged up on but even people at Cedars were telling me I was not wrong to be suspicious about Don seeing another woman. Eventually, I was proved right. And there was this person coming in to my home having an affair with Don. I knew it was going on even though he denied it. My anger and frustration had nothing to do with Cedars. I absolutely never resented Cedars or the people Don was helping but I could see a pattern happening all over again. I thought no, I don't want this. No more. Not again. It was the same nightmare."

It was not an unfamiliar feeling and even though the people coming to their home were decent, respectable people, it harkened back to the days when bikers and their ilk came to their Windsor homes at all hours of the day and night and life had an air of insanity. In December, just before Christmas, after six years together in Africa, Tait asked Johanna to leave the house.

"We had been arguing and at some point, Johanna said to me 'You know Don you're nothing but a nuisance.' And to me, here it was again, that huge feeling of rejection." To Johanna, it was Tait's rejection of her. With a ghastly sense of déjà vu she prepared to get out, to escape. She found herself an apartment, a car, became a qualified trainer and worked at gyms in Scottburg and Durban. She was determined to move on and build a life on her own, yet again. Tait admitted to her that he was having an affair.

"I wanted to get all those things I kept losing on account of him. Every time I let my guard down I got shot down and I was fed up with it. I wanted us to work this time but I took a chance and it blew up in my face."

Their friends on both sides of the ocean were disappointed the two had split and quietly hoped they would eventually get back together. However, while they may have wanted the relationship to work out, Tait's behaviour, the unresolved issues between them and anger simmering beneath the surface, seemed to make it highly unlikely. However, yet another health catastrophe in Tait's life and a lot of talking and healing old wounds, would slowly, eventually bring them together again. For Johanna, one big issue in the relationship was trust. She was fed up never being able to trust him and wondered if she ever would.

"He used to tell me he was the best friend I would ever have, but I knew he was not my friend. He wouldn't treat a friend like that. He always broke any trust between us and even when I came here I don't think I really trusted him. In my heart I wanted to, but he made it really difficult."

Despite their estrangement they kept in touch. To those watching it seemed as though an invisible force conspired to bring them together. Within a year, in November 2011, she moved back in and their lives were soon to change course, an apparent ill wind of change that was to have unexpected consequences.

In late 2011 Tait had been complaining about having a sinus problem, a sensation of "something stuck in my nose" and a sore throat. It became an aggravation, so he went to the doctor hoping to get some relief from the incessant "tickle." The doctor thought it was an infection and prescribed an antibiotic. The problem persisted so the doctor sent him to an ear, nose and throat specialist. During that medical visit in mid-January, 2012, Tait received a lot more information than he bargained for. The specialist, after scoping Tait's throat, said he was concerned about a "growth" which could be benign but he wanted to do a biopsy. The results revealed a malignant cancer.

"Is it serious?" Tait asked. The answer was devastating.

"Very, very serious."

Tait's growth was a lethal form of cancer at the base of his tongue and throat. He would need extensive, invasive surgery, followed by radiation. In typical Tait fashion he acknowledged the diagnosis and said, "Let's get on with it and get it over." An appointment was made for him to see one of the country's leading ear, nose and throat cancer specialists. He confirmed the diagnosis and as soon as Tait got home he immediately consulted Dr. Google. The ENT specialist was quite correct. He had the misfortune to have developed one of the most aggressive, lethal types of cancer to attack a human. What saddened him more than anything was learning that he had brought it on himself because this type of cancer is most common in people who are chronic alcoholics and heavy smokers. It's also most common in men, something he couldn't control.

Yet, despite the high recurrence rates, poor survival and significant alteration in speech and swallowing with this type of cancer, patients are potentially curable. There is always hope. Surgery was scheduled for February 15. As he did when he thought he would die following his heart attack, he turned to what always gives him hope.

"I am in your hands God. I know I am in good hands. Whatever happens it is what I am supposed to experience." He reminds himself that God is not cruel or vindictive. "Who says a person is not supposed to go through hardships?"

Throughout this process his constant companion is Johanna. She becomes his rock and his solace. One side effect of the surgery could be the loss of his voice. It's an irony that's not lost on Tait. It was the loss of his voice so many years before that led to his ultimate downfall. While it may have been tempting to see it as a deadly organ, a body part out to cause him more torture, he saw it differently. This time, he says, it was very different.

"There are similarities but the reason I wanted my voice back then was for the glory of being Don Tait, big shot lawyer. Now it is for a different purpose. There is no ego driving me. I just really enjoy trying to spread the message about recovery and the very real solutions we have to help addicts lead contributing, meaningful lives. No bullshit. No empty promises of gaining fame and fortune and becoming big shots. Just the truth about what works and how to get there. That would be the biggest loss if I lose my voice."

The last time Tait lost his voice he turned to alcohol. This time he turned to his relationship with God. "If my voice goes, then it's in the plan. It's what my experience is supposed to be."

At 6 a.m. on Wednesday, February 15, he is prepped for what was expected to be an eight-hour surgery. During the procedure the surgeon skillfully removed a chunk of flesh at the base of the tongue and lymph nodes on the side of Tait's throat. He was taken to intensive care and maintained in an unconscious state for four days. He would remember it later as one of the worse surgeries of his life. When he woke on day four he couldn't speak and had a feeding tube in his abdomen. The surgeon told him he was pleased with the result but the bad news was that the cancer is stage four. There is no stage five.

"If this is going to incapacitate me, I don't want treatment. I am not a person who will go to any means to cling to life unless I have the ability to be useful," he tells the doctor.

"Things look good and I think there's a good chance you will do well," he was reassured.

Tait agreed to follow up the surgery with radiation. From the time of the surgery to the beginning of the radiation sessions at the beginning of May he made a great recovery. The oncologist marked out a plan of treatment - thirty sessions at five sessions per week. He was to wear a mesh-like head, face and neck-type mask through which the radiation would be directed.

In the early days of the treatment things were going well, but soon worsened. The pain in his throat and mouth became intense. Eating was impossible and he continued using the feeding tube. He lost thirty pounds off his already thin frame. Talking became too painful. It was sometimes difficult to believe or to hope. He reminded himself there would be an end date to the treatments but for now, it was one painful week after another.

Thirty treatments later it was difficult to remember a time without pain, a time when his mouth and throat did not feel full of broken glass. He wanted to feel better before the arrival of Canadian guests in three weeks. He isn't confident.

SOUTH AFRICA – So much pain

June 20, 2012

IT'S BEEN ALMOST THREE years since my first trip to visit Tait. Because of the cancer, his life had taken a dramatic turn. Because the type of cancer he has is so often fatal it was important to make another trip to get a first-hand observation of what was happening to him.

I seem destined to be taken aback by my first sightings of visits with Tait. This time I am shocked by how pale and diminished he appears. He can barely talk and does not come to the arrival area with Johanna to greet my husband and me. She explained he was feeling too nauseous and was sitting in the waiting area. She looked worried. On the drive home he was as friendly and welcoming as his pain allowed. We tell him not to try to talk, that we can catch up when he feels better. There is a general air of concern among all of us and no one says very much.

It's almost 9 p.m. when we arrive in Scottburg and after a very brief conversation everyone took to their beds. What, I wonder, will he be like in the morning. I am not hopeful he will be much better than what we've seen so far. And, in fact, that turns out to be the case. His condition is even worse than the night before.

In the den, Tait sits in a comfortable chair with a backdrop of tropical greenery and the Indian Ocean. He grimaces and leans forward, his hands cradling his head. The nausea and acid reflux has returned, and it is relentless. It defeats even the stoic Tait who never lets any expression of pain pass his lips. But this is different. He can't will this pain away like he has so many times before. This is a pain associated with the toxic bombardment of radiation. It has given him a raw mouth. On

248

this day it's the blister along his gum line causing the grief. That, and the dreaded nausea.

We all snack on nuts and Fritos. Tait half-heartedly laments he cannot join us. The rawness in his mouth and throat has prevented him from having a meal for several weeks. He has a feeding tube in his abdomen – his only source of food. He occasionally attempts to eat scrambled egg but it hurts too much. Every drink of water and every bite feels like glass and fire ants crawling down his throat. A sun worshipper, he would prefer to sit outside in the warmth but there has been a steady rain all day preventing him from leaving the house. He retires by 7 p.m.

Thursday, June 22

Tait has had a trying day. There is no change in his condition. His pain is palpable and Johanna feels helpless. His state of ill health is evident when he uncharacteristically opts to lie down for a short period in the afternoon and then retreats to the bedroom to sleep. In the early evening he returns to the den hoping to be able to chat with us and watch one of his favourite television shows. But he says little. He is in pain and constantly rests his head in his hand, his lined face ruddy and contorted. He closes his eyes in an attempt to keep the pain and nausea at bay. It clearly is not working. Even a comedy routine can raise only a grimace of a smile.

He leaves the room to get water and medication. His thin body, having dropped considerable weight, moves slowly. He drags his damaged legs along as he mounts the three steps into the next level and out of the room. He returns wearing a warmer blue and white jacket. He is extremely sensitive to temperature changes and is most often cold and shivering. He sits, trying to pay attention to the news while we sit and eat dinner. Tonight he is too ill to sit and keep us company. The rain has continued in a steady downpour which again keeps everyone inside. Johanna remarks on how uncommon it is to have several days of constant rain without a break in the clouds.

249

Sunday, June 25

 Each morning Tait says he feels "a bit better," but by late afternoon the nausea and burning return with a vengeance. Not able to eat, he mixes a special milk shake filled with nutrients to pump into his stomach feeding tube. To add to his misery, ulcers appear on the roof of his mouth and again along his gum line. The pain radiates into his left jaw and eye – the side targeted by the radiation. The effort and pain of speaking keeps him mainly silent. He worries that he is neglecting his guests and his clients at Cedars. He refuses to believe that his determination to carry on work as usual has put added stress on an ailing body that needs more rest.

"I'm sure the reason for this pain will become clear. I'm not complaining."

Sunday night is one of the worst yet. Even the ever-optimistic Tait has grown worried about what is happening to him and tells Johanna he wants to go to the doctor in Durban on Monday. Johanna's worry and frustration had reached its limit. During the day she tried to contact the oncology group which, she had been told, was always available. However, a voice on an answering machine told her someone would "get back" to her. No one ever did and she was to subsequently discover the number she was given was actually a discontinued number they had not updated. She couldn't sleep and knew there would be no rest until she got him to the doctor.

It has now rained non-stop for three days and it feels as though the soft, gentle, warm rain has a purpose. A strange, healing purpose and when it stops so might Tait's pain.

Monday, June 26

Tait is feeling better, but he typically feels better in the morning. He and Johanna set out for Durban with him driving. At the clinic they didn't learn much, but the oncologist told Tait his mouth and throat problems might continue for several more weeks. He didn't appear concerned about the weight loss and reminded him to continue to add to his diet which would eventually help put back the weight. Tait was delighted. For him it was an affirmation that things would improve and he would continue to recover his strength. Johanna, who worried constantly about the amount of pain he was suffering, was frustrated that there didn't seem to be anything the doctor could do to ease that pain.

But, overnight a miracle seemed to have happened. After dropping Johanna off at home, he drove to Cedars feeling better than he had for many days. During the day he managed to eat rice, peas and corn and three slices of ham – a feat if there ever was one – and the nausea didn't return. Tait is grateful. He hopes the end of the stomach tube is near.

And so, the pattern of the next few months is set. Some days are more bearable than others but even the good days are not great and it becomes clear that the promise of "it should be fine" is not going to materialize. Eating becomes a steady diet of protein shakes, nutritious cereal, pancakes and eggs. He wonders if a steak is something he will ever enjoy again. But whatever the downsides, the upside is the removal of the feeding tube from his abdomen. He also continues to go the gym but not at the frenetic pace he had always set for himself. Letting his body be his guide he works out three to five times a week and on mornings when his body screams for him to stay in bed a couple of hours past 4 a.m. he forces himself to stay there.

"I can't walk very well but I can bench press 250 pounds," he says laughing.

CEDARS

July 2012

NO MATTER HOW BADLY his body is wracked with pain, Tait does not miss a meeting at Cedars. His pain, he says, is nothing compared to what many of the addicts are experiencing. His being there is important to them, so he pretends he is doing fine. The applause that greets him when he walks into a room is not just the residents greeting the day, it is filled with a special warmth for Tait. They see through his pretence.

A typical day at The Cedars starts with counsellors arriving at 7:15 a.m. for an 8 a.m. meeting, led by Keith. Over mugs of coffee they sit in a small office and review each resident, discussing their cases in detail. Most are making good progress, a couple are having privileges revoked, several new people are struggling, one is not fooling anyone with his pretence of following the rules, one is expected to leave even though they are all convinced he will relapse in short order and they expect another to get a royal drubbing from the group when they hold the Concerns meeting later in the morning. Concerns, Tait explains, is a time when everyone weighs in on behaviour they see in each other that is of "concern" and might stifle the person's chances for success in the program.

They are excited on this particular Tuesday morning because the first Zulu man is graduating from the program and they expect he will be successful in his sobriety. Many of the young Zulus who come to Cedars leave before the recommended time and none to that point in 2012, had been successful. They all agreed this was a huge step and hoped the man would be an inspiration to other Zulu men and women. There are a couple of patients who have to be evaluated by the medical team. They have arrived with a bag of medications and diagnosed as bi-polar. Keith suspects neither will actually suffer from the illness.

"They are never bi-polar. They are suffering a drug-induced psychosis. In ten years we had only one person with genuine depression and eventually she got off her meds but it took a long time. So many of them come in on multiple prescription meds besides their illegal drugs of addiction and it takes the first twenty-eight days to get them off meds and find out if they have true mental illness. Almost all get off meds.

When someone is admitted and the doctor here says they are in bad shape we send them to hospital if necessary. There is little that can be done to help an alcoholic whose perceptions are blunted by multiple prescriptions of psychiatric drugs. We don't take anyone if they can't get off the meds."

While the shortest length of stay they recommend is three months, it depends on the individual. Many require a longer stay, especially older addicts who have become set in their ideas and are "conditioned" addicts. It is recommended they stay at least six months, if not longer. Particularly vulnerable are addicts who, like Tait, relapse after very long periods of sobriety. One woman in her sixties, who lives with an alcoholic, relapsed after twenty years off the booze. The advice to her is to "get rid of him" and remain for long term treatment. According to what Keith has observed, there is little hope of success for someone who relapses after a long period of sobriety.

"It is very different for people after a long term absence. In all my years being an addict and in the rehab business, Don is the first person I've seen be successful after relapsing following a long time sober. The odds are a million to one. They always need long term treatment and that gets harder as they get older. Caleb was here twelve months before he got sober. But it can be done if they really want it and are prepared to work hard at it, and it is bloody hard work. That's why it is great to have Don here because he is a rare one who is successful, but he can show them it can be done with hard work and commitment to it."

253

Word about The Cedars is spreading, mainly from people whose lives have been saved and changed. There are people seeking help from this unique program from all over the world, including Canada, the United States, United Kingdom, Zimbabwe and all neighbouring South African countries.

But make no mistake about it, this is not a five-star, Hollywood-style rehab. Similar to Brentwood Recovery Home in Windsor, Ontario, it is based on the principles of spirituality and the 12 Steps of AA. The first two months are spent working through the Steps, then a month of making them part of life while still at Cedars. On average there are thirty-five or thirty-seven people in the house, broken down into two-thirds men and one-third women. They range in age from eighteen to people in their sixties. It's a kind, supportive, gritty, no bullshit, no frills environment designed not to make people feel better, but rather to help them find a better life.

Because of his own experience in a number of rehabs, Tait knows only too well that there is no easy way to not only get sober but also to continue to live sober.

"Most rehabs know people are looking for an easier, softer way with big rooms, TV in every room, medication, pills and pampering, but that doesn't get you well. This is not an easy program, but it gets you well. Those who get it have been beaten to a pulp, have nowhere else to get well and will do anything but they have to be desperate or the Steps won't work. Some people just can't be honest. So many alcoholics get primary treatment for bipolar illness but the alcoholism is not a secondary disorder, it is the disorder. Treat the alcoholism and, from our experience, you can often fix the bipolar illness diagnosis."

As the meeting winds down, they all make recommendations about which patients should be partnered with others, depending on their personalities and the place they've reached in the program. The counsellors enter the main meeting room where everyone in the program is already seated. The first order of business is to elect a new house leader and an assistant. Approving applause greets each of the elected leaders. The focus then turns to Simphiwe Mhlongo, the 38-year-old Zulu who is leaving. He expresses his deep gratitude to the counsellors and fellow addicts. The affection they have for Mhlongo is evident in their farewell messages.

"You are sensitive and aware and you will carry a strong message to those who need it on the outside."

"You are a very loving man with a big heart and the way you are able to get through to others is very special. I want what you have."

"There is something inside you that oozes out even when you have to give hard advice. You do it with ease and grace."

"I can see you are passing on the message. The world is lucky to have you coming its way."

Tait and the other counsellors are optimistic that Mhlongo will be able to convince other Zulus who come in to the program to stick with it until they are in recovery.

"We are very proud of you and know you will be successful in your recovery," Keith tells him with affection. "I also know you will be a great influence on members of your community who need help. We all wish you well."

The conversation then turns to the young Zulu woman who has decided she should share her HIV positive status with the group. She fidgets and is obviously embarrassed but finds an inner reserve and, in a barely audible voice, explains her precarious health condition. She is being supported by a young man with advanced cancer who understands the physical and psychological challenges of living with a life-threatening illness. As the information is digested by the men and women in the room there is a sudden outpouring of concern and offers of support.

"You have the love and support of members in the house," she is told. "If you can come forward with what you have I can only admire and thank you. You have great courage."

The morning has been emotional and everyone takes a break before getting together again in the afternoon. There is a camaraderie evident among them and it is rare to see anyone walking or sitting alone. They are more often in deep conversation or talking in groups.

The Concerns meeting that follows lunch is no nonsense and its participants tough talking. On the hot seat, everyone receives them badly, according to the counsellors. At first they try justifying their behaviour but soon realize it's a learning experience. Some people find it scary to bring Concerns until they realize the exercise is a two-way street – helping them and the person in the hot seat. The no bullshit discussions are brutally honest, almost like tattling. They can become confrontational, especially if there are harboured resentments. If these are not resolved in the group, the two people involved have a one on one, where there is usually a resolution. If the one on one is not successful, the two people meet with their sponsors.

Consequences depend on the rules being broken and the time frame varies. Communication bans can last for two to three weeks and if the ban is broken, the consequence can extend for a longer period. Someone who is being lazy and not completing chores will get the cup station - pots and pans washing detail. The house monitors have the responsibility of checking on the job completion status of each member of the group and must bring Concerns to the meeting.

In this Tuesday morning group many cite concerns about one young man who clearly came in to get detoxed but not necessarily to become a sober and contributing member of society. It is his third time in the program.

"He was on kitchen ban but he was in the kitchen area asking others to get him food."

"Instead of discussions on the Steps and recovery, he was telling jokes on the morning contemplative walk."

After four or five other Concerns, the young man tries to interject to defend himself.

"I just want to ..."

"We don't want to hear from you. Continue." Keith's patience is wearing thin.

"He was making farting sounds with his arms during one of the meetings and distracting others."

Keith has heard enough. Turning to address the man in the hot seat the no-nonsense Brit pulls no punches, confronting him and his inability to see beyond himself.

"We all get tired, we have all not wanted to do what's demanded. I'm still questioning if you are mentally sound or if you just don't care. We tell you over and over what you need to be doing and over and over you end up leaving and sponging off relatives. Then you come here and piss away their money when they're trying to help you. You should be grateful to be here and doing more than anyone else in this room, but it's always a joke to you. You're always pushing the boundaries, like you have to be weird in some strange way, always trying to beat the system. If I had been here when you were admitted this time you wouldn't be here. They told me you were different and I wanted to believe that but bang! Here you are. You are not different. Coming from the streets you should be doing everything you can to change. You spend four or five months on the streets then come here for a month using us for a place to stay and get meals. I'll give you a week. But just one more concern or consequence and you're gone. I don't want to see you irritable or treating this like a holiday place. You will abide by the rules of this house and respect the people in it. Otherwise, go. Unless we see a major change in you, just go. So many need help here and we spend too much time over and over on the same shit with you. Do I make myself clear?"

"Yes Keith."

"Right then. Anything else?" There are several more Concerns raised that are dealt with and the meeting ends.

KEITH

KEITH WILKS COULD HAVE walked straight out of a Humphrey Bogart movie. In his sixties, he carries 20 extra pounds, is balding and has the air of a man who knows how to take charge. There is something about him that's hard to put your finger on until you've heard his story.

Born in Barrow Inverness, a town in northwest England on the Irish Sea, his early life was tainted by his working-class status in a working-class town. With a father who was a shunter for British Rail and a stay at home mother, he passed the Eleven-Plus exams and attended grammar school. The school housed many clever kids, but he never considered himself one of them. His problem wasn't lack of potential, it was his "bone laziness." He liked pleasure and shunned anything that required effort – including school and sports.

He was tossed from the grammar school at 13 and sent to a Secondary Modern school in a rough area run by hooligan mobs. They seemed to always be having fun and he gravitated to their lifestyle. At 16 he left school with no qualifications whatsoever but, with an uncanny ability to promote himself, he headed for London.

For three years he worked in publishing as a copy boy and in sales. It was the 1960s and the drug culture was pervasive. His preference was amphetamines. He returned to Barrow and partying with his mates. He lived for weekends filled with "sex, drugs and rock & roll." It cost him his assistant transport manager job at a cereal mill and an uncle arranged for another job in the office of the shipyards. LSD and other psychedelics made it virtually impossible for him to work. He was 22 and married to his 17-year-old pregnant girlfriend Susan.

After his marriage to Susan, with whom he had three children during their 14 years together, he left the shipyard and opened a boutique. That financial disaster led him to 14 years following in his father's footsteps – working on the railway. His 12-hour shifts were followed by equal hours of heavy drinking in the ale house. He drank at work every day and was drugged out on weekends. A drug bust netted him a suspended sentence but didn't change his addicted lifestyle.

His wife was drinking and doing drugs and the marriage was imploding. She finally decided to get it together and to do that had to get out of the morass, so she left with the children. One morning, in a silent and lonely house Keith woke up to a brutal truth – he was a dirty, bearded, down and out drug and alcohol addicted lout. His parents had left Barrow because of the shame he brought them so he called his sister in Hertfordshire and asked for help. Thus began a long journey on the rehab circuit. The first two years in and out of rehab centres did not compel him to stay clean – not even a pleading letter from his daughter. But one June afternoon, sitting on a bench across from his three children who had come to visit him, he had his awakening.

"I looked at their little faces crying and I thought 'I can't do this (to them) anymore. I want to commit to being a father.' I knew it was my last chance. I made peace with their mother and told her I wanted to be a proper father. After much yelling and screaming at each other, we declared a truce."

Focused on getting well, he faithfully attended AA meetings and supported his children initially from welfare payments, then part-time jobs. He sold cars, sold meat door to door and eventually struck up a friendship with an antiquarian book dealer. He also qualified as an addiction counsellor. Using everything he learned from the book dealer, he opened a second-hand book and music shop and was soon making a more than average living. Then he met Julia, an upper class, grammar school-educated woman who was "exceptionally bright and astute."

Julia was studying psychology at Lancaster University and life was looking up so they decided to buy a house together. They were to buy and sell many houses over the course of their marriage. Julia graduated, became a prison psychologist and they were soon in the money. Julia drank, but while she drank a lot, it didn't at first appear to be a problem.

A holiday in Mombasa began Keith's love affair with Africa. Later, a chance meeting in Cape Town with a woman named Shelley, newly out of rehab, was to eventually lead him to a counselling job offer. He turned it down because he realized he did not want to work for anyone.

Returning to England he found Julia "in a mess." Her drinking had become out of control and caused her to be fired from her prison job. She was now on the unemployment roll. They decided to sell up and move to South Africa to start a rehab centre of their own. In the remote area of Dududu they found a neglected plantation home which turned out to be exactly what they were looking for. Networking with Rotary and the Chamber of Commerce, they began to get clients.

Julia developed a program that saw people in recovery teaching illiterate women to read and write. One of the men in recovery began to help a young man they had come to know who suffered from a severe form of schizophrenia. Life was good. Just when they thought they had life by the tail, Julia, her immune system weakened by her addictions, fought a valiant six-week battle with pneumonia. She lost. She was only 48.

Today, Keith lives with Sam and her young daughter with whom he shares a happy life. He and Tait are the heart and soul of Cedars. They have much in common.

THE NEARNESS OF DEATH

IN THE YEAR FOLLOWING his surgery the nearness of death for Tait is omnipresent. The mortality of it all is so much more real, as is the idea of dying. He begins dreaming of people he has not thought about in years. He has a new attitude towards most aspects of living and has also developed a new and fatalistic attitude to the "damn throat thing," not expecting it to ever get any better so that he never becomes disappointed. He philosophizes that it is a lot easier to accept things when you ascribe an importance factor to them. The least importance you place on hardship, the more likely you are to be able to cope with it.

"It's like at Cedars. I keep it down to the things I absolutely know are true. For example, I absolutely know that I, personally, am not important. I am as or more defective than I have ever been, it's still there. Mostly I don't act on it, sometimes I do. It's something I have to work on until the day I die."

He carries a bottle of water with him, something that once caused him to laugh or scoff at those who did, deriding its "pretensions." With no saliva, the bottle is an essential appendage. At times he feels much more aware of life's nuances than he has ever before. The classic playboy doesn't socialize much, except time he spends with colleagues and clients at Cedars.

He tries not to have expectations. Now, in his seventies, and a cancer survivor, he is letting go of things, realizing, he says, that everything is transient and that everything is going to change. Whether you want it to or not it will change. He tries not to live in either the glorious or painful parts of his life. He is convinced that whatever is to come will give him the experience he is supposed to have and he will accept whatever that experience is.

The cerebellar ataxia is causing his legs to steadily deteriorate and walking is becoming a huge challenge. He has to drag his legs along in order to walk and has to accept the use of a wheelchair at airports because of the incredible effort it takes to walk any distance. He refuses to dwell on the knowledge that a timely prescription of vitamin B12 would have prevented the condition. The effects of the radiation still make everything he swallows feel like acid or broken glass in his mouth and throat. His symptoms are steadily getting worse. Despite consulting with specialists and every Google posting about others who suffer a similar affliction, there seems to be no solution to the pain in his mouth. He is still working out at the gym and rebuilding his strength. However, since his cancer diagnosis and radiation treatments his life has been filled with many health challenges.

In August 2012 Tait's feeding tube caused a large hernia to develop in his abdomen. Once it was repaired doctors removed the tube and told him to try to eat normally but the constant pain in his mouth, throat and tongue made it very difficult to chew and swallow. He can manage to eat small amounts by drinking water with each bite. Radiation has destroyed his salivary glands leaving him without the liquid that helps keep germs and infections at bay and this causes fungal growths to develop in his throat. One was so large it severely constricted his voice box and not only was he finding it almost impossible to breathe, it brought on anxiety attacks that became so acute Johanna was afraid it would cause him to have another heart attack. During a stay in hospital surgeons scraped away the fungus but it is something they say will return and require more surgical intervention.

As if he wasn't struggling enough, the morning after this surgery he awoke in such a bloated state he couldn't fit into one piece of clothing. His entire body, except his face, had increased by about four kilograms. Johanna had to buy him elastic-waist workout pants and an oversize t-shirt because he had nothing to wear. Another admission to hospital and a battery of tests could not find the cause of his sudden bloating but doctors suspect it was an unusual reaction to one or some of the medications used in the previous day's surgical procedure. Once the reaction wore off his body returned to its normal size. Because of the lethal aspect of his cancer, he is also admitted to hospital on a regular three months schedule to have an MRI or PET scan and a biopsy of his tongue and throat.

SOUTH AFRICA

May 19, 2014

IN THE TWO YEARS SINCE I've seen Tait, everything that's been happening to him has been relayed via telephone and email by him or Johanna. In order to finalize some of the stories for this book we all agreed it was time for another visit. I am anxious to see him face to face and again and wonder about the shape he will be in this time.

Unlike our visit in 2012 when Tait was too ill to greet us, he was in good shape and spirits. For some inexplicable reason the pain in his mouth, throat and tongue had disappeared two days before and for the first time in more than two years, he was pain free. The doctors had no answer, but Tait doesn't care about the why, he is revelling in being able to eat and drink without grimacing – when he is able to eat at all.

Over the next week we spend many hours revisiting various periods in his life and every conversation is laced with lessons he has learned along the way, the spirituality that has changed his life and the importance he places on working every day to be a better person. His mantra Bring It On is written in bold ink on the inside of his left arm. He takes it very seriously.

Just a week after the pain disappeared, it returned. At dinner one evening Tait refuses the meal and says he is having oatmeal and everyone asks why? He has shown no signs of his throat pain having returned. He admits the pain had started the night before and was growing progressively worse. He shrugs it off. "Oh well, at least I had a week without it. Perhaps this is a sign it will continue to come and go so that I will at least have some days when it's not bad. I'm lucky."

The next morning at Cedars he met with his group of more than forty men and women. I note that the number of black South Africans in the room has increased considerably which is something Tait and Keith were hoping to see. Tait talked to them about the importance of welcoming the experiences they have, embracing them and understanding what they mean in their lives. Experience, he told them, is what you get when you get what you want, and it's not what happens to a person it is what a person does with what happens to him or her.

"We choose the experience. Life is difficult but once we accept the fact life is difficult, it ceases to be difficult. We are in charge of the experience. We are not powerless. You ask 'Why am I so angry? Because I choose to feel that way.' The truth will set you free but first it pisses you off. And what is my responsibility? Constantly thinking of others. Nothing is bad out there. Nothing needs to change. I need to change. What an opportunity we have in this place...all of us needing each other. Start on your knees. God works through people. I was a total atheist and now fourteen years later I don't think there is a God, I know there is a God. I don't know why it works, it just does. This can't be a blame game. Forget about self. When something is wrong with me it can't be fixed by something outside of me. The buck stops here," he tells them, pointing at his own chest.

Many of the men and women share their own stories about how they've experienced life after starting every day on their knees in prayer. Some who fought it, who thought it was "hogwash," talk about how shocked they were to find that when they started their day on their knees in prayer it effected an unexpected change in the pace of their recovery. There is a warmth in the room that comes from a group of people focused on each other, all united in being more giving and less self-centred and selfish. Tait also talks about the parable of the Prodigal Son – it's one he brings up constantly

266

in these sessions.

"The Prodigal Son tries to fill the hole inside himself but eventually he gets on his knees and he goes home. The Prodigal Son illustrates the unselfish act of forgiveness of the father, to show that when you hit rock bottom, when you think there is nowhere else to turn, there is repentance and forgiveness. But the addict has to be stripped bare. The alcoholic will look everywhere else so everything has to go in order that there is only one place left. The alcoholic has to be willing to be accepted back into the fold and to develop a relationship with the God of his or her understanding."

Throughout the hour Tait drinks copious amounts of water in order to continue talking. No one comments on his hoarse voice and he offers no explanation. The pain is not important to him, as long as he can be heard and understood. No one knows he is in pain.

As I watch Tait, I cannot help but marvel at what I have witnessed in this man over these many years since my interview with him in Costa Rica. I ask myself 'Where is the insecure Tait of childhood? Where is the Tait of those celebrity days in Windsor? The Tait of those down and out days in Costa Rica? Who is this Tait humbling himself before a group of addicts in Africa?'

Listening to the exchanges between them, I realize he is, in fact, the sum of all he has been but this transformation happened because he has ultimately found a way to use the best of himself from those experiences. As a journalist, it is an extraordinary opportunity to follow a human being through such a journey. It is also humbling. It would also not be possible to imagine this part of Tait's life without Johanna. Tait's health trials and tribulations have caused a significant change in their relationship.

"I must say out of all of this I have become a pretty independent person, self-assured with respect for myself. I'd lost a lot of that living with Don and I was always terrified, mentally and physically, never knowing what to say, never feeling I had the freedom to speak for myself. I can do that now. I can deal with things. I'm on equal grounds with him. So, I guess good things can come from bad situations."

While the road to redemption has been long, arduous and rewarding for Tait, it has been an equally long and difficult journey for Johanna. I often wonder if Tait really understands the depth of love she must have for him to return time and time again, when most woman would have let him rot. If ever a woman loved beyond all measure, it has been Johanna's often baffling love for Tait.

"In 1980 when he came out of Brentwood things were really good for us. Then his practice took off and the money started rolling in. By 1992 we had big houses, expensive cars but it was never enough for Don. He also stopped going to meetings and hardly ever went to Brentwood. He had the disease of always wanting more. It was all 'morether,' meaning I need more and more. That's when things started falling apart. Then he had an affair with one of his secretaries and started seeing another woman. He wasn't drinking and doing all this, he was just doing it, so I left. So much has happened between us over the years, but here we are."

So many years later, Johanna says she finally has peace of mind.

"It's taken a long time for him to regain my trust. In this last year or so since his illness I have come to trust him and I truly love him. We are closer than we ever were. He let his guard down and he knows I really do love him. I always told him the prestige and money was never important, it was only the love between us."

And, when people ask why she would keep going back to Tait, why she would forgive him when most women would probably have given him the boot and moved on, she says it is and has always been about the love, and ultimately the understanding of his disease.

"From the beginning he was my soul mate even though I knew it wouldn't be easy. When we would split I would say 'That son of a bitch, never again. I despise him and I will never let him do that to me again.' Then, inevitably, we would be in contact, talking on the phone, then meeting for lunch or dinner and we'd want to get together again. During the good times we did have it showed me the good, human side of him that I was crazy about. Those times gave me hope that someday, somehow, we would be together and be happy together."

After more than thirty years, Johanna says she understands Tait's never-ending struggle to stay sober, that it is a continuous journey of daily living that means ongoing therapy and treatment. It is something that is never cured. And, she says, for Tait it is a pervasive family disease that affects him, his children and grandchildren.

"The more you understand about AA and the disease and the longer you spend around that lifestyle, you begin to really understand what that life is all about. We have made a life here together. It's still not always easy but we make it work. We don't have a lot of money and it's not a life of luxury. We have a very quiet life and spend our evenings enjoying TV, watching our favourite series and having friends come over for coffee. We go to dinner once a month if Don can eat. People in Canada sometimes ask why he doesn't pay back Revenue Canada, well get over it, he can't."

While she admires the work he is now doing, Johanna laments, somewhat, that he will never be able to play a role where she believes he would have made a significant contribution to society.

"I always tell him he would have made an amazing Supreme Court judge. I really wanted that for him. He loved practicing law and as a court reporter, I was there when he received his QC. I watched and was so impressed by him in the courtroom. I also saw the torment of him not being able to practice and it affected me too. But I now believe this is how it was supposed to be, that he had to take this journey so that he could help so many others get back their lives. They are alive and doing well because of him and I've seen that happen so often over these past years at Cedars. "

Johanna also says Tait's journey and his years in Africa have made him the man he is today.

"The human being he is today is more human than I've ever seen him. I believe it was always there, but he never expressed who he is today because it wasn't the most important thing to him. But he is where he is supposed to be. He gave up something so that he could save others and in the end, it saved him."

While he spends many hours working at saving the lives of addicts at Cedars, he is also trying to change the lives of his two daughters. Both have spent time with him in South Africa. Melanie, now in her forties, also spent time in Cedars during an eighteen month stay in Scottburg. She returned to Windsor pregnant and two months later while Tait was in the city, she went into early labour. Tait held his daughter's hand during the 16 hours she was in labour and was with her during delivery. She continues to live in Windsor with her son Jack and while they did not speak for almost two years, Melanie and Tait are once again in touch and talking. Barbie, as Tait calls his older daughter, was deeply moved by her weeks in Africa. Tait cherishes the letter she sent to him during one of his hospitalizations. It provides an insight into the profound effect Tait's meteoric rise and fall and his addictions had on his children.

Dear Dad:

I wanted to send flowers to the hospital. I've been calling there and checking on you before work and after work. It just doesn't seem to convey how much I've been thinking about you. This 10,000-mile distance was always kind of blown off by saying "I'm just a phone call away." No matter how far technology advances, it won't take the place of skin to skin contact. Phone conversations are kept short and sweet and to the point. I miss so very much sitting on your back-deck area, coffees in hand, musing on the mysteries of the universe and our important places in it.

Stuff I remember, that I want you to remember, too...the stuff that wasn't scary or bad and contributed so very much to who I am and why I am the way I am:

When I remember who Barbie Tait was, the potential she had and the feeling that I had the RIGHT to be loved. Sure, there are some typical Tait endings to the stories but they make me smile in that oh so typical nothing ever is normal with the Tait's kind of way. (laugh).

Some of my very first memories of my life - they may not be 100 per cent accurate, but they are 100 per cent the way I remember them:

I remember you and me outside in the summer. I was walking down a little dirt trail kind of thing behind an apartment building. You were there smiling at me and singing the theme song to Miss America...my very own Burt Parks: Here she is...Miss America. And I was walking and preening. My daddy thought I was special enough to be the most beautiful, smart, talented woman in the world. And then? In typical Tait fashion I stepped on a piece of glass or something. Reality always did kinda suck for me. But what did I take from that snippet of a memory? My father loved me. I was very special.

I remember you and I outside with some friends from law school. We were entering the Ox Box. We were going to have lunch. Who was? Well, my Daddy and I and his friends. Why? Because even as a child my father was proud of me and loved to show me off to his friends. I was, in fact, one of the guys. My daddy was my daddy...and my best friend. He liked me more than all the other friends he had. I knew that already. I was his Miss America, after all.

I remember getting to stay up late to watch Star Trek with my

Daddy. Sure, the mother was there but it wasn't a special thing for her. I got to break the rules and stay up late to watch TV with my Dad. Because we liked the same things - my father, my friend - and he genuinely liked my company and wanted to hang with me. We did the same things on lazy Saturday afternoons, too, when he could. We'd hang in your bedroom on an ugly green and yellow bedspread watching a teeny, tiny black and white TV and watch scary (?) movies together that weren't scary at all...ummm...except Bette Davis movies and the Birds. They scared the hell out of me, but I always put on a brave face.

Oddly enough, the majority of my dreams ended when yours came true. You became Don Tait, this mythical man of gigantic proportions. You had the houses, the cars, the clothing, the esteem of colleagues, the fame and fortune. And like most people who "hit it big," the little people who were there on your way up didn't seem to be a priority anymore. It seems when you became HIM, you lost the real Don Tait. I've always been a daddy's girl and will be to the day I draw my last breath. During my rebellious years, it wasn't YOU I was angry at it was Don Tait. I still hear about him, even from you when you say: I USED to be Don Tait...google me! That wasn't really you. The period of time when you went from being Daddy to Don Tait? I know how important that image was to you. You felt justified and important and adored. But just so you really know? That's the way I felt BEFORE you became Don Tait. I meant what I said when I visited you in South Africa: I'm more proud of what you do now, who you ARE now, than I ever was with the image of you. I know that when the real Don Tait stands up, he won't be a criminal lawyer, or an addict, or fearing loss of control. The real you was the man singing my praises, the real you was the man confessing a love so strong about Johanna that you were torn between your children and the woman you loved. The real you was the man crying in the den after Brentwood when watching The Champ and worrying that Don Tait may have stolen the love of your family.

From you and Dorothy, I learned how to love my children unconditionally, through all their faults and tribulations. From you, I learned that I have importance in the grand scheme of things. From you, I learned the weirdest thing about forgiveness: I have no need to forgive anyone. My love for them forgave them long before my brain caught up with my heart. I always felt, after Don Tait, that I would never amount to anything to be proud of. Those were huge shoes to fill and quite another set of shoes than what I learned about as a child. I felt small, insignificant, scared - a disappointment. Life has a way of making us crave that which we don't have. In my case? A real mother - the universe sent me Dorothy to show me how a mother should be. I had money growing up. Money was never a priority. Fame was all over our house. I had no need for it. I wanted "normal" but had no idea how to go about getting it.

I'm now at yet another crossroads in my life. I am without those things that defined me, much as you were when you arrived in Africa. I am faced with just "me." And even now, I am trying to follow your example: to shed Barb Ray and all that accompanies that and become Barbie Tait again. She was who I was supposed to be. I work for no other reason than to achieve the goal of maintaining myself, helping my sister and going home to my family. I have discovered that it's all external and that everything and everyone who surrounds me can add to my joy of life, but is NOT my life. I need my Daddy. You centre me. You remind me of Barbie. You are so very important to me. You've shown me everything: who I am, who I am meant to be, how I get there, what is important and what is not. You've even given me a religion that is not yet on a map. Part mystic, part science, part Vedic - and all you. The truths you have shown me are as important as the truths you showed me as a child.

Your life story should be a book (although many would think it was fiction or embellished...hahahaha). You hit the pinnacle of a glorious law career. You travelled the world. You owned the nicest homes, cars and yes, women's hearts.

How do I fill 48 years' worth of lessons into an email? How can I possibly let you know the impact you have left on my heart, mind and soul? As much as I hate the fact you left us, I know that the result in your life (and therefore in mine) returned my father and got rid of (mostly...haha) the Don Tait who wasn't you anyways. People have asked how I can possibly love/forgive a man like that. Or, conversely, how LUCKY I was to have lived with the benefits of you being Don Tait. Before you take this as castigation, you have to remember I grew up with the alcoholic you. There was only a very short time in sobriety before I was an adult. The answer has always been this for me: you and Don Tait were NOT the same person. My father was loving, affectionate, funnier than a comedian, quick to anger - quicker to forgive. Don Tait was an image that he couldn't ever seem to live up to or accept. Obviously, because that man wasn't the Daddy. Not the real Donald Hawkins Tait. And it's THAT man, the man you were and the man you became again, who has taught me the most important things in my life. It is because of Dorothy's influence on Donnie Tait and what she gave to him that is the part of you that I take with me.

This letter isn't about how my kids are or how Mel is doing or how things are with you and Johanna. It's not about how the effects of your disease affected me. It's not about exchanging pleasantries or knowing how you're doing after surgery or where it will lead to. I need to let you know how much I love you, have always loved you and what I carry of you inside me all the time. It's about you and me, our relationship. It's about me letting you know how important you have been to me and will continue to be to me. It's letting you know that my childhood sense of awe at the world and the universe was reignited thanks to you. It's letting you know that the lessons you taught me as a child and again when I returned to you completely broken inside a few years ago have had a profound effect. I love you, Daddy. Barb"

Tait is trying to make up for lost time with his daughters, at least as much time as they will allow him. His granddaughter Courtney, Barb's daughter, has made multiple visits to see her "Faffy."

"I want to be here for her and Melanie and Barbie. This

journey hasn't been easy for any of us. I can't change the past, but I am trying to leave them with happier memories."

May 28, 2014

ON A SUNNY WEDNESDAY afternoon we are sitting on a sidewalk café in Durban. The conversation is lively and Tait is explaining that the radiation treatment for his cancer has loosened his lower teeth. He finds it quite concerning and says he has an appointment with a dental specialist in the coming week. Then, half way through the meal, a dental bridge on the lower right side of his mouth falls out. He is mortified but it was not unexpected. He just didn't think it would start happening so soon.

It is obvious that this worries him but he does not utter one word of complaint, demonstrating his philosophy that it is just something else he has to learn to live with. We finish lunch and nothing more is said about the teeth. The following day his dentist, knowing he would soon be seeing the specialist, cemented it back with a very light adhesive.

Only a week later when we are at the Hluhluwe Game Reserve and having dinner just outside the small town, another dental bridge on the other side of his lower jaw fell off. Tait handles it with aplomb. Nothing can be done at that moment in time to change anything, so he accepts it and moves on. To him it is all part of what he is supposed to experience. He does not complain but wonders out loud "What the hell is next?"

For Tait now, every day is a bonus and a new opportunity to do something good for someone else. That may seem excruciatingly corny to people who have known Don Tait only in his high-flying courtroom or addiction days, and they would find it equally difficult to believe that a man could change so dramatically. He has. But the change in Tait came as a result of being beaten down more times than most people could stand in a lifetime.

He has been sober for more than sixteen years and remained sober through great trials and tribulations. People who are still angry with him will never be convinced he has truly embraced a spirituality that he hopes not only brings him closer to God, but is allowing him to learn to be less selfish. Tait says he is now able to see life more clearly and to finally learn what it means to love and be loved unconditionally – but admits this is still a daily struggle and makes it clear that a path to redemption never gets paved. As incongruous as it will likely be to someone who has not had contact with Tait since his flight from Canada, there is no doubt that the path he has chosen is deeply, truly spiritual.

Looking back, Tait says he could not have lived his life any other way if he was going to find the truth and find out what the truth was not. If he had stayed or returned to Windsor he would have continued his addicted-style life because he was powerless to do it any other way.

HOME AT LAST

THE END OF TAIT'S STORY is drawing to a close. Hopefully, the cancer that will kill him is kind enough to remain at bay for many more years. For every year it does there will be more men and women in Africa and beyond who will be glad and grateful that he lived. For the addicts of the world, Tait hopes the lessons he has learned and is passing on will help them stay on that long and often treacherous road to sobriety and redemption.

"Everything I was using to make me happy I lost. Everything. And I put everything ahead of God. That's when you get to the Prodigal Son...who am I? Not the lawyer. And not the guy with everything I thought made me happy. It was all going and I knew it was going. There was always this big hole inside me and I was trying to fill it with everything I could find. And for a moment, when I thought I had everything that made me happy I would feel whole, then the emptiness returned and I would need more and more. I didn't know who I was.

Everyone is addicted to something – alcohol, drugs, money, work, sex – there's a long list. I think every human being comes to a spot that's overwhelming, whether it's death, divorce, bankruptcy, or illness and disease. Overcoming them means coming to an acceptance that this is what life is about. Jung said we all have a thirst. We have a thirst for a relationship with God and once we find that, we find a solution. My thirst was greater than most. But this has been a wonderful ride. Even with all that's happened, with the heart attack and the cancer. I'm grateful for the whole thing."

While he has embraced the life he has found Tait nevertheless has struggled with the intrusion of the past. He has oftentimes feared that too much of the old Tait survived and could threaten to draw him back into the abyss. But a letter addressed to Cedars that arrived in April, 2015 had an unexpected benefit that, while it filled him with emotion and much sadness, helped Tait truly understand the man he used to be and why that person had to exist.

The letter came to Cedars from a woman now living in Michigan in the U.S. but who had been a juror on one of Tait's trials in Windsor. It reads in part:

Just a short note to remind Don Tait (if he is employed with you) that he still has many people who respect him in the Windsor & surrounding areas. He may have made some mistakes...OK he did! But who hasn't? He was a phenomenal lawyer at a level that was previously unheard of. I happened to be on jury duty and had the honour of watching the man at work. He had razor sharp wit and was mesmerizing. I remember him walking into the courtroom and letting a long list of his client's former crimes (68 or so) roll all the way down to the floor. HE READ THEM ONE BY ONE. He said, "My client's no angel, but he has never committed a crime similar to the one he's been charged with today." The jury gasped at the audacity and realized right then that Don Tait was a master! It was amazing to watch how his mind worked. I could have listened to him all day! If he had any insecurities he hid them well. When he was speaking you could hear a pin drop. I'm so happy he's doing well. I wish as a community we'd have known of his problems and maybe helped him out, but I guess at his level he couldn't risk showing any sign of weakness. I am still at a loss understanding just how he became so insecure. The pain and pressure he was under had to be excruciating for him to suffer so deeply as an adult. I don't get it. He worked so hard to achieve what he did and then sabotaged his career & life. People dream of attaining the dizzying heights he attained yet it didn't make him happy. But I do know that there is nothing he could ever do to make Windsorites turn their backs on him. No matter what, we miss you Don!

After a first read, Tait worried he would start wishing he could go back to that old life, that the stirrings of longing for past glories would be too strong to resist. But that letter unexpectedly helped him to finally mourn, then come to terms with, that man he left behind.

"That's still me. I will not regret the past and that guy got me to this point in my life. If not for him I wouldn't have found what's so important to me now. You can call him self-centred and everything else, but if not for the journey and that guy who was on the journey, I wouldn't be here. I no longer look at him and say, 'I wish he had been different.' I've found my peace with him. I'm not saying I'm not responsible for him and what he did but life is pain and pain leads you to a journey of discovery. I looked at that guy who certainly had his faults, who certainly gave me an experience and acknowledged that it was my life. We all have experiences and that was mine. I don't regret the past, nor do I shut the door on it.

Even though I have now, in 2017, been sober for more than sixteen years, my life has not been easy and it still is not easy. Whatever I'm experiencing in my seventy-fourth year, I should probably be dead. Pain causes us to eventually change. Most of it is caused by trying to avoid pain, which in turn causes pain. Life is difficult. No matter how spiritual you become the shit is still there. My experiences put me where I am today. I don't regret how I got there. They were the experiences I needed. The more I accepted that truth the easier it became. As long as we resist we live in the problem. The whole purpose in life is to wake up. My purpose in life is to give the best of myself to the best of my ability with no expectation of anything in return.

My end is coming. It doesn't scare me, it's just a reality. I try to give this message to anyone who asks. I try my best to live that way, trying to help, whether it does or not. To anyone who reaches out, the hand of AA is there to help. At times it can be frustrating to see someone causing pain to him or herself but I can't make someone happy. They have to want that. My definition of gratitude is an action, a love that won't give up. It's saying 'I'm here. If you want it you can have it.' I go back to the visit from the two cops when I was at Homewood. It was an enjoyable break in my terrible life. They didn't say the words but by their actions it was clear they were telling me 'We love you as you are Don.' No one was trying to change me. The gratitude they had was a love that didn't give up. I believed, as I was sure many others did, that I was a piece of shit. But they didn't say that.

I realize I couldn't have done it any differently than I did. I used to wake up and remember I'd done something terrible and would tell myself I would never do it again. But I always did and because of the addiction I was powerless to change my behaviour, no matter how much I wanted to. I accept my life and history as it happened, so I don't regret the past. The solution is to welcome life as it is, not as you think it should be. I try to make amends to people, hoping they will forgive me, not for a pat on the back but for themselves, freeing them from anger, resentment and self-pity.

I remind myself, when five out of forty-five recover, that love is not conditional, not that I will love you but you must be well. No. My job is not trying to change them. Life is about trying to give, to be able to say I couldn't have done better, I did the best I could. It's giving them the freedom to be who they are. I can see myself in them and I am constantly reminded this is a two-way street. It's me giving but I also receive. It's just a reminder, all the time, that there is a beast and an angel, and I am both.

Every morning on my knees I say Bring It On. My relationship with God it what gets me off. The truth of who I am. Every day I need my fix. My fix is life and God comes to me disguised as my life. That life has been a hellava ride and I wouldn't change any part of my journey because I can't."

Tait's request for his tombstone: What a fucking ride!

Epilogue

MANY YEARS HAVE PASSED since the day Don Tait called me from Africa. As I close this last chapter, I am acutely aware of how much I've learned personally from this part of Tait's journey. While my daily news reporter brain has often been frustrated by the slow pace of the book, I now realize there was no other way it could have been written.

All writers can ask good questions and write in elegant prose. However, being able to take some part of a man's journey with him, to witness life bring him joy and torture and be moved to tears by his obvious excruciating, physical pain, brings a different depth of understanding.

Enduring a personal journey of my own that included a near death experience also helped me get inside the emotion and acceptance of the life-death cycle Tait has so often described. Listening to him, I always thought I understood it intellectually and found the right words to represent his experience. Yet, I was to discover that no matter how cleverly a writer can interpret another's suffering, there is nothing as sobering and enlightening as a shared experience. Even in the throes of my own medical crisis I was strangely, acutely aware of how superficially I understood Tait's brush with death. Conversations we shared played in my head and I drew on many of those life and spirituality discussions to help me accept where my crisis might take me.

Once I recovered, it was clear to me that this telling of Tait's journey is a tale for all people. Tait represents something that each and every one of us has experienced, is experiencing or will experience in some way. Tait's was a life of excess and catastrophic loss, of success and failure, of rejection and hope, hatred and love, banishment and acceptance. Somewhere on the continuum of life that represents all of those experiences is where we all land, eventually. Tait so often has reminded me that addictions are ubiquitous and not limited to alcohol, sex, money and drugs. Throw in work, sports, cosmetic surgery, food, idleness and hypochondria and many more of us emerge as addicts.

I am convinced it was ordained that this book not be written on my imposed deadline of two years, because I would not have been able to represent Tait's journey adequately had I not landed on several places in that continuum. That unique awareness allowed a powerful life force from the brain and heart to find its way to the keyboard.

Because of this I am getting my work addiction somewhat under control. Don Tait, aided by the constant intervention of Christopher, may have also inadvertently saved my life.

BROWN COUCH SURVIVORS

There is no more important evidence on which to judge the impact one human has on another than to hear it from the person on the receiving end. These stories from people whose lives have been changed by their interaction with Tait are often spellbinding. It is easy to see why they identified so closely with his life experiences and respected his advice.

They share their own experiences to pay tribute to Tait and the team of counsellors at Cedars and to continue to fulfil Step 12.

People who ask for treatment at The Cedars are given several residential options with the least recommended being the twenty-one or twenty-eight-day stays. All of the counsellors agree, because of their personal experiences, that addicts barely get detoxed from alcohol and drugs in that short time period. Those who are serious about changing their lives and learning to live well in sobriety never leave before ninety days. It is not unusual for even the most determined addict to relapse and return to Cedars multiple times. In fact, most people don't make it the first time around but the gates and arms are open, as long as counsellors see a genuine desire to succeed.

No one knows better than senior counsellor Caleb Atmore how important it is to never give up the fight for sobriety. It took seven tries at Cedars before he succeeded. Atmore entered his first rehab when he was seventeen years old. Born in Klerkstorp near Johannesburg, he spent much of his young life in and out of a dozen rehabs in South Africa and other countries including Israel. He was kicked out of most of them.

"I got kicked out of a lot of them because I wasn't ready and many because the treatments are not successful and consist mainly of psychiatrists giving you medication and labels. Bipolar is the most common and easy label they stick on you. Once you've been in a few rehabs you learn to be institutionalized and start telling them what they want to hear. It's one of the reasons why there's a revolving door of people going in and out of these places. They get detoxed, get labelled, get meds and get out. But they are still not sober so it's just a matter of time before they are back in another rehab."

Atmore says his body was a "trash can" of prescription and illegal drugs, primarily opiates and alcohol. By the time he found Cedars he had destroyed a four-year relationship, a business and his family. He was isolated and suicidal and in a "very bad place." He was also taking four medications prescribed by a psychiatrist from one of the rehabs who had labelled him "Bi-polar."

"I am not bi-polar. The symptoms of addiction are similar to mental problems and when an addict describes those symptoms, including that you are suicidal, they look for labels to stick on you. But addicts are also to blame because we are able to manipulate them."

His first stay at Cedars lasted three months. He was just not willing to follow suggestions from the counsellors and left. He soon relapsed and after his family intervened returned for one day, and left again. The next admission lasted six months. During that time he was able to progress to tertiary care, where clients have progressed to a trusted position and are allowed off-premise privileges. However, he would bend or not stick to the rules and would get knocked back to secondary care which is more restrictive.

During his fourth relapse his consumption of large quantities of drugs caused him to become paranoid, psychotic and suicidal. He had teeth missing, weighed less than a hundred pounds, had sores all over his face, was jittery and nervous and suffered blackouts. He was afraid to live and afraid to die. Then, one day, when he saw no hope for his life he got in his car and drove to Cedars.

He stayed one year. In his second year he came back to do voluntary work with the clients and in his third year he began doing counselling work. He discovered he was not only very good at it, but found it fulfilling and rewarding work.

"I never imagined myself doing this kind of work. I thought IT or because I'm a guitarist, becoming a rock star. But then I met Don. As a counsellor he wasn't as harsh with me as some and there was this great warmth in him; and he was always so insightful. He also always, always had patience with me and never lost hope in me. Plus, it was the way he looked. He was cool, had tattoos like me, was well built from working out and I gravitated to him."

Atmore and Tait began scuba diving together, taking dive masters and instructors courses. He was finding a new life and says it would not have happened without Tait.

"His story is incredible and for us addicts being able to identify is really important. He showed me that I am not better or worse than anyone. And, I felt if someone like him could be where he was and became the kind of man he is, then there is hope for me and all of us. As my sponsor and mentor he showed me that surrendering to God is not about religion, that spirituality is a way of life. Religion is in a box but spirituality is open and that's how I live my life, working towards selflessness and self-sacrifice for people around you, built on trust and loyalty."

One special moment in Atmore's life was having Tait perform the marriage ceremony at his wedding. In this new life he says he is also a better son, husband and father to his daughter. He has a good life and a future and says without the Cedars program and Tait, he would be derelict or dead.

"There is no question about it. I would probably not be here if not for this program. I couldn't hide here and I couldn't get away with anything. The counsellors here have seen and heard it all and, most importantly, they've done it all themselves. It is a very real program and Don, Keith and Julia all had vital roles in my, and everyone else's, recovery. Keith is very direct and knows the Steps and how they should be used; Julia was compassionate and caring and had a way of telling you the raw truth and you still liked her. She could be confrontational and you still loved and respected her. She was a mother figure in recovery and left a big void when she died. Don has the more spiritual side of things and it's spirituality for different views and different styles. It doesn't matter in the least what religion you practice, he combines it all and makes it work for anyone. He has a great gift for doing that. His group is the most insightful here.

So, the three of them - two recovering alcoholics from England meet a recovering alcoholic lawyer on the run from Canada - all meet here in Umkomaas, then find this house in the middle of a cane field in Dududu and create this amazing program. So many things came together at the right time. And I can tell you there are so many people who are clean and sober out there because of them. It's a miracle what's happening here. Cedars offered me happiness and freedom in sobriety. There's a big difference between being sober and being free and happy in sobriety."

Atmore says none of the many rehab programs he tried could come close to offering addicts the hope of recovery they get from the Cedars program. Everyone, whether the person is a multi-millionaire business tycoon or a poor prostitute, are treated exactly the same. They all have to obey the same rules and the rules are brutally stringent, with consequences attached. It's a boot camp but the difference, according to Atmore, is that they are enforced with genuine kindness and caring, not in the cold and unfeeling sterile manner of most rehabs he has frequented.

Andre

Andre Redinger grew up in South Africa during the time of apartheid, deeply believing that society was "structured against the will of God." He felt as if humans were "alien" to his world, his world being a deep connection to nature and the beauty of creation. He felt safest on the family farm, in the forest, on the plains, among the sugar cane fields and with the animals and insects.

He grew up in a strict household where they spoke German and maintained a strong German culture. The focus of his life was the Lutheran church and school. His parents struggled in their relationship and he found that his mother depended heavily on him for emotional support. They were ambitious and therefore financially well off. His father became a successful politician and his mother's role was managing the family affairs.

Adding to his alienation, he knew from a very young age that he was gay and different from anyone in his circle of friends. Terrified he would be "found out" and "literally sent to hell," he kept to himself as much as possible and immersed himself in his studies which also allowed him to escape from reality.

That escape started during orientation week at university when he was 18. He had his first drink and its impact astounded him. It lessened his fears and isolation.

"From then on I would drink heavily when having to socialise and until age 27 I was able to study and work without alcohol impairing my productivity. In character, however, I was a difficult person to live with and work with. To cope with life, which I only came to understand in

recovery, I was using my character defects which included resentment, anger, people pleasing, manipulation, dishonesty, self-pity, intense selfishness and denial of my homosexuality, which I was living out in a 'secret' world of prostitution. I realized but didn't accept that alcohol had become a crutch."

After earning a master's degree in psychology he joined the family sugar cane business and helped grow it into one of the largest private primary sugar producers in the country. By the time of his forced resignation as CEO in May 2008, they had just fewer than 1,000 employees, an "insane" amount of debt and outstanding court cases, primarily because of his attempting to run a company in "full-blown addiction."

"Drinking at lunch and evenings was essential to cope with the mounting work pressure and the insane relationship with a paid lover. At 30 I had moved onto a family estate thinking a geographical change was what I needed and I ended my six-year relationship with my expensive lover. The result was an acceleration of my addiction. From age 30 to 37 my life became more and more unmanageable – poor business decisions, many sexual encounters, mounting debt, increased anxiety attacks and a break down in relationships with my family. To seek a solution I consulted many doctors, psychologists and psychiatrists who prescribed me a variety of mind altering medication which I used together with my ever-increasing alcohol consumption.

A friend with whom he had been in rehab in another city had gone to Cedars as a last resort and, in an email, talked about how grateful he was to have found the program. In April, 2008, Andre found himself in his Durban apartment, completely broken and wanting to end his life. He called the friend who gave him the Cedars' telephone number.

"By the time I arrived at Cedars in May 2008 I had spent short stints in another rehab which had diagnosed me as Bi-polar, ADD and over worked. On entering Cedars I firmly believed in these diagnoses and did not view alcoholism as my disease."

Andre's first encounter with Tait was in his group.

"In character I found him to be strong, even forceful at times when it comes to his message. I met a man who was very passionate about his subject – recovery in the AA, spiritual growth and working on a relationship with God. He inspired me, immediately creating a willingness to at least listen as I sensed a strong spiritual presence and hunger in Don. I have always been seeking spiritual growth and here was a man who seemed to talk some sense. I certainly felt a bond before I got to know him personally. I believe that the main reason for this bond was knowing that he accepted me unconditionally and his actions and words showed no judgement."

Andre says Tait played an integral role in his recovery because he felt safe to expose his feelings, defects and secrets. A key moment in his recovery, he says, came when doing Step 5 for the first time with Tait as his sponsor.

"I was unable to accept my homosexuality and he told me that this would keep me sick – self-denial of who I truly am – all of me in God - would inevitably cause me to drink.

I walked away believing I could deal with this matter at a later stage and on my own. I did not and Don was right. I relapsed a few weeks later. After my relapse, however, which lasted for seven days, I had the courage to come to Don knowing that he loves me unconditionally, knowing and having faith that he could help. He did help me by taking me back to Cedars and walking very closely with me through the 12-step program. I would not be in recovery today experiencing an amazing life if it were not for God working through Don. Don is an example to me as to how this program works in action. I am growing in recovery by following Don as my sponsor and guide."

Andre stresses that it is this unconditional love that mattered most and is something he is learning to give to others.

"It is difficult to put in words but I never imagined a man who can come across as typical alpha male, to accept all of me, especially my homosexuality and addiction. Through Don I am learning to love myself and am able to say today that I am grateful to be a gay man. Gratitude I never imagined possible.

We are now great friends and part of my quality of life is due to spending time with him and Johanna. Spending time with Don is spending time and growing in recovery. Don has taught me that recovery is even more amazing than not having to pick up a drink; it is about actually living a life with purpose, service and having some fun. Ultimately, I am having an incredible spiritual journey. Don opened the door to this and continues to inspire and challenge."

In following Step 12 – passing on the message of recovery – Andre said this is possible because the foundation of what he learned is love.

"Don showed me that love is acceptance, allowing, patience, compassion, truth, courage and service. My reward now and in the future is in what I do and in service to others. A foundation in fellowship, recovery is about relationships and working with diversity. It's ok that we are different, it actually is exciting. Accepting this diversity allows me to take on opportunities and experience situations always seeking what God aims to teach and grow in me. So many situations in the future I now know I don't need to avoid. To always remember what I am – an alcoholic. With this comes humility, faith and service. To never lose my desperation to grow in recovery and attend as many AA meetings a week as possible – around this I can do life on life's terms. To meditate and grow in my conscious level with God. In this growth I am presented with many opportunities to do things God's way and grow or to take my will back and regress. I owe this to Don."

Walking through her flower gardens on a warm March afternoon, Andre's mother smiles when asked what Don Tait has done for her son.

"Don has not only given my son back his life, he has given us back our son. He is a remarkable man. I am so grateful to him."

Benton

"Benton, you want to share?"

All eyes in this rehab session travel to the 32-year-old with thick dark hair and a handsome face marred by a roadmap of hard times. He exudes warmth of character and a calmness that belies the carnage of his life, prior to finding Tait. Today, it is his turn to share his story with his group.

At 14, a young man with tremendous potential from a good, staunchly Catholic family, he ran away from Johannesburg to Durban – moving from one drug dealer to another. Eventually his parents let him come home and he entered a rehab centre. Intelligent and talented, he entered university and studied design. Following graduation he worked for a design firm where he was being groomed to become creative director. His ultimate downfall began with a woman with whom he was besotted and for whom he would "do anything," including becoming submerged in a life of drugs and alcohol.

While he used ecstasy and drank heavily, he shied away from crack and other similar drugs, but the girlfriend wanted to try them. Thinking this might solve their relationship problems, he agreed to "hit up" with her.

"It grabbed me immediately and created a whole new world. I just knew it would solve all my problems."

Far from solving his problems, the following six years were a roller coaster. They were arrested many times, often nearly killing each other and made half a dozen stabs at rehab. The final straw for both of them came the day he began selling her for sex to pay for their drugs. Her parents kicked him out and in desperation he called his parents to ask for help. He tried. Got a design job and maintained for five years – until the ultimate experience of his life. Heroin.

"I used to think it was a dirty street drug but from the very first moment I tried it I knew I would be on this drug for a very long time. I didn't know how I could ever live without it."

He began showing up late for work and falling asleep on the job, became dirty and dishevelled, began stealing and embezzling and turned to petty crime to feed the heroin demon. He was fired.

His friends began dying from overdoses – some choking on their own vomit. He was down and out and there was nowhere further to sink, or so he thought. He began attending AA meetings at an Anglican church but soon stopped showing up and couldn't "keep it together."

At one meeting he saw Don Tait.

"A breed unto himself. Tanned with a baseball cap and Gucci man bag. He appeared intimidating."

He had also switched from Heroin to prescription drugs. Doctors began cutting him off. Then one day he went to a clinic, the only man at an HIV clinic for pregnant mothers. A neighbour was there with her housekeeper who was sick with AIDS.

"She came over and grabbed me and said, 'this is the end of your life,' and took me to see Don. He met my parents and explained how the rehab would work – with the 12-step program – and my parents became quietly optimistic. I think they had resigned themselves that I would be a down and out addict forever because my track record was not good. Yet, they never lost faith in me and paid for the whole rehab."

For two months he did well. Tait took him to the gym to train with him and became his sponsor. He also was given a job in Durban in a design firm where the owner was also in rehab. He shared an apartment with his friend Caleb and one evening they decided to go to a nightclub together "just to see..." They went a couple of times but found it "boring" and went home by 11 p.m. The third visit to the club ended his umpteenth, albeit brief relationship with sobriety.

He was fired again. He didn't tell Tait. He spiralled out of control. Tait eventually found out and convinced him to go back into rehab, even arranged to get his old job back. Within months he was back on the drug circuit and the nightmare began all over again. But he was worn out.

"I went to sit on Don's couch. I spent a lot of time on his couch. He would lose his temper sometimes but he was always there – either at his home or on the phone. He is one of the few who never gives up on you. He said he saw something in me."

Tait had plenty of time to see what that "something" was during his six admissions to Cedars.

In 2007 he entered and stayed seven months. Things were going well until he met another woman – a fellow alcoholic. Tait advised him against the relationship and recommended he concentrate on recovery. He didn't and relapsed into what he hopes now will be his last waking nightmare. In 2008 he finally had enough and went back to Cedars. In March 2009 he celebrated a year of sobriety, something he never dreamed he could ever accomplish, not after 15 years in an almost constant addicted, addled state. Those years saw him pull a knife on his father to get drug money and stealing antipsychotic medications from the rehab. At one point he became cadaverous, existing on drugs and little else which saw him whittle to 90 pounds and spending three days in the intensive care unit fighting for his life – such as it was. He spent a year on meal replacements. Tait again took him back to the gym and had him enrol in a trainer course. He was soon offered a full-time trainer position. He gave up smoking. It took him three weeks to be able to lift a two-kilogram weight.

"I'm fitter than I've ever been and I'm happy, most of the time. It's different now. I don't expect things to happen overnight. I still have some days of self-pity"

He was 32, living with his parents, and says he has learned a new respect and gratitude for them. For the more than five years Tait has been in his life he says Tait's been like a "second dad."

"He gives me shit but if not for Don I wouldn't be alive. When the shit hit the fan I ended up on his couch. He's been there and knows what he's talking about. I had to really hit bottom. I love him. I can tell him anything."

One thing Benton says he has learned is that addictions are no respecter of status in society.

"I've been in rehab with celebrities, counsellors, professionals with a dozen letters after their names and people living on social services."

Today Benton is a personal trainer at a Scottburgh gym and is mentally and physically healthier than any time in his life. He says he has found something precious and important – a life worth living - and he credits Tait.

"There is something about Don and Cedars. There is a powerful fellowship here. I never thought I'd come back. I did. But Don carried me a lot of the time."

Peter was born in Johannesburg in 1952 and has spent most of his life in South Africa. He left for two years in the mid-1970s to study hotel management in London, England. Returning to South Africa, he worked for a large hotel company and in 1975 had an opportunity to buy the Cutty Sark Hotel in Scottburg. On his first visit to the town he says he was dismayed.

"I flew to Scottburg and thought 'this is a one-horse bloody town. How can I survive here?' I knew it would be a challenge."

Over the past 34 years since he bought the Cutty Sark he has mostly prospered through hard work and good management. A drop-in business following the 1994 post-apartheid elections in the country was short lived, mainly, he says, because of the leadership of Nelson Mandela and Bishop Desmond Tutu who helped ford a period when people were frightened that South Africa would erupt in a bloodbath. But his success came with a price. The job involved a lot of drinking and being a social fellow with his guests, so he drank constantly and soon couldn't survive a day without a drink.

He was able to hide his alcoholism for many years but eventually the cracks began and he couldn't hold it together. His marriage was on the rocks and the future looked bleak. A chance conversation between his wife and a couple who knew about a new rehab that was opening called Cedars, was to eventually lead him to recovery, but it would be a struggle. He was also to be the Cedars' first client. At AA meetings he met "this Canadian guy" who had recently arrived from Canada. They hit it off.

"I liked the way he talked. I was his toughest customer because I wouldn't go to rehab." One day Peter arrived at an AA meeting "drunk as a skunk" and Tait realized not only was he in a suicidal drunken haze, but seriously ill. He was taken from the meeting to hospital where he spent 17 days in a coma. From hospital, he went straight to Cedars where he became Tait's protégé.

"Don is a phenomenal speaker and especially when he is on the topic of addictions. You can hear a pin drop at his sessions. There is never one person who is not blown away by his story – it is so compelling. When he talks about his last days in Costa Rica, the despair and hopelessness. To hear his success story is so powerful, how this man was overcome by this disease yet was able to overcome it in the end. I was in the same situation and could not control the damn disease. I'd had four back operations and couldn't walk."

Peter extols Tait's character.

"I don't think I have known anyone else with the strength of character he has. I could take things from Don I would not have taken from anyone else. The magnetism of the man is huge. The way he puts things together – there's drama and theatre in the way he speaks. Then there's his compassion in what he does every day up at Cedars. He has taken so many and turned their lives around. So many of them had been in and out of institutions, but in Don's presence they flourish. When he did not see me for a while he would phone me or just show up at my place."

Without Tait, says Peter, he and so many others like him, would not be alive.

"What he is doing here in South Africa is giving hope back to people who had none left and saving our lives. Wow, now I have this new, sober life. I have three kids I am very close to and my wife and I are friends and together again. I wouldn't change anything. I have gone through that hell and have the spirituality to continue. Don and I see each other. We have a huge bond and friendship. There's no one closer."

Like Benton, Peter has spent many hours on Tait's brown sitting room couch. His visits to the home have not been without incident. Often arriving inebriated, shrubs and driveway construction have often fared badly when Peter was at the wheel illegally. Tait remembers one occasion when his friend and client took out half the plants on the driveway and nearly took out the gates on another. Their friendship endures.

Until she was twelve years old Casidy's home life was as normal as most families. But all that changed as her mother became mired in alcoholism and depression and her father was rarely at home. She had no guidance and, out of necessity, became pretty self-reliant.

She attended a small German public school and high school but says she had few social skills. Because of that she was bullied and followed her father's advice "don't slap them, punch them."

She earned a notorious reputation and was respected by her peers only because they were scared of her. Her mother's alcoholism was to have a devastating effect on her and her younger brother. They were not close but she looked after her mother the best she could and says in spite of it all they loved each other.

After high school Casidy headed to college in Durban. There she met her first fiancée who had been to rehab nine months previously but introduced her to alcohol and weed, which she didn't particularly like. Her father told her if she married the guy he would not attend the wedding and would, in fact, disown her. "If you can tell me you love me maybe I won't marry him."

Her father responded, "If you can tell me what love is."

The fiancée soon showed himself to be a physically abusive womanizer and she left him. Her life became a merry-go-round of drugs and drinking and meaningless one-night stands. Her cocaine addiction was severe and the only job she could get was in her father's business, which she hated. She overdosed but instead of going to hospital she went to a friend's uncle's home, and survived it.

She then met a guy who worked in a restaurant who seemed

to be able to calm her down somewhat. During the time she was living with him she went for a pap test to find out she had dysplasia and would undergo two years of laser treatments. Doctors told her if she wanted a child she should have one immediately before it was too late. She had a son but by the time he was born her relationship with the boyfriend was over. The responsibility of a child was overwhelming, so she had her mother come to live with her for three months and calls them the three worst months of her life. She started drinking again. She worked for her father from home but began drinking and sleeping and not doing much of anything else. Her son was in play school until noon. She would look after him until his 6 p.m. bed time, then drank until she passed out.

Soon, she began drinking earlier in the day and was terrified for her son. Her parents forced her to marry the father which turned out to be a big mistake. Her drinking intensified and she began to have memory lapses from the blackouts. She didn't want to lose her husband and son so attempted AA and Narcotics Anonymous but couldn't stay sober for long. She had an affair with a guy she met in AA and they relapsed together. She was sixty-nine days sober when she began smoking weed because it "took the edge off" her alcohol cravings. Her weed smoking became so intense she would smoke while driving her son around in the car. A trip to the hospital had her diagnosed with a sleep disorder and bi-polar illness. She was prescribed Zyban and says she became alternately like a zombie or manic. She asked her husband to move out and started leaving her son home alone – rationalizing it was better than leaving him in the car while she went in to a bar to drink.

Christmas 2010 she went to Johannesburg to visit her parents. Her mother had been in recovery for five years and they could see she was "destroying." On Christmas Eve her mother told her to change her ticket and leave their home, now! She left, dropped her son off at his father's house and spent the rest of Christmas alone on a "serious bender." She attempted suicide by swallowing pills, smoking as much weed and drinking as much alcohol as she could consume. She awoke in a drunken stupor and called her former sponsor.

Keith told her "Come into treatment."

She told him "I don't do the God thing, I don't get along with women, I'm arrogant and throw my weight around." Keith replied, "Come into treatment."

Her withdrawal was painful, as were the times in the Concerns group when she was told she should change her dress and behaviour and that she was selfish.

"Don's group made me stay for the three months. Because of the spirituality part of the program I wanted to change. I would stare at him in awe. He knows what I need to hear, when he speaks about souls and that you can't use life as an excuse. Nothing that happens is because God hates you or life is unfair. If not for Don's enlightenment I don't know how I would have gotten through it all. I come to his house or we talk on the phone. He would talk to me for hours. I am so afraid of what will happen if he dies. Don is the person I wanted dad to be. He pushes himself too hard for us. He gave me faith in faith. To know what he has gone through and manage to apply spiritual principles, it showed me that this is not crap. It's true stuff. He inspires me, like Keith. They are so honest. I can't thank Don enough. The things he does are a life saver for me. My rock bottom happiness is inside the walls of Cedars."

I was born on 22 June 1982 in Pretoria (now known as Tswane), South Africa.

My early life was as far as I recall pretty content. My folks had me at an early age and were quite occupied with their studies, building their careers etc, which left me to the care of a carer and school during the day. My folks went to great extents to ensure that I never went without. I built a very strong bond with my mother and had a rather distant relationship with my father. I grew up in a very nice area, went to good schools and we went on holidays. All the makings of a normal, happy, young life were there.

My folks were divorced when I was 12 and my mom remarried when I was 13. There was conflict in her second marriage and I recall my high school years as challenging. My relationship with my mother became quite co-dependent and my relationship with my father became even more distant. I was an average student, due to a lack of interest in my studies and half-hearted efforts. The unmanageability started creeping in during my high school life, even though I kept it together to some extent. Other than occasionally going out and from time to time getting drunk, I did not party or use, as yet. This only came after school, when I was away from home and left to make my own decisions.

By the age of 21 my drinking and using had brought me to me first rehabilitation centre in Johannesburg. It was already identified by my family that I had a problem. I was still far from realizing this myself. My mad addiction journey from there took me to the Drakensburg, then abroad to Dar es Slaam and eventually brought me to Durban, where in another treatment facility, I had met Annie, whom I at first lost contact with and then saw at a Narcotics Anonymous meeting. She was, at the time, at Cedars. Between Annie, my mother and another friend of ours they "captured" me and convinced me to go to Cedars. This was in March 2007. I clearly recall seeing Don for the first time on the day of my arrival at the Wednesday Scottburgh meeting. I had heard about his groups but had a strong attitude of I do not do God and I certainly do not do religion.

As mentioned above, I arrived at Cedars and attended Don's group, very anti-God or any form of spiritual living. Don certainly has a way about him to capture his audience for regardless of myself, I was gripped by his experience, his views on spirituality and his life in recovery. I was rather fearful of this man, with his powerful voice at first, but somewhere along the line, I began to make a lot of his teachings my own and I found a certain clarity around the aspect of a spiritual life, which I lacked before. Don became my first proper sponsor and a close friendship formed. Don has always felt like an extension of my family, that's how dear I regard him. He certainly played a massive role in my continuing fight for recovery which at times I succeeded at and at other times failed at. But regardless, Don remained a presence throughout the past nine years of my life and is certainly still one of my greatest spiritual guides in recovery.

What I believe makes Don effective is that he has such varied experience as an active alcoholic, as well as his experience in recovery. He has an extremely spiritual outlook on life and recovery. However, through his own experience, he shows how attainable a spiritual life and a relationship with a God of my understanding could be. Don's presence in my life and his guidance has had an enormous impact on my life, without which my life might have turned out very differently today.

ACKNOWLEDGEMENTS

This has been a long journey and could not have been completed without the help and cooperation of everyone I have interviewed for the book during the past decade.

My most special thanks, of course, to Don and Johanna Tait who have had the courage to share the privacy of their lives in such a public way. Painful though it is, they both do this hoping their story will make a difference in the lives of others who might see a parallel with their own. I also thank their daughters Melanie and Barbara.

Thank you to my editors and those who read the manuscript and provided insight and critique. I am so very grateful to Rebecca Wright, Vanessa Shields, Diana Mady Kelly, Ashley Ann Mentley, Julianna Bonnet, Brian Sweet, Larry Forsyth, Shelley Divnich-Haggert, Angelica Haggert, Angelo Montilla and Peter Hrastovic. I extend a special thanks to Marty Beneteau and my colleagues at The Windsor Star who helped in any way with the production of this work.

Thanks also to the many people who shared stories about Tait and their observations of him personally and professionally. I am sure there are many more than those I've included.

Since their reading of a draft of the first chapters, I have been hounded by my sisters Leona, Pauline, Marilyn and Beth to "Get it finished. We want to know the whole story." It never hurts to get pushed along and I appreciate their encouragement. I would also like to thank the talented Jessica Jagmin for her wonderful cover.

Thank you to supportive friends and family; to Christopher whose support and love never falters and my sons Rajesh and Bijan.

Other work by Veronique Perrier Mandal

Chasing Lightning ~ History of gambling in Canada
Written with Chris Vander Doelen

The Adventures of Poff and Balloonman
~ children's musical

The Pink Hat
~ A romantic mystery

Heart's Return
~ A musical

Praise for **GETTING OFF ~ A Criminal Lawyer's Road to Redemption**

It's a powerful piece of work and one that shall interest and inspire many. I see it as a biography, of course, but also as a powerful docudrama; epic theatre piece; audio book; movie. I also see it as a road to recovery documentation of Don Tait's life and the tremendous influences he's had on the lives of so many.

Its appeal is wide. I felt the hunger of those who struggle; the gift of unconditional love. The characters' journeys made me question my own ability to love, accept etc. etc. So, your work is a valuable experience for me.

Diana Mady Kelly, former director, School of Dramatic Art, University of Windsor.